The Ancient Art of Northern Asia

The Ancient Art
of Northern Asia

Anatoly I. Martynov

Translated and Edited by
Demitri B. Shimkin and Edith M. Shimkin

University of Illinois Press   *Urbana and Chicago*

Publication of this book has been supported by a grant from the National Endowment for the Humanities, an independent federal agency.

This book is printed on acid-free paper.

Library of Congress Cataloging-in-Publication Data

Martynov, Anatoliĭ Ivanovich.
    The ancient art of Northern Asia / Anatoly I. Martynov;
translated and edited by Demitri B. Shimkin and Edith M. Shimkin.
        p.   cm.
    Translated from Russian.
    Includes bibliographical references.
    ISBN 0-252-01219-4
    1. Art, Prehistoric—Russian S.F.S.R.—Siberia. 2. Siberia
(R.S.F.S.R.)—Antiquities. I. Shimkin, Demitri Boris, 1916–   .
II. Shimkin, Edith M. III. Title.
N5310.5.S65M37   1991
730'.0957'0901—dc20   89-20686
                                                            CIP

From history we should take fire, not ashes.

Jean Jaurès

As long as mankind is in the world, there will also be art.

Vladimir Stasov

Contents

List of Illustrations

priests). Gold plaques from the "Treasure of the Oxus," an Afghan hoard supposedly near Kunduz in Afghanistan. About fifth century B.C.

134. The Tree of Life linking the living and the dead. Gold open-work belt buckle. From the Siberian collection of Peter I. Scytho-Siberian, perhaps from the Altay.

135. Horses tethered to the World Tree. Petroglyphs, Tepsey, Yenisey. Tashtyk period.

136. "Woody" bronze cast objects of the Kulay culture. Western Siberian medieval forest art. First millennium A.D.

137. Images of an Earth Mother with emerging shoots: (1) Tazmin' ulus, left shore of the Bira [Byura] River, Minusinsk Basin; (2) Uybat chaatas, Minusinsk Basin. Okunevo Eneolithic.

138. Fertility deities: (1) Tazmin ulus; (2) Chernovaya I, stela incorporated into Tagar-period *kurgan*. Okunevo Eneolithic.

139. Fertility deity, "Deity with Spears," from Chernovaya 8, Kurgan 4. Okunevo Eneolithic.

140. Fertility deities with trees growing from their heads: (1) sandstone gravestone in Khakasia; (2) Terentiy ulus, Khakasia; (3) Mount Chiti-Khys, on left shore of Askyz River, on top of a Tagar *kurgan*. Okunevo Eneolithic.

141. A deer in the maw of a griffin, with antlers tipped with griffin heads as a sign of regenerated life. Kurgan 2, Pazyryk. Scytho-Siberian.

142. The Tree of Life in the form of a ram. Mongolian. Scytho-Siberian.

143. Exaggerated, luxuriously branching antlers as the Tree of Life. Altay, primarily Yelangash. Scytho-Siberian.

144. Images of ancestral mothers: (1) Ust' Tuba 3, Yenisey (from a tombstone); (2) Chernovaya (from a tombstone); (3) Syda, Minusinsk Basin (petroglyph). Okunevo Eneolithic.

145. Images of half people, half animals: (1) Myandash-deva (half woman, half reindeer); (2) Myandash-paren' (half man, half reindeer). Ural Animal Style. First millennium A.D.

146. Gold diadem from the Novocherkassk burial in the Ukraine. Tree of Life with attendant deer and a ram. Sarmatian (third-second century B.C.).

147. The solar cart of Strettweg, Graz, Austria. Hallstadt culture, sixth century B.C.

Foreword

The Ancient Art of Northern Asia describes systematically, analyzes stylistically and historically, and interprets iconographically the basic genres of Siberian archaeological art from the Paleolithic to medieval times. It is a unique work, Formozov's selective and purely descriptive volume (1969) being the sole extant comparable study. The present volume comprises, in addition to a brief introduction and concise, philosophical conclusion, six substantive chapters. Five deal with culture-historical periods, the Paleolithic, Neolithic, Eneolithic-Early Bronze, Scytho-Siberian, and Medieval. Each of these chapters provides a basic politico-economic background and then systematically covers the major genres of that period. Iconographies are emphasized with the aid of extensive reviews of religion and mythology, among both north Asian and ancient Near Eastern and Indo-European peoples. The sixth chapter, on the Tree of Life, seeks to integrate a good part of the preceding material. It explores how this concept, in plant, animal, and human manifestations, has been handled in north Asian prehistoric art.

This study is the fruit of prolonged research in the field, museum, laboratory, and library. It is based on Anatoly Martynov's firsthand investigation of virtually all the materials discussed. It is also a most thoughtful and original work. Dr. Martynov, a Marxist and a student and close colleague of the distinguished archaeologist A. P. Okladnikov, has formulated many new and significant ideas on art history, and on the cognitive world of ancient peoples. His work also adds much to the general culture history of northern Asia through succinct reviews of major events and cultural configurations, and through many detailed treatments of practices related to art. One such practice is the manufacture of Tashtyk burial masks, which illuminates technology, social organization, and belief systems. As a whole, *The Ancient Art of Northern Asia* represents both scholarship and passion, for it communicates the author's deep identification (as in his treatment of Neolithic petroglyphs) with the hopes, fears, and problems of *taiga* hunters. This is a pioneering study rich in interesting, perhaps speculative, interpretations, and indicative, in the inherent tensions of his abundant materials, of many research problems yet to be investigated.

Translating and editing the volume presented many challenges. Our intent was to convey accurately and to make understandable the materials and theories advanced by the author. To a secondary degree, we were also concerned with communicating Dr. Martynov's style. Our problems were both linguistic and contextual. Russian and English have important differences in the scope of words, syntax, and accepted style. Because of these differences, it was necessary, for example, to translate the Russian *obraz* by different English words, notably "image" and "icon." More than this, clarity sometimes demanded fairly substantial paraphrasing rather than close translations. Correspondingly, some levels of repetition quite acceptable in Russian had to be replaced by more varied synonyms to reflect English usage.

The contextual problem basically reflected the need for supplementary information, often only a few words, to define specialized data for nonspecialist readers. There was also a need, in a few cases, to add more recent data. All except trivial supplements have been enclosed in brackets.

In particular, we adopted the following usages. Following the Soviet distinction between the areas west and east of the Tien Shan-Altay line, we used "central Asia" for the former, and "inner Asia" for the latter. Again, to distinguish allied cultures in central Asia, south Siberia, and inner Asia from the Black Sea Scythian culture described particularly by Herodotus, we used "Scythic" or "Scytho-Siberian" as a more general term. Finally, the term "Old Turkic" refers, in accordance with linguistic practice, to the period in which epigraphic materials in Runic letters were made. While its absolute chronology varies from area to area, "Old Turkic" generally encompasses the years 550 to 1000 A.D.

Our translation has used the transliteration system of the U.S. Board on Geographical Names, retaining, however, palatalization symbols. We have used the author's illustrations, except for a few that seemed extraneous or presented severe technical difficulties. Color photographs were unavailable. We used the author's captions with some augmentations, primarily of references. We are responsible for the specific placement of references to illustrations in the text. We are also responsible for the location maps. The bibliography includes all works that could be accurately identified in the Martynov citations, plus a very few others.

It is our hope that this work is of good scholarly standard. But we know that errors and omissions have resulted from translation and editing. Unfortunately, great difficulties and the unreliability of the international mails precluded a highly desired review of our work by the author. The entire effort has proceeded over a period of nearly ten years under a number of difficulties. Edith Shimkin and the illustrator, E. I. Bigler, died; Anatoly Martynov and Demitri Shimkin had periods of severe illness. Other work competed for priority. This particularly included the joint effort on "Studies in North Asiatic Archaeology, Neolithic to Modern" (*Arctic Anthropology* 25[2]: 1-100 [1988]). Finally, many delays resulted from the communication difficulties already mentioned.

This collaborative effort was made possible, above all, by the Fulbright program of the United States Information Agency. Through this aid, Dr. Martynov traveled to the University of Illinois in 1980, and Demitri Shimkin went to Kemerovo State University in 1984. In that latter tour, the help of the Ministry of Higher and Specialized Education of the Russian Soviet Federated Republic (Minvuz) was most valuable. The All Union Agency for Author's Rights (VAAP) kindly granted permission to the University of Illinois Press to publish Dr. Martynov's manuscript. Finally, support came from the Department of Anthropology, University of Illinois at Urbana-Champaign, and the Wenner-Gren Foundation for Anthropological Research. Mr. Robert G. Carlson aided in this task.

DEMITRI B. SHIMKIN

Introduction

General Overview

The history and culture of mankind, in spite of all their diversity, are basically unified. Over the course of thousands of years each region of the globe and its inhabitants have brought a unique contribution to the common history of all mankind. The experience accumulated over thousands of years, basic discoveries, and inventions always have become the property of all people. Ancient art is also such a general human property.

This book is devoted to one of the regions of human history, northern Asia, i.e., Siberia and the Soviet Far East. These are Asiatic territories of the Soviet Union, extending from the Urals in the west to the shores of the Pacific Ocean and the Bering Strait in the east; from the stormy, eternally cold seas of the Arctic Ocean to the mountain massifs of the Altay, Sayan, and Khingan, which separate northern Asia from the remaining parts of the continent.

Northern Asia is a considerable portion of our planet, with an area of more than ten million square kilometers. But other factors are more significant. Great events of world history are connected with northern Asia: the settlement of the American continent during the Paleolithic; the formation of many ancient and contemporary ethnoses [sociolinguistic groups]; and the events of the Great Migration of Peoples at the beginning of our era, i.e., the first centuries A.D. In northern Asia, in western Siberia, proceeded the primal formation of the peoples of the Finno-Ugrian language group; this was also the region where the Samoyedic group of peoples originated. And southern Siberia includes the zone where the numerous Turkic-speaking peoples of the Middle Ages arose. The settling and dispersal of the Tungus-Manchurian peoples occurred in the eastern portion of northern Asia. Their descendants—the Evenki [Tungus], Eveny [Lamut], Nanay [Goldi], Ul'chi, Orochi, and Oroki—reside even now in the territory of the Soviet Far East. Here too, in northern Asia, live the Paleo-Asiatics: Chukchi, Koryak, Itel'meny [Kamchadal], Yukagir, and Eskimo of the Arctic zone of northern Asia and North America.

The history of northern Asia is ancient, interesting, and important.

The culture of the forest hunters was formed in the boundless forests of Siberia as early as the Neolithic and Bronze ages. In the south, in the steppes, the culture of the herdsmen arose, forming the basis of the unique nomad civilization.

At the same time, we must not forget that northern Asia is basically a zone of unwritten history. Everything that has been revealed of the ancient history of this region has been disclosed by archaeologists, ethnographers, and physical anthropologists. At the dawn of Russian control of this area, this was a country of "twilight." In the seventeenth and eighteenth centuries, and even toward the middle of the nineteenth century, no one knew or even guessed how ancient the history of this mysterious region was, nor how deep and intriguing the cultures of the tribes and peoples inhabiting it.

The artistic monuments which form the subject of this book are interesting and unique in themselves. In addition, they are irreplaceable sources for the reconstruction of the lives and worldviews of the ancient populations of northern Asia. These monuments are meaningful to us, not only for these reasons—their local significance—but also because they are part of worldwide human culture.

The ancient peoples of northern Asia have, in fact, bequeathed to humankind magnificent memorials of their spiritual culture, inimitable works of ancient art in varied forms: depictions on cliffs, works in bronze and precious materials, and primitive sculptures of small dimensions.

The Genres of North Asiatic Art

Metal work, rock carvings and paintings, small carvings of the Paleolithic, and Turkic statuary comprise the principal artistic genres known in northern Asia.

The ancient art of Siberia was first known long ago, as early as the seventeenth century. The first written reports about excavations of Siberian *kurgans*, or burial mounds, for the purpose of obtaining gold and silver objects and vessels date to 1669 (Radlov 1891:21). At the beginning of the eighteenth century, a significant number of art objects from Siberian *kurgans* were collected by the Siberian governor, M. P. Gagarin, who, in 1716, forwarded 222 gold objects to the Emperor, Peter I. Still another shipment of antiquities—two silver and sixty gold objects—was sent to Peter I in 1717. This formed the basis of the remarkable Siberian gold collection, which was enlarged in subsequent years. These magnificent artistic objects constituted the basis of the first Russian museum, the Petrine Kunstkammer (Zavitukhina 1977:63–69; Rudenko 1962b:71).

Some of these art objects from Siberia were, at the beginning of the eighteenth century, available to Nicolaas Witsen, a former member of the

Dutch Embassy and friend of Peter I, for study. Subsequently, Witsen published on these objects.

In January 1722, D. G. Messerschmidt and P. I. Stralenberg excavated several *kurgans* of the sixth through the third centuries B.C., not far from present-day Abakan [on the Abakan River, in the Minusinsk Basin of the Sayan region]. These were the first systematic excavations of Siberian *kurgans*, the beginning of Siberian archaeology (Kyzlasov 1962:43–52). Since then there have been excavations of hundreds, even thousands, of *kurgans* in the Yenisey steppes, in the mountain valleys of the Altay, in the Transbaykal, and other localities in northern Asia. They have provided first-class scientific material, including magnificent examples of Scytho-Siberian art, the so-called "Animal Style," which arose in the milieu of the herding populations of the Eurasian steppes from the Black Sea in the west to central Asia in the east. These are preserved in major museums in the Soviet Union and abroad. I had the pleasure of studying some of them in the Buffalo Museum of Science and in the Metropolitan Museum of Art in New York. These brilliant, unique examples of the "Animal Style" art date to the first millennium B.C.

In this century, the world has been astounded by numerous and varied art objects from the *kurgans* of the ancient Altaic nobility. In 1928 and in 1947–49, five huge *kurgans* were discovered in the Pazyryk Valley of the Gornyy Altay (High Altay). In subsequent years, *kurgans* were excavated in the settlement of Bashadar and at the village of Tuekta. Under huge stone mounds, immense crypts in the permafrost preserved magnificent objects of wood, leather, felt, and carpeting, objects of a kind not usually encountered by archaeologists (Gryaznov 1958; Rudenko 1960).

The spiritual life of the ancient and medieval populations of northern Asia cannot be imagined today without taking into account their astonishingly graphic art, the so-called Siberian pictographs (*pisanitsy*), which reveals the artistic world of ancient hunters and herders. Many Siberian pictographs were discovered long ago. Copies of rock art were made by members of expeditions sent to Siberia in the eighteenth century by the Academy of Sciences. Messerschmidt (1962), Stralenberg (1730), Gmelin (1751), G. Miller (1937), and Pallas (1771–76) made major contributions. In the nineteenth century, Radlov's discoveries (Radlov 1891, pls. 8, 13–18; 1894:68–71; 1895) were also noteworthy. Most significant were the many finds along the banks of the Yenisey River made by I. Aspelin, I. T. Savenkov, and A. V. Adrianov (Savenkov 1910).

At present, Siberian petroglyphs can be found at hundreds of sites comprising thousands of components. These are literally scattered over the entire huge territory of northern Asia. In western Siberia, there are the Tom' River pictographs (Okladnikov and Martynov 1972). In eastern Siberia are those on the Lena River (Okladnikov and Zaporozhskaya 1959;

3

Okladnikov 1959, 1972a), on the Angara (Okladnikov 1966), on the shores of Lake Baykal (Okladnikov 1974), and in the Transbaykal (Okladnikov and Zaporozhskaya 1969–70). Large aggregations of cliff representations have been discovered in recent years in northeastern Asia (Dikov 1971; 1977:134–61; Okladnikov and Mazin 1979). Until recent times, the remarkable sites of ancient art of the lower courses of the Ussuri and Amur rivers in the Far East were enigmatic, unexplained, mysterious. But numerous, most interesting, and unexpected findings were revealed by a remarkable accumulation of primitive representations of the ancient Nanay village of Sakachi Alyan on the Amur (Okladnikov 1968, 1971, 1981).

Finally, it is necessary to mention two additional ancient art forms of the Siberian peoples, both connected with major historical periods. These are the Paleolithic art at the beginning of the mastery of northern Asia by man, and the unique art of the Old Turkic tribes of southern Siberia.

The Paleolithic statuettes of Siberia were first discovered at the end of the nineteenth century, subsequent to the Paleolithic sculptures of western Europe. Since that time, the number of sites with Paleolithic art has grown in northern Asia (Abramova 1962, 1966).

In addition, the monuments of art of the Turkic peoples of southern Siberia are directly connected with ethnographic materials. Examples of this art have long been known. The most impressive examples, at isolated sites in the steppes and mountain valleys, are stone sculptures representing girdled men in a defined pose, primarily sitting or standing, with a saber or dagger in one hand and a vessel in the other. These silent guardians of the steppes are basically concentrated in two regions of northern Asia: in the Altay, and along the upper Yenisey, in the Khakas-Minusinsk steppes and valleys of Tuva (Sher 1966).

Thus, the art of the ancient peoples of northern Asia is diversified. It takes many forms and is an integral part of the history and development of the world outlook and esthetic viewpoints of the ancient populations of this region over the course of thousands of years, from the depths of Paleolithic antiquity up to the formation of the first state systems in northern Asia.

The Art of the Mammoth Hunters

1

The Paleolithic Era

More than a hundred years ago it became known that the most ancient traces of human activity in northern Asia extended far into the past, to the Paleolithic epoch, when a considerable portion of Asia, Europe, and America was covered with layers of ice. On the ice-free areas herds of mammoth roamed, and reindeer, musk-oxen, and wild horses grazed. In 1871, at the time the Irkutsk Military Hospital was under construction, reindeer bones were discovered. Along with them lay stone and bone tools as well as art objects made by Paleolithic man (Cherskiy 1872:167–72). Some years later, the Paleolithic settlement at Afontova Gora near Krasnoyarsk and the Paleolithic campsite in Tomsk were discovered. As a result, it was clear by the end of the nineteenth century that in the Upper Paleolithic, around 25,000 years ago, man already inhabited northern Asia, in the basin of the Yenisey, on the Angara, and on the Ob' (see map 1).

For a long time, the tens of discoveries and investigations of the Paleolithic sites in northern Asia made since 1871 could not shake the opinion that northern Asia had been settled only in the Upper Paleolithic. Now we know that this is not so. In 1961, on the outskirts of the city of Gorno-Altaysk in the center of the Gorno-Altaysk (High Altay) Autonomous Oblast', the most ancient Paleolithic site in northern Asia—Ulalinka—was discovered. There has been controversy about its age for many years. People have expressed the opinion that the site dates to the Middle Paleolithic, or even earlier—that it is around 300,000 to 400,000 years old. One geologist, L. Ragozin, an investigator of the Altay, estimates that the upper stratigraphic boundary of Ulalinka campsite can, on the basis of the overlaying layer of ashy-yellow clays, be determined to be more than 300,000 years old. The lower chronological boundary remains still to be ascertained (Okladnikov 1964a, 1972b; Pospelova, Gnibidenko, and Okladnikov 1980).

Excavations at Ulalinka have yielded hundreds of worked stones and tools made from yellow-white quartzite. In the general mass of finds, as

5

A. P. Okladnikov has noted, coarsely split pebbles, made from quartzite split lengthwise into two flat oval halves, predominate. Nothing exhibiting this technique of working has been discovered at other campsites known in Europe or Africa. These artifacts resemble "orange segments." At one end, the surface of the spine is blunted, while the other has a thin blade suitable for cutting or chopping. Flat pebbles with traces of smoothing blows can be placed into a special group. There are also pebble tools specially formed by trimming with retouch on the edge; these are pebble-choppers with a protuberant worked blade, placed across the long axis of the pebble at its end.

This site is not the only one. Pebble tools have been found at the village of Bogorodskoye on the Amur, at the village of Ust'-Tu, at Filimoshki on the Zeya River, and at Ust'-Kanskaya and Strashnaya *peshchera* [cave] in the Altay. Probably these sites, as well as those now discovered in Mongolia, in the Gobi, in the region of Sayan-Shanda and Mandal-Gobi (Maydar 1981:19–20), constitute one whole. Only now has the work which was begun in the 1920s by the Central Asiatic Expedition of the American Museum of Natural History, under the leadership of Roy Chapman Andrews, been crowned with success. As a result, a new map of man's pre-history in northern Asia is being drawn.

It might appear that these far-distant epochs do not relate to our theme, but without knowledge of these new discoveries it is not possible to trace the complex processes which spread over huge expanses of northern Asia during the Paleolithic.

No less significant have been recent discoveries of the Paleolithic in the very center of northern Asia, on the Lena, in Yakutiya, at Dyuktay Cave. The site, with well-studied stratigraphy, has given much new material to science, clarifying our suppositions about the Paleolithic of northern Asia (Mochanov 1969a:235–39; 1977; Mochanov et al. 1983). And, finally, there have been Paleolithic discoveries at the northeastern extremities of the Asiatic continent, in Chukotka, and in Kamchatka on the shores of Ushki Lake, near the American continent (Dikov 1977, 1979; Mochanov 1969b, 1978:54–66).

Thus, the Paleolithic in northern Asia can now be clearly divided into two major chronological periods: the Lower and Middle Paleolithic, consisting of sites and isolated archaeological finds, basically in the southern foothill portions of Siberia, and in the Soviet Far East; and the Upper Paleolithic, known from sites distributed over a large periglacial territory in the basins of the great rivers of northern Asia.

Materials on the Upper Paleolithic attest to a complex process of settlement by *Homo sapiens* and the formation here of his culture. The complexity of this epoch is attested to, first of all, by the fact that in the Upper Paleolithic, as is now clear, there was not just a single archaeological culture in northern Asia, but several cultures with their own traditions of stone working. There are clearly delineated sites of the so-called Mal'ta culture (Mal'ta, Buret', Achinskaya campsite), with characteristic tools of narrow, thin, knifelike blades and stone-working methods of the European Paleolithic. Complex dwellings and realistic art are characteristic. Near the region of Mal'ta culture lay those of the Afontova Gora and Kokorevo cultures on the Yenisey, and also the Lena Paleolithic. All were quite distinctive.

It is well known that with this epoch is connected a great event of world history: the penetration of the American continent by the inhabitants of northern Asia. It must be presupposed that the first wave was connected with the very beginning of the Upper Paleolithic, with the general process of development of man of the species *Homo sapiens*, with diffusion into, and mastery of, new territories. Then, undoubtedly, there were other waves of migration throughout the Upper Paleolithic and in the Mesolithic. In all, this migration was scarcely a single process.

The Siberian Area of Paleolithic Art

The sites of Paleolithic art in northern Asia are not numerous. They are, however, clear examples of primitive creativity, and occupy a deserved place in the general corpus of man's ancient artistic efforts. Most noteworthy are the finds from the Irkutsk Military Hospital, Mal'ta, Buret', Krasnyy Yar, Afontova Gora II and III, Oshurkovo, Sokhatino IV, Berelëkh, and Shishkino (see map 1). Overall, however, these artistic productions appear to be limited to east-central Siberia.

Irkutsk Military Hospital. In 1971, near the city of Irkutsk, in the loessy loam deposits, among animal bones and tools, excellent sculptured objects were found: rings of various sizes, a ball, a disc, and small cylinders, polished and decorated with rows of incised parallel lines. All were carved of mammoth ivory. Among these objects, the small cylinders were encircled with stripes of incised concentric lines.

Mal'ta. This remarkable site, located eighty kilometers west of Irkutsk, gave science a basic collection of north Asian artistic treasures. Around thirty unique female statuettes of varying shapes were found in Mal'ta. Anatomically, the figurines are of two types: full-figured women with strongly hypertrophic forms, and women of thin, delicate form (fig. 1). Some of the figures are nude; others have peculiar incisions, evidently imitating clothing. Finally, most of the figurines have modeled faces, significantly differentiating them from analogous European figurines.

In addition to the female statuettes found at Mal'ta was a series of bird sculptures (fig. 2). In all likelihood, these sculptures represent water birds, both in flight and in a resting position, evidently in imitation of birds floating on water.

7

An engraved representation of a mammoth appears unique (fig. 2, bottom). The engraving is on a convex slab of mammoth tusk measuring 8.2 by 3.6 centimeters. The figure of the mammoth was executed in profile by means of thin hatchings. The trunk, both tusks, and the thick, firmly planted legs of the animal can be easily recognized. On the mammoth's body, straight hatchings are closely placed, evidently intended to indicate its long wool. The drawing convincingly renders a likeness of this powerful Paleolithic animal (Z. Abramova 1962:43). Another slab of mammoth tusk is quite unusual. Three engravings of snakes appear on one side. All have puffed-up heads turned to one side. It has been surmised that they are similar to cobras (Z. Abramova 1966).

Among the objects from Mal'ta are apparent bracelets, mostly found in fragments. However, plaques and clasps predominate in the collection (fig. 3). A flat rectangular bone plaque with representations on both sides is especially famous. Spiral rows of round pits appear on one side, and on the other are engraved representations. A large number of beads, in addition to the bone objects and ornaments, were also found at Mal'ta.

Buret'. This site was studied in 1936–40 by A. P. Okladnikov (1945). The settlement is located on the bank of the Angara River, not far from the mouth of the Belaya River. Materials obtained in the course of excavations are similar to the objects from Mal'ta. Five female sculptures and a series of bird representations come from Buret'. The statuettes differ in their state of preservation; the best-preserved was obtained from Dwelling No. 1. It is a carefully formed sculpture of a woman, 12.2 centimeters long and 1.9 centimeters at the shoulders (fig. 4). The figure has somewhat distorted proportions. The head is oval, narrowed at the crown; the face is well modeled with excellently delineated cheeks, cheekbones, and chin, but somewhat asymmetrically placed eyes and nose. The statuette's shoulders are narrow, frail, and rounded, and the short arms lie along the torso. The torso itself is narrow and flat-chested; the thighs are prominent, the spine smoothly curved and the legs compressed. The figurine differs from the majority of Siberian and European statuettes in that it has clearly delineated clothing. Except for the face, the statuette is almost covered by half-moon incisions arranged in vertical rows. The ornamentation possesses a distinctive rhythmic regularity independent of the contours of the statuette. It is as though the figure was clothed in a hooded fur garment of a "combination" type (Okladnikov 1945:104–8; 1960:280–88). There are also similar incisions on objects of uncertain significance at Mal'ta.

Krasnyy Yar. This site is located on the right [north] bank of the Angara River, two hundred kilometers down river from Irkutsk. A unique sculptured article, evidently representing a seated person, was found in the cultural layer. The article is 3.7 centimeters high, 1.1 centimeters wide, and 0.8 centimeters thick. It represents a human figure in a somewhat simplified form. Along the back there are short, uneven lines across the figure. Similar, although deeper and sparser, lines are distinctly marked on the left side of the figure (Petri 1927:44).

Afontova Gora II and III. These campsites are situated along the bank of the Yenisey River, in the environs of the city of Krasnoyarsk. In the lower cultural stratum of the Afontova Gora II campsite, scores of various ornaments were discovered. Among them is a famous disk of *agal'matolit*, a variety of pyrophyllite, with a hole in the center. Along its edges and flat surfaces are dents and strokes. Also found were flat circlets, some made of soapstone, others of bone, pierced with apertures measuring from one or two millimeters to one centimeter. There were also perforators of hare long-bones with cut-off epiphyses, and pendants made from perforated teeth of reindeer and polar fox. In I. T. Savenkov's find at Afontova Gora III (Savenkov 1910) one can single out a large unpierced *agal'motalit* disk, the flat surfaces of which were decorated with incisions radiating from the center to the edge. Presumably this disk had some sort of cultic meaning. The remaining objects were analogous to the finds at Afontova Gora II. These were a small ball of mammoth tusk, punches made from long bones, flat pendants and beads of *agal'motalit*, and pendants made from the pierced teeth of arctic foxes and deer.

Oshurkovo. This campsite lies on the south bank of the Selenga River, eighteen kilometers downstream from Ulan-Ude. At the time of the excavations in 1958, a unique stone pendant of triangular form with rounded edges was found there. The pendant is flattened, its edge covered with deep slanting cuts two to three millimeters apart. There are light, thin strokes going randomly in different directions on both flat surfaces. A small hole had been drilled in the upper part of the pendant. A fragment of a bone insert tool was also found; zigzag ornamentation was cut into its surface.

Sokhatino IV. The site is located on the Ingoda River in the Transbaykal. Some pieces of animal-rib bones with stroke ornamentation drawn on them were found there. On the flat surface of one piece was ornamentation consisting of "bunches" of cuts. One "bunch" placed in the center appears to be a representation of a person, in the opinion of Okladnikov (Kirilov 1980:239–40, n. 10). The remaining three fragments are thickly covered with strokes.

Berelëkh. This find consists of a slab of mammoth bone bearing an engraved representation of a mammoth (fig. 5). It was obtained in 1965 by V. Flint in Berelëkh, a village located on the river of the same name, a left tributary of the Indigirka River. (Berelëkh is located at approximately 71 N, 146 E, north of the Arctic Circle.)

The mammoth is shown in profile, facing left. The long trunk descends in a straight line to the legs. Two barely curved tusks are shown by two intersecting lines. The figure has two legs of uneven and disproportionate length, one of which is slightly thicker than the other. The characteristic hump on the animal's back is clearly shown; one little line delineates its tail. The entire figure, rendered by engraving, is thickly stroked over, evidently representing the animal's wool. Short dashes are drawn on the belly, representing bits of pendent wool (Bader 1975:30–33).

Shishkino. Pictographs of animals—wild horses and bison—discovered by Okladnikov on the Shishkino cliffs on the right, or east, bank of the Lena River occupy a special niche in Paleolithic art. The drawings were applied in outline with red coloring, and are of rather large proportions. Thus, one horse is 2.8 meters long and 1.5 meters high. It has a massive torso and pronouncedly hanging belly. A second drawing is analogous in style to the first, but decidedly smaller in size. This horse is also outlined and in profile. Its torso is heavy and massive, the belly defined by an arched outline (Okladnikov 1959:23–25). Without question, these are the oldest cliff representations in northern Asia. However, their attribution to the Paleolithic is not indisputable.

[Over more recent years, examples of Paleolithic art have been discovered at the settlement of Malaya Syya in Khakasia, and in various other sites. Particularly notable is the discovery at Mayna campsite, in the Minusinsk Basin (Yenisey River), of a ceramic female statuette, a truly unique artistic object (Vasilevskiy 1983).]

Within the Siberian context, the art of Mal'ta and Buret' constitutes a true artistic school, with its own basically representative traditions and aesthetic ideas. The art of Mal'ta reflects a rather complex spiritual world of the peoples of the glacial period. One sees in the art of the people of Mal'ta evidently keen observation, high artistic skills, and fantasies. This art and indeed the entire culture have a definite similarity to the culture of Kostenki and Mezin in the European part of the USSR, and to the traditions of western European culture. Western analogues to the culture of Mal'ta can be traced here not only in art but also in small tools made from chips and thin knifelike flakes.

This similarity is not absolute, however, and the Siberian culture does not appear as a simple analogue of the European; rather, it shares only the general traditions and technical attainments of the Upper Paleolithic epoch. In it there is much that is *sui generis* and specific. There are unique sculptures of water birds, most likely loons. There are no such birds in other collections of Paleolithic art. Exceptional local masterpieces are the clothed female statuettes. Here, in Siberia, building on the common basis of realistic creativity of the glacial epoch, an artistic school arose, the leading images of which were the woman and mother, and the animals of the era.

Basic Elements of Siberian Paleolithic Art

In more general terms, Siberian Paleolithic art can be distinguished as a stylistic school comparable to that of Paleolithic western Europe principally through the characteristics of its portable art. Siberian anthropomorphic representations, engraved zoomorphic representations, and bird figures in particular should be noted.

Anthropomorphic Representations

A study of east-central Siberian and European statuettes shows that in spite of their general similarities, there are very substantive differences between them. This enables one to single out a Siberian style of female statuettes (Z. Abramova 1962:46–56). First, the Siberian statuettes differ from the European ones in their artistic approaches (*traktovka*) and proportions. The European ones, as a rule, have emphasized sexual features: pendulous breasts, thick hips, and bulging stomachs. The Siberian ones do not have such clearly enlarged forms; they are well proportioned, in the majority, lean, with correct masses for the separate parts of the body. One of the basic differences to be noted between the two groups lies in the treatment of the face. Not one European statuette has a molded face; only the head from Brassempoui in southwest France could serve as an exception. But all examples in the entire series of Siberian statuettes have defined faces, that is, a modeled chin, delineated brows, a nose, and at times, even eyes and a mouth. Finally, a distinguishing detail of Siberian statuettes is what appears to be the presence on the figures of a distinctive ornamental covering, representing clothing. Analogues to this phenomenon do not exist in materials either in western or eastern Europe (Z. Abramova 1969:103–7).

Engraved Zoomorphic Representations

Attention must be drawn to the engravings of mammoths on slabs from Mal'ta and Berelëkh. They have no analogues in the European part of the USSR. However, the engraved representation from Berelëkh must be placed in the category of dubious finds, in view of the fact that it was not found in a stratigraphic context. It is necessary to note that sculptured representations of mammoths are known in other Paleolithic sites in the Soviet Union. Almost all of these sculptures come from the Kostenki region: Kostenki I, Aleksandrovskaya, Anosovka II. However, as an engraving, the mammoth from Mal'ta is similar to various other representations known in the Paleolithic art of western Europe, in particular, the engraving of a mammoth on a Magdalenian cave wall in the Dordogne, France (Wymer 1982:256).

Bird Figures

These representations must be noted especially. The bird figurines from Mal'ta and Buret' are not like any others in European Paleolithic art. They are very realistically executed, in spite of a certain conventionality. It is notable, also, that they seem to represent a series. There are also bird heads from Kostenki I, but they are peculiar, since their shape often depends on the natural form of the concretions of marl, the material from which they were made.

While these three groupings of art objects—anthropomorphic representations, engravings, and figures of birds—command attention, they are not encountered in all Siberian Paleolithic sites. Thus, in the materials from the Irkutsk campsite and at Afontova Gora, one finds a somewhat different, abstract world of art. These objects are puzzling balls; long bone rods (sterzhni) with cuts on the ends; short cylindrical rods made of mammoth tusk, and ornamented; stone disks and circles, decorated with linear cuts; as well as other items. Undoubtedly, we have here a unique, intellectualized world of the Upper Paleolithic, which arose from a distinctive material culture.

The Meaning of Paleolithic Art

It is impossible to approach this art, so far removed from us, with the values which we apply to contemporary art. There are many theories explaining this ancient art. Whether it is necessary for us to recount them all is doubtful. Paleolithic art, and Siberian art in particular, is a complex phenomenon, and, most important, does not have a single meaning. Therefore, it seems that theories explaining it from a single viewpoint, either aesthetic or magical, are unfounded. In my opinion, this art does not yield a single explanation, although this does not appear conclusively so at first sight. A common aesthetic undoubtedly underlies the expression of images, the canons, the traditions of small plastic art and engravings, and the distinctive artistic means that can be characterized as the Upper Paleolithic Siberian artistic school. In the depths of this set of aesthetic principles lie aesthetic ideas, moral and social canons, formed in the womb of Paleolithic societies generally.

However, another vitally important side of this art is no less significant: its semantic content and the concrete purposes of creative works. Yet it is difficult to determine the purposes of objects of Paleolithic art because of the fragmentary nature of the finds. It is possible that the statuettes are only portions of some sort of distinctive "altars" to ancestral spirits, protectors of clan and tribal societies. They may be only a part, in their artistic embodiment, of complicated ritual-mythological complexes.

Rational aspects, magical activities and aesthetic norms, and rituals were in antiquity parts of a general system of ideas about the surrounding world and about the people themselves in this world. Such a system, in opposition to later religious systems, can be characterized as a ritual-mythological model. Paleolithic "artists" and "sculptors" scarcely distinguished between the "truth of life" and the "truth of art," that is, between reality and imagination. In this sense, Paleolithic art was an important component of social and ideological life. It is true that realism in art intertwined with mythology in semantic content. Hence, in explaining the semantics of primitive art, one should not choose between alternatives, between the "truth of life" and "myth." Myth originated out of the elements of the "truth of life," but the combination of these elements surely must not be mistakenly subordinated to the logic of our natural perception. Such a concept stems from the fact that in essence the behavior of primitive man was rational. The basis of this behavior was, by necessity, the efforts for adaptation to the outer world and for control over it. This behavior included both pragmatic activities, and this connected with ritual-mythological traditions and inherited norms, in which it was necessary to believe and observe unconditionally. The Paleolithic art of Siberia also was a part of such ritual-mythological traditions and norms.

Sacred Animals and Solar Symbols

Neolithic Art

In Eurasia, where the realistic art of Paleolithic hunters had existed, a sharp break in artistic creativity took place about seven to ten thousand years ago. The little paths to hidden cave sanctuary-temples grew over; bone and stone figurines of women disappeared. The descendants of the Paleolithic master craftsmen lost interest, as it were, in the real-life subjects that had concerned their ancestors. Replacing Paleolithic realistic painting and sculpture, there ensued in the Mesolithic era a full, puzzling schematism in ornamental, decorative, symbolic art. This transformation took place primarily in the regions that became the zone of agriculture and animal husbandry. The change from foraging to food production brought about a basic change in world outlook and human sentiments. The new era generated an "ideoplastic" art.

However, this sharp break did not take place everywhere. There still remained vast territories worldwide where climatic conditions either did not permit a quick transition from hunting and gathering to new sources of subsistence, or else fully blocked the rise of the new type of economy. This was the case, on one side, in the far south in Africa, where traditions of realistic art persisted for millennia among the hunters of the Sahara, and among the "Bushmen" (Khoi San–speaking people). The same was true for the other extreme of the Old World, in northern Asia and in the north of Europe. There, hunting, fishing, and the pursuit of mammals continued into the Mesolithic, Neolithic, and Early Bronze ages. The living forms of animals, related in spirit to Paleolithic representations, long were dominant in art. The hunting magic and the distinctive understanding of the surrounding world, the special philosophical world-perceiving system of hunters, remained alive and continued to motivate this art.

The Neolithic art of the Siberian hunters was consequently a continuation, under new historical conditions, of the basic traditions of Paleolithic realistic art. It absorbed the artistic attainments of the preceding era. Here we find the representation of animals in profile, a convention that was formulated in Paleolithic art. Certain images and "actors" also persisted: bears and water birds. However, in this new era the moose, which appeared in the Holocene environment, became the major image of north Asiatic art.

It must be emphasized that the basis of Asiatic thought and style remained as before in the north Asiatic Neolithic because the basic economy and lifeways of the hunters changed little. True, there were external discontinuities in the beginning of the Holocene. Glaciers and mammoths disappeared; the Siberian forests filled with moose, the tundras with reindeer. Hunting conditions changed. But hunting remained the base of the north Asiatic foraging economy.

The Neolithic art of northern Asia which has survived to our times is represented basically by three creative genres: ornamentation, sculpture, and numerous depictions on cliffs. The subjects of this art reflect the economic evolution of this era and, as a whole, have the following fundamental traits: (1) animals take a primary role in petroglyphs, while man is clearly secondary; (2) an interesting combination of live, dynamic realism and conventionalism may be observed in the artistic communication of images; and (3) the ideational, semantic bases of this art are the world outlook of hunters and primitive hunting magic. (See map 2.)

Ornamentation

Neolithic ornamentation is basically associated with ceramic wares. Unquestionably, objects which have not come down to us—clothing, wooden objects, and birchbark—were decorated to the same degree. Thanks to the mass scale of its use and its ties with objects of daily life, this ornamentation had a practical function. Decorating various articles, it served as a kind of "calling card" of one or another primitive social unit. Made up of rhythmically repeated conventional elements, the patterns of ornamentation distinguished Neolithic provinces, cultures, and chronological periods. At the same time, the semantics of ornamentation are very difficult, in most cases impossible, to decipher.

The Neolithic ornamentation of northern Asia was quite varied. It has never been dealt with in the scientific literature as a separate topic. Yet all Neolithic pottery is decorated, with external surfaces fully covered in most cases. It thus constitutes a massive body of material testifying to the definite aesthetic tastes of northern Asians and to the meaning of these aesthetic elements in their daily lives. Ornamentation was thus associated with people's lifeways. In contrast, petroglyphs and sculptures developed under the influence of religion and worldview.

In northern Asia, ornamental motifs are remarkably numerous. We will deal here only with the most basic, most common elements. But it is these that permit us to differentiate separate ornamental areas. Two large zones, the Siberian and the Amur–Far Eastern, may be distinguished in the ornamental art of the north Asiatic Neolithic. Each differs fundamentally from the other.

The Siberian Neolithic Zone

A horizontal placement of strips of ornamentation and a rhythmical repetition of the same initial ornamental pattern is characteristic of this extensive region, notwithstanding a great variability in details. Such ornamentation produces a showy, tapestry-like surface for the vessel and transmits an excellent feeling of rhythm and balance. At the basis of ornamentation in this zone lie the simplest initial decorative designs and symbols. Such designs are the inclined cross, the impressed pit, the broken zigzag line, and the wavy line. Hundreds of different combinations are formed from these basic elements on vessel surfaces in different Neolithic territories.

The elements were marked on the pots in different ways, and with the aid of various tools. In some cases, the ornament was drawn with the help of a small, blunt stick or shovel-like instrument. With these instruments also, patterns could be impressed. Somewhat different patterns resulted when a sharp object was used for drawing or impression. Another instrument was a special, small-toothed comb used in making cross-shaped or zigzag imprints. Thanks to the different tools used, the same design might be drawn, impressed, or incised. A symmetrical and rhythmical execution of the design lent beauty and finish. The initial elements came in groups of four or five, which formed an ornamental band encircling the Neolithic vessel. Several such bands usually covered the vessel surface. Between the bands were delimiting zones of lines, strips of designs with different compositions of elements or pits.

More rarely, another system of design layout was used. It was, in a sense, complementary to that of horizontal banding. In this case, the entire vessel was covered in checkerboard fashion with rectangular fields of horizontally and vertically placed designs. The lip and bottom of the vessel were often decorated in a special way, separated from the body pattern by some other design. All this created a unified, finished composition. The decorative elements of the Siberian zone, which arose as important accessories (in a representational way) of pottery, can later be traced through the Bronze and Iron ages, up to medieval times.

The Amur–Far Eastern Neolithic Zone

Ornamentation of a fundamentally different composition arose and developed during the Neolithic period in the Amur and Far Eastern regions. An enormous quantity of pottery has been accumulated from settlements on the Amur and Ussuri rivers. These collections permit us to trace the rise of a distinctive decorative art in the Neolithic of this area, its connection with petroglyphic art, and, what is very important, its direct ties with later and even contemporary ornamentation among native peoples of the Far East, the Nanay [Goldi], Orochi, and Ul'chi.

This ornamentation, as executed in the early Neolithic, was first encountered in pottery from a settlement on Suchu Island of the lower Amur (Derevyanko 1970:74–75). The ornamentation consisted of vertically placed stamped zigzags (fig. 6). On the surface of the pottery, as well as on the background, wide, deeply incised spiral lines were placed freely and in a flowing manner. In the intervals between them were triangles. The decoration of a vessel combined incised and stamped elements with painting. This also differentiates the art of this region from that of the forest.

The vessels had a lustrous pale dull-red background coloration, while the deeply incised strips of ribbonlike pattern (spirals) were filled with saturated black paint. In this way, the design became sharp, its surface convexity emphasized. Such ornamentation is encountered at Khabarovsk, at Vozeneskoye, and in the region of Sheremetyevo and Kazakevich villages (all on the lower Amur). This ornamentation is conventionally termed "ribbonlike" or spiral. (See fig. 7.)

A second kind of Amur ornamentation is a pattern of interwoven lines, which forms a handsome solid network of diamonds, the so-called "Amur wicker."

Finally, a third type of pottery decoration is the unique representation of masks on sherds from sites near Voznesenskoye and Kondon (fig. 8). This type permits us to establish a direct tie between Amur Neolithic pottery and petroglyphic representations. The masks are executed in a specific manner, with a high degree of conventionality in execution, and with unusual expressivity. The face is a heart-shaped oval; the lips are barely everted, the mouth deeply incised. The most expressive feature, the most striking for the beholder, is the disproportionately large eyes, formed like enormous commas. These large eyes are further distinguished by their coloring, which gives them an illusion of projecting outward. The nose, finally, is presented in an artistically original way as a thickening above the upper lip.

The surface of the face, except for the eyes, is covered by fine, netlike ornamentation. Next to the face are representations of sharp-clawed paws. The sherd from Voznesenskoye is painted a bright crimson.

The representation closely resembles the masks found on boulders near the village of Sakachi Alyan on the bank of the Amur (figs. 42–46). In its emotional perception, the facial type is unquestionably frightening; threat and frozen cold emanate from it.

The complex of materials from the Lower Amur or Kondon culture is dated by the radiocarbon method at 4520 ± 20 B.P. [uncalibrated]. Another unique artistic product of the Amur tribes can also be attributed to this era. This is a clay figurine of a person discovered by G. S. Martynova in one of the semisubterranean houses in the Kondon Neolithic settlement (fig. 9). The length of the sculpture is 17 centimeters. It is made of compact clay, with a polished surface. The entire sculpture transmits, in a conventionally realistic way, the image of a young woman, a girl. Her frail body is simplified, with the slope of the shoulders and the projection of the arms barely shown. The neck and head are, conversely, elongated. The lovely, well-executed face blends into a long, flattened, backward-sloping forehead. A tender beauty and grace are suggested by her face: the little projecting chin; the very small, slightly chubby, tender lips; the thin, slightly aquiline nose; the softly projecting cheeks; the characteristic Mongoloid cut of the eyes; and the eyebrows arched over the face as a whole.

Unquestionably, the figurine was furnished with accessories that have not survived, probably clothing and some sort of stand. In the expanse of the almost flat forehead is a small spot. It is likely that a head ornament was attached here.

Primary attention in this sculpture was given, not to sexual characteristics, but to the beauty of the young feminine face. In its artistic finish and expressiveness, the figurine is one of the masterpieces of Neolithic art.

As a whole, the decorative art of the Amur, born in Neolithic depths, survives to our day among native peoples of the area, the Nanay [Goldi], Ul'chi, and Nivkhi [Gilyak] (Okladnikov 1968, 1971, 1981). The basic ornamental design, the spiral, still persists. A distinctive pattern of spiral tendrils covers the national dress of the Amur tribes, women's robes of fishskin, as well as domestic utensils of birchbark, and surfaces of funerary structures. This pattern is so widespread and common among the peoples that it forms their basic, contemporary ornamental characteristic. It is a fundamental element, from which other patterns emerge. On its basis, stylized representations of living subjects—fish, frogs, snakes—are also formulated. The second motif, the patterns of Amur "wickerwork," also persists, but retains only a simple initial form, a checkerboard of diamonds and stamped zigzags.

This uninterrupted artistic tradition is associated not only with a continuity of style, subjects, and artistic form, but with a continuity of ideas linked to these subjects. The mythology and folklore of the contemporary Nanay and other Amur peoples retain the ideas that brought this mysterious world of art to life.

Having sketched the nature and development of this art, another question arises: What were its origins?

This question was asked more than a century ago by the academician L. I. Shrenk (1899:89–90). In the 1850s, having gathered materials on the art of the Amur peoples, he expressed a number of uncorrelated ideas. He noted the distinctive character and tastes of these peoples, which were totally different from those seen among Siberian "natives" (inorodtsy).

And these distinctive ornamental tastes did not diminish, but rather increased with distance from the Chinese.

At the end of the nineteenth century, a major American scholar, Berthold Laufer, worked along the Amur. He was especially attracted by the art of the Amur peoples, rich in content and original in execution. He concluded that their rich and complex decorative art was not their creation but borrowed. He reckoned that its form and conceptions were saturated with a Chinese spirit. From this, the origin of Amur ornamentation was judged to be late, from the medieval Jurchen period (Laufer 1899).

But at that time these problems of origin could not be solved. Materials were few, while the ancient archaeological art was totally unknown. And without that, the art of the "backward" Nanay and other nineteenth-century Amur tribes were an enigma thought to have been borrowed from elsewhere. The archaeological materials alone showed that this decorative art had developed locally over at least five thousand years. Developing continually, it had its own particular roots, its sources and developmental traditions.

Of course, one must not insist that these ancient artistic forms came down to our time fully and unchanged. The Amur people have gone through a long and complex pathway of development since Neolithic times. The Liao and Pohai states—the Jurchen empire—have risen and fallen. These historical events could not fail to influence the art of Amur peoples. However, it is more important for us to establish the fact that the basis of this art and its mythological coloring had its local origins since most ancient times. [It was a regional development paralleling others in east Asia from Jomon in Japan to Yang-shao on the upper Hoang-ho.] At the same time, the fact must be noted that certain ornamental designs, specifically the masks, have ties to a wide circle of cultures. A certain broad similarity to the Jomon culture of Japan and to Oceanic decoration can be observed; A. Middendorff (1860–69:I 747) remarked on this in the nineteenth century. The skull-like mask representations have explicit resemblances to the archaic style of petroglyphs of the northwest coast of North America, specifically, those of the British Columbia sites of Cape Midge, Venn Passage, Return Channel, Torkelson Creek, and Fort Rupert (Okladnikova 1979:151–52, pls. 12–13). These petroglyphs are quite heterogeneous and of varying age. Yet clearly dominant among their subjects are anthropomorphic representations, especially masks, which would warrant detailed comparative study with Amur materials (Meade 1971; Lundy 1974).

The Neolithic Sculptures of Siberia

Neolithic sculptured objects are few; they come basically from burials in the Siberian forest zone. They are small, and executed in bone or stone.

I. T. Savenkov discovered the first such objects at Bazaikha near Krasnoyarsk (Sawencof [Savenkov] 1893:323–30; Okladnikov 1969:pl. 19). Three small bone figures of moose were found among other objects. One figure had bent legs; another had two forelegs and incompletely rendered haunches. The peculiarities of these sculptures are the massive, somewhat exaggerated heads with open jaws, as though the animals were bellowing (fig. 10). The nostrils and eyes are shown by a few strokes. In general, the heads are executed gracefully, only the jaws being somewhat carelessly done. This sculpture is realistic and has a definite resemblance to representations on petroglyphs.

The most vivid examples of realistic sculpture are the bear figure from Samus' and the birds from the Yaysk cemetery (Matyushchenko 1963:102, pl.2; 1961). The bear figure is carved from sandstone (fig. 11, no. 1). The animal is seated. Its snout is realistically rendered; the lips, nostrils, and sharp bend of the forehead are shown. The eyes and ears are made by a sharp instrument. The entire figure is executed with a soft plasticity. The bear figure from Burial 6 of the Old Moslem Cemetery near Tomsk is entirely different. The animal is shown running (fig. 11, no. 3).

Among the Neolithic works from the forest and forest-steppe zones of the Ob' are a swan figurine carved from bone (Ordinskoye cemetery) and a fish figurine, the latter from the Baraba steppe. Miniature figurines were discovered in the Neolithic burials of Vas'kovo cemetery in the Kuznetsk Basin (Borodkin 1967). Among these were a bear figurine of bone, a very small animal head carved from a (bird) long bone, an equally miniature moose head, and the figure of an unidentified animal with two heads turned in opposite directions. The last represents something between a bear and a moose.

The little bear and the moose head are executed with special feeling, quite realistically and expressively. The soft outlines of the snout and eyes are communicated by barely noticeable depressions; the ears protrude, while the mouth is delineated by an almost straight line. These figures are among the artistic creations of Neolithic tribes. In contrast, the two-headed figurine from Vas'kovo, among others, is executed in a conventionalized way.

High convention governs the stone and fired-clay bear figures from Neolithic settlements of the Far East (Vasilevskiy and Okladnikov 1980). The animals are shown in various poses: standing, sitting, or holding a fish in their paws. This development is not accidental, for the bear cult is brought to its greatest development on the Amur. It undoubtedly arose in the Neolithic and continued, with some changes, to the nineteenth century. Among the Nivkhi [Gilyak], Ul'chi, Orochi, Nanay [Goldi], and Sakhalin Ainu this ceremonial complex is known as the "Bear Festival." It consists of a series of activities: The captured bear cub is fed in a cage for three or four years. Then, in winter, a grand celebration with ritual games and contests is organized. At the end of the festival the ceremony of parting with the animal is performed. The bear is refreshed and informed of the good care it has been given. The celebrants march in solemn procession. Then the bear is killed by an arrow. The bear is honored as a holy animal, as a tribal ancestor, as half beast, half person.

Ethnographic materials show multiple levels of meaning in this ritual. At one level, it is an expression of the battle of the cosmic forces. Divine properties are attributed to the bear, while his origins are tied to the concept of the "Son of Heaven." Light is thrown on this by the interesting investigation of words for "bear" in Siberian languages made by G. N. Potanin. Evidently, among a number of Turkic and Mongolian peoples, the meaning of "bear" embodies the words "thunder," "mountain," "sky," and "shaman's drum." Most frequently, there is a blending of "bear" with "thunderer," the personification of the thundering sky.

The bear figurines and the bear figures on petroglyphs show that deep in the Neolithic forests, beliefs about the bear and his mythic powers were being formed. This included the bear epic and cult retained in historic times by Amur peoples and the Evenki [Tungus]. According to one legend of this epic, the bear in ancient times preferred earth to heaven. His heavenly father was angered by this attitude, so that he ordered his son to remain forever on earth, and covered him with an animal's hide.

On this mythological basis, the bear was reckoned to be the totemic ancestor of many Siberian peoples. According to the report of V. G. Bogoraz-Tan, the Lamut [Eveny] of the last century called him "Grandfather," more exactly the brother of the remote ancestress Dantra. Thus, Lamut hunters would surround a bear den and, before frightening him, hold hands and sing: "Grandfather Bear! Our Grandmother, your older sister Dantra, has commanded, saying to you, 'Do not fight us. Die!' "

Ritual relationships to the bear were expressed in the past by many Siberian people. For example, the Ostyak [Khanty] would skin a bear most carefully, since this was his fur coat (*shuba*). The Lapps would thrust a piece of salt fish in the mouth of a slain bear. They would ask him not to say that he was not fed. If other bears came, they too would be fed. The dread, carnivorous power of the bear was the basis of various superstitions. Bears were surrounded with more mysteries than moose. Among the Orochi, for example, everything connected with the bear was taboo, for bears were believed to be former people.

Moose and bears were the basic artistic subjects in a wide area of forested Eurasia during the Neolithic. Such a wide distribution and representational uniformity suggest the presence of a most ancient philosophical-mythological substratum to the art. Evidence to this effect may be found in animal sculptures from Scandinavia (Hällström 1938), in the Olenostrovskiy cemetery of northwest Russia (Gurina 1967), in Neolithic sites of the Urals (Eding 1940), and in Siberia. This unity is also observable in the ways of artistic execution of the basic images. Here was a distinctive, fully determined school of artistic creativity, with its own techniques and expressions for sculpture. At the same time, it is important to note that Neolithic sculptures, in their subjects (moose, bear, birds) as well as in their artistic forms, closely resemble petroglyphic representations. Both are embodiments, with different artistic means, of one school of art. The basic difference lay in the different types of objects that were created. Drawings on cliffs created immobile, stable spiritual monuments, clan and tribal sanctuaries within nature. The small sculptures were mobile; it was always possible to have them with one. These were amulets, receptacles of desire.

North Asiatic Petroglyphs

Northern Asia is a region where more representations on cliffs are found than anywhere else in the world. They form a considerable part of world artistic culture. They are distributed along the banks of Siberian rivers and on rocks in the mountain valleys of the Altay and Tuva. Many relate to the Neolithic and Bronze ages.

Contemporary knowledge of North Asiatic petroglyphs permits us to delineate several large culture-historical and artistic zones: (1) the forested regions; (2) the Sayan-Altay uplands; (3) the upper Yenisey and Khakas-Minusinsk regions; (4) the Baykal and Transbaykal; (5) the Amur; and (6) northeast Asia. The subjects of art in each of these zones differ. In general, these zones coincide with the large culture-historical areas currently defined for the Neolithic, areas which differ largely in their historic patterns of economic development. Within each, there unfolded embryonic ethnic groupings which created the differences reflected in petroglyphic art.

Forest Zone

This was the most widespread and perhaps most typical of the north Asiatic zones. Here, over an enormous area, in the sixth to third millennia B.C., was formed the distinctive economy of forest hunters. It was perfected over several millennia. In the deep forest, this type of economy continued with little change up to the first millennium A.D. Its basis was the hunting of the moose, the basic dweller of the Siberian *taiga*. For thousands of years, moose meat served as the main source of subsistence, moose hides and sinews went for clothing, while arrow points, harpoons, awls, needles, and various household artifacts were made from the bones. In fact, this animal played about the same role in the lives of Neolithic inhabitants of northern Asia that the mammoth had in the Paleolithic period. This economic peculiarity was reflected in the art and the world concepts of the forest hunters. That the moose was the primary subject of art was therefore to be expected. The north Asiatic petroglyphs are de facto illustrations of a moose epic. These animals were shown in various poses, in real-life situations, such as scenes of hunting and reproduction, and in mythic contexts.

The most typical sites of the representative art of the forest zone are the petroglyphs on the banks of the Tom', Angara, and Lena rivers. In the western part of this territory is situated a famous assembly of representations, the Tom' River petroglyphs (fig. 12). Interest in this site, which has achieved worldwide notice, has not abated in the three hundred years since its discovery by Russian people. As early as 1730, P. J. Stralenberg had published in Stockholm the first drawings of the Tom' River petroglyphs. Since then, many scholars—G. F. Miller, S. P. Krasheninnikov, J. G. Gmelin, P. Pallas, V. V. Radlov, and others—have engaged in studying this outstanding site. Currently, it is a protected national monument.

In Neolithic antiquity, this cliff was a cultic place. At its base, on a stone ledge, the ancient hunters evidently conducted clan festivals in honor of their ancestors, spirits protecting the clan animals, and the omnipotent sun. They represented the reproduction of animals, scenes of successful hunts, and the gaining of spirit favors in religious spectacles, dances, and songs. Evidently these festivals took place in the spring, since concentric circles representing the sun are found among the drawings (figs. 50, 51) (Okladnikov and Martynov 1972:255; Martynov 1966:33; 1970:22).

The drawings, pecked by an able human hand and incised into the rock, are simple and truthful. They transmit in lively fashion the image of the basic *taiga* dweller, the mighty moose. In these drawings, the animal's fundamental features—the immense chest, the characteristic hump of the muzzle, the fleshy lips, the long thin legs, and the distinctive back hump—are brought out with amazing skill. Many drawings are distinguished by masterly execution. Among them are the remarkable depictions of lightly, timidly treading moose, and of bounding deer on the upper rock of the Tom' River assembly. On this upper rock, too, are pecked drawings of an owl and a crane. These are so correct and precise that even their feathers can be sensed (fig. 33).

On the Lena, the most remarkable assembly of representations is on the Shishkino cliffs, a true "picture gallery" of ancient *taiga* art. It is a site of unique culture-historical importance, with over a thousand representations and extraordinary compositions (fig. 13) (Okladnikov 1959, Okladnikov and Zaporozhskaya 1959). Lower on the Lena, from its juncture with the Olekma, Markha, Markhachan, and Sinyaya down to the Aldan, is another province of petroglyphic art, the Middle Lena (Okladnikov and Zaporozhskaya 1972). (See map 2, A.) In all the art of forest-zone petroglyphs, moose representations greatly predominate, numbering thousands. Along with them are depictions of bears, anthropomorphic figures, masks, and birds.

Petroglyphic sites are known at twenty places on the Angara River, from its sources to the mouth of the Kamenka River, almost at the juncture with the Yenisey (figs. 14, 15). Noteworthy are the drawings at Verkhnyaya Buret' village, at the town of Svirsk, on Maraktuy Island, and on the so-called Kamennyye ostrovy (Stony Islands), the last being the largest assembly. On the Lower Angara, petroglyphs are known at the village of Manzi, on Ushkaniy island, and elsewhere (Okladnikov 1966:321) (see map 2, B.)

Each great group of representations of this zone has its own, inimitable appearance, indivisibly tied to the past of a particular population. At the same time, all are united by the predominance of moose representations.

Altay-Sayan Province

In the villages of the Gornyy Altay [High Altay] and Tuva, the distribution of petroglyphs differs from that of the forest zone. Large surfaces covered with representations are rare here. Instead, drawings are scattered on boulders in secluded places, often far from water or river banks. The most significant of the known assemblies are in the Yelangash Valley and in the huge complex of representations on the cliffs of the Karakol river valley, both in the southern High Altay (Okladnikov et al. 1979:135; 1980:139; 1981:145). In the latter area, groups of representations are scattered on separate boulders for many kilometers. Pecked and incised representations are also known in other localities of the High Altay: at Kuyus'; at Belyy Bom, where figures of goats and other animals are preserved; on the northern slopes of the Terekta ridge in the Ursul river valley; in Dyan-Del canyon; and near the village of Kulada (Khoroshykh 1947; Minorskiy 1951; Frolov and Spiranskiy 1967). (See map 2, C.)

The basic peculiarity of this artistic province is the predominance of representations of goats (ibex) and sheep (fig. 16). Also typical for this region are representations of yaks, cattle, horses, and deer. Moose representations are rare. Among carnivores, wolves and panthers are shown. Male and female anthropomorphic figures and depictions of hunters are especially interesting. In drawings from the beginning of our era, herdsmen, horsemen, various symbolic marks, and battle scenes are shown.

The petroglyphs of the High Altay are part of the spacious central and inner Asiatic (Mongolian) province of rock art (Novgorodova 1984). Its representations differ sharply from those of the *taiga*, and are linked to the living conditions of ancient hunters and pastoralists of mountain valleys, steppes, and deserts.

The Upper Yenisey

The petroglyphs of this zone were first given monographic study early in this century (Savenkov 1910). On the Yenisey, bordering Khakasia and the Minusinsk Basin, the most significant ancient assemblies are known in the following localities: Shalabolino (figs. 17, 18, 19), Oglakhty (a complex of several large assemblies), Ust' Tuba, Cheremushnyy Log [Ravine], Tepsey, and Sukhanikha. In the upper reaches of the Yenisey [within Tuva] are well-known pictographs on the Kemchik River, at the mouth of the Malyi Bayan Kol, Synn Chyurek; in the Sayan Canyon (Mugur Sargol); at the mouth of the Chinga River; and at other places (Devlet 1976b:119; 1980a:264; Sher 1980:185–94).

The petroglyphs of this region are rather numerous yet difficult to categorize. They do not express such sharp differences in subject matter as those evident between the petroglyphs of the Altay and the forests. The variety of these sharply different regions can be sensed in the upper Yenisey but, at the same time, there is much that is inherent only to this region. The representations found in the upper Yenisey, where masks, goats, and anthropomorphic figures predominate (fig. 20), can be differentiated from those in the Minusinsk Basin, in which moose figures prevailed in early Neolithic times. Yet both sub-regions have much in common with the Neolithic representations of the Angara. In later times, in the Bronze Age, new subjects appeared in the upper Yenisey: masks, carts, fantastic beings, and bulls. Analogous representations on early Bronze Age slabs date this material.

Transbaykal

Like the Altay-Sayan upland, this large region of rock art lies on the borders of northern and inner Asia. It comprises the steppes of the Transbaykal (fig. 21), and should include the representations on the cliffs of Lake Baykal, at least in part (fig. 22) (Okladnikov 1974:125; Okladnikov and Zaporozhskaya 1969–70). In general, the petroglyphs of this region cluster in geographical groups, especially within the Selenga River basin (Dzhida, Kyakhta, Selenga, Uda, Chita, Bichura). These groups have only a topographical significance; stylistic differences cannot be traced.

In this region, among a mass of different representations, drawings of birds are particularly characteristic. Although somewhat schematic, they show accurately the images of falcons, eagles, kites, and hawks. These petroglyphs show simplified body treatments; quadrangular enclosures ("courtyards"); groups of anthropomorphic beings, often schematic; crosses and circles. Analogies from ethnographic materials establish the special religious function of the petroglyphs of this region, their association with the cults of predatory birds (eagle, falcon) and fertility rites among steppe herders of the Bronze Age (Okladnikov and Zaporozhskaya 1969–70:II, 90–128).

Lower Amur

A special province of primitive art is represented by the drawings pecked out of basaltic blocks along the lower course of the Amur and Ussuri rivers, and on the Razdol'noye River west of Vladivostok. Assemblies of drawings have long been known in this region. For example, Richard Maak investigated, in 1855, depictions on the rocky shores of the Ussuri, and at Sheremetyevo. Also in the nineteenth century, the orientalist P. Kafarov, as well as F. Busse, L. Kropotkin, and P. Vetlitsin, studied the Amur petroglyphs. The rock representations at Sakachi Alyan village and Kalinovka were studied at the end of the nineteenth century by the American orientalist Berthold Laufer and by Gerard Fowke, a member of the Jesup expedition of New York's American Museum of Natural History (see map 2, F).

Laufer published the first note in the scientific literature on the Amur petroglyphs in 1899. In it, he wrote that at the Goldi hamlet of Sakachi Alyan, on the Amur, were found many boulders covered with representations. The pictures, in Laufer's words (1899:746), depicted "human faces . . . animal bodies." Laufer also mentioned three dragon figures and made the first reference to the Nanay (Goldi) legend of the three suns and the Great Archer, which is directly tied to the Sakachi-Alyan cliffs. The valuable drawings at Sakachi Alyan were fully studied and published by A. P. Okladnikov only in our time (1968, 1971, 1981).

The Sakachi-Alyan petroglyphs are original both in subject matter and style. Here, on the banks of the Amur, the distribution of realistic art typical of the neighboring forest zone ends. For Amur art, a tendency toward ornamentalism is characteristic. Spirals, concentric circles, and plain circles are the typical component parts and most important formational elements of rock art of the Amur and Ussuri.

The representations are pecked and then smoothed in grooves of varying depth. The drawings, therefore, have the appearance of bas relief and high relief. Images executed in this way, further smoothed by time and water and blended in color and texture with the rock itself, appear as though made by a blunt tool on soft materials. This recalls the Nanay legend celebrating the first appearance of these remarkable representations. It states that, in the distant past, there was not one sun but three, which generated so much heat that the rocks were soft as wax. It was possible to draw on the surface with a finger. A mythical ancestral hero drew these rock pictures. This continued until another mythical hero, a giant, shot out two suns with his mighty bow. Only one luminary remained, nature quieted, and the rocks cooled, retaining forever the representations borne on their surfaces.

The subjects of the Lower Amur petroglyphs are remarkably stable in image and style. Five basic subjects can be isolated: masks, birds, snakes, boats, and reindeer. The central place in the Sakachi Alyan representations belongs to the mysterious facial images or masks, which are of a unified style and form (fig. 23). These are not true faces, but conventionalized, abstract depictions that are quite varied in their combination of different signs. They can be grouped only by the form of the facial features: oval; egg-shaped, with a narrowed end downward; heart-shaped, with a bent upper part; or circular. Masks of trapezoidal or, very rarely, quadrangular form are encountered. Masks with an oval upper part and a straight-sided base can be distinguished. Many masks are greatly widened at the top, where large circular eyes are found. Some resemble ape heads; some, skulls. Finally, so-called "partial masks" can be identified. They lack an outer perimeter and have only such details as eyes in the shape of two circles or ovals.

The masks are compiled of different elements, which are arbitrarily called "eyes, mouth, and nose," and which are communicated by various means, creating faces that range from realistic ones—almost portraitlike in extreme cases—to very abstract ones, simplified to mere circles and stripes. Fundamentally, realistic anthropomorphic masks are lacking at Sakachi Alyan.

Animals are represented by several strange figures which are difficult to identify. Figures that might arbitrarily be called tigers are most noteworthy. Their bodies are marked by transverse stripes. They have long tails. An important place among the representations unquestionably belongs to snakes with flexible, wavy or spiral bodies. They are incised on rocks separately from other drawings or also become part of larger compositions.

As mentioned earlier, primacy on Amur petroglyphs belongs not to animals but to man or, more precisely, anthropomorphic images—masks—which comprise the distinctive feature of this region. The bulk of these representations, it is now known, relate to the Neolithic. This deduction is the result of extensive archaeological excavations. Analogies to the Amur petroglyph masks appear, unexpectedly, on Neolithic pottery from sites in this region.

Northeast Asia

In recent years, petroglyphs have been discovered in the northeastern part of the Asiatic mainland, in the Aldan River basin, and in Chukotka at Pegtymel' (fig. 24). These are distinctive. In them are shown scenes of sea-mammal hunts and mysterious anthropomorphic figures with mushroom-shaped headgear. As a whole, they resemble mushrooms and there-

---

fore have received the designation of *mukhomory* (*fly agaric*, the narcotic mushroom utilized to induce visions by shamans throughout northern Eurasia) (Dikov 1971:131; 1979:157–59). In fact, this rock art is part of a circumpolar, arctic zone.

Petroglyphs of the interior of this zone, which have been discovered in the Aldan River basin, display a closeness to those of the Middle Lena. [Recently discovered sites and their locations are given below (Mochanov et al. 1983).]

River	Site	Mochanov Number	Location	
Amga	Siibikte	153	59° 45' N	128° 45' E
	Tyympy	154, 155	59° 55' N	129° 00' E
	Munduruchu	156, 157	60° 02' N	129° 10' E
	Ilim-Orgu-Yuerkh	158	60° 05' N	129° 50' E
	Ukaan	159, 160	60° 08' N	129° 50' E
	Onneyu	163	60° 15' N	130° 15' E
Aldan	Suon Tit	11, 12	58° 05' N	123° 35' E
	Yennyuyes	42	58° 55' N	128° 20' E
	Balaganaakh	43	58° 58' N	128° 20' E
	Tympyya	77	60° 03' N	133° 50' E
	Ust' Maya	84	60° 28' N	134° 30' E
Maya	Talaya	102	58° 35' N	134° 35' E

Investigators have attributed the ancient layer of these rock drawings to the Neolithic period, the fourth to third millennia B.C. (Okladnikov and Mazin 1979).

Realistic representations of moose, with a tendency toward an exact rendering of the animal's body, are present in the art of this area. Associated with them are generalized anthropomorphic figures, shown standing and frontally, with outstretched arms, and forked lines on their heads. Boats accompany these representations. Also encountered are plus marks, stripes, crosses, and vertical stripes in groups. The last evidently are enclosures for the capture of animals.

These Yakutian petroglyphs reflect complex cultural and ethnic contacts with an extensive area of the forest, reaching from the Lena basin to the Amur, and with the south from the Pacific Ocean to Lake Baykal.

The Style and Technology of the North Asian Petroglyphs

A well-defined art style was developed in the north Asian Neolithic. The ancient master craftsmen achieved considerable perfection in representing the profile silhouette of animals. At the same time, we are convinced that these artists did not know many other ways of representing animals.

Such stylistic paucity was characteristic of ancient art in general, including the colored murals of ancient Egypt and the drawings on Egyptian papyri. Yet, the ancient artist skillfully and in his own way used the contrast between the pecked surface of the rock and the untouched base rock. He used color differences and lines in relief, taking into account the illumination of the drawings and even cracks in the rock. In this fashion, simple, cartoon-like drawings received traits of three-dimensional representation, reminiscent of contemporary high relief.

It is essential to note that these representations were literally fused with the background cliff. They would be difficult to tear out of their natural surroundings. The creators of the petroglyphs adapted the images to the bends and projections of the rock, skillfully using the color and lighting of the cliff. Sometimes they used the natural flaws of the cliff for intensifying, for example, the representation of an animal's eye, mouth, or antler.

The creators of the petroglyphs overwhelm us with the freshness of their world perceptions, their capacities to seal in rock concisely and accurately what they saw and experienced. In most petroglyphs, a single line traces the outline of the animal, yet its essential features are transmitted. Moreover, a third dimension is often suggested in animal representations. Such a harmony was achieved by a deepening of lines for those body parts which had to be shown projecting outward, or by the widening of contour lines wherever massiveness and volume had to be emphasized. Through such simple artistic means the massive lips of a moose, for example, were shaded. Or, desiring to show the depth of an animal's jaws, the ancient master craftsmen would leave a contrasting bulge in them.

In certain cases, for example, in the Tom' River petroglyph, the neck and chest of an animal would be shaded by transverse, somewhat oval stripes. This produced a clearly perceptible feeling of mass and power in a straining neck. The artists would use similar methods to emphasize another feature of the animal's figure—its loose-hanging, capacious belly. For this purpose, semicircular stripes descending from the spine were drawn on the upper part of the flanks. It is possible that this signified a pregnant moose, emphasizing the protruding, heavy belly. The thin, long, yet enormously powerful legs of the moose were drawn in the Neolithic period with equal attention. Many animals were shown running lightly. This was conveyed by a defined artistic manner: the head is shown raised and leaning forward, the neck stretched out, and the legs slightly extended.

Unquestionably, before us are real, in most cases highly artistic, works of representative creativity. Here a definite style of art is noticeable, a manner which contemporary artists might envy. In this connection, the central composition of the Tom' River petroglyphs is dynamically expressive and most interesting. The animals move in a solid mass with raised heads, as though climbing a hill. Their movement is majestic and unhurried, yet their entire pace is witness to the tension of a cautious animal (fig. 12). The ancient hunter of the Siberian *taiga* most likely saw them in such a state.

Seeking to transmit precisely the image of an animal, the ancient craftsmen sometimes created true masterpieces that were full of charm and distinctive beauty. These images convey, as it were, not only the animal's body but its soul, its fearful alertness and mood. Certain depictions deserve attention in this regard. First is that of the galloping, leaping deer on the Tom' River petroglyph. This can be compared with the best examples of Assyro-Babylonian art. Its economical, expressive quality has no equal in primitive art. Second, the owl figure, majestic and still, communicates wisdom. Its feathering is shown with unusual artistry by small triangular dents (fig. 33, no. 2). And third, the crane is expressive and graceful. It is true to life and charming, with a jewel-like, thin, long beak, equally thin legs slightly bent at the knee, and a gracefully bent neck. The slightly wavy line of the spine indicates the bird's feathers. The drawing can indeed be felt (fig. 33, no. 1).

The principal creative object of the Neolithic forest artists was game. For this reason, the drawings represent the world of the hunters, basically moose hunters. But human representations, or even figures in which something human can be surmised, are rare. Their execution, when it occurs, lacks realism as a rule. Human traits can barely be caught in them. Many are allotted animal or bird characteristics, for instance, heads with projecting ears, sharp snouts, or three-clawed bird legs.

The Petroglyphs as Vignettes of Life

The petroglyphs of the forest zone and the upper Yenisey are particularly interesting for the portrayal of key activities and typical events. Two ideas vital to life are basically communicated in early Neolithic representations: animal reproduction and successful hunting. It is therefore not coincidental that, within the mass of animal drawings, there is a predominance of those of hornless females in whose wombs new life is being created. Among the drawings are those which show animal copulation rather prosaically and in customary ways. Often, however, an anthropomorphic being is shown in the petroglyphs taking part in this act so important to life. Man, attracted by his desires, filled with concern for good fortune, takes part in this process himself—or, more exactly, it is an anthropomorphic being, an ancestor and protector of the clan that does so. Before us are quite realistic vignettes of a cult of fertility in a distinctive incarnation of the consciousness of forest hunters.

Among these depictions a scene of reproduction on the Tom' River petroglyph stands out (fig. 25, no. 1; see also a comparable drawing from the Angara, fig. 25, no. 2). A female moose stands in a typical copulating position. Behind her is an anthropomorphic figure. They are in a sexual act. The anthropomorphic being has thin, almost beast-like legs, and a head quite unlike a human's. One fact is important: the anthropomorphic being fertilizing the moose cow is holding in his hand a heavy wand (*kolotushka*). The image of the god Thor comes readily to mind. Here, in any case, is an ancient divinity, a protector of animals, who is capable of joining their reproduction and preservation. These strivings, embedded in religious cults, have vivid reflections in other petroglyphic drawings.

The simplest and most explicit of these is a very interesting composition, also from the Tom' River petroglyph. A solid mass of moving and bellowing moose cows is represented on a small, smooth surface. Only one moose is crowned with bifurcated antlers with small spikes. The moose are shown impetuously, boldly, without special detail. However, the principal figure here is again an anthropomorphic being who lifts himself over the cows. A male being with a blob for a head and protruding abdomen is shown. His arms are spread out widely to the sides. One arm terminates in a huge three-clawed bird appendage. This is a dynamic, naively simple scene (fig. 26).

No less expressive and simple in execution is a comparable scene: On the Fifth Rock among a multitude of animal and bird figures, one can distinguish a hornless female moose with open, roaring maw and ears laid back. The cow's legs are at once the legs of a man pictured in a lively and distinctive manner. Moose and man flow together in a sexual act (fig. 27). These figures have rather many analogies. Figures very similar in detail and fully analogous in interpretation are known from the Shishkino cliffs (Okladnikov 1959: figs. 23, 25), near Svirsk on the Angara, near the village of Srednyaya Buret', and also on the Angara (Okladnikov 1958:26).

The image of the squatting man is known in stone renditions as well. Among the full-relief animal figurines in the Neolithic burials at Bazaikha near Krasnoyarsk is such a representation. The same bending of the legs, but more fully expressed, characterizes figures in a series of Neolithic sculptures from north Russia and Finland (Foss 1952: 198–99, fig. 101), as well as the Urals (Eding 1940).

The idea of reproduction is expressed in various ways in the petroglyphs. Realistic scenes of the sexual act were not the sole means of expressing this. Often the male sex organ alone was pictured; often, female organs are shown in the form of an oval, narrowed below with a dot in the center and lines radiating out from it. To explain such ambiguous signs, it is important to note that unexpectedly close analogies to them are found in the classic sites of Paleolithic art. For example, almond-shaped ovals are known from La Ferrassie in France and other Paleolithic sites. Evidently such mysterious signs transferred from Paleolithic art to that of the Neolithic Siberian petroglyphs. (This conjecture becomes more plausible when cave paintings of Paleolithic type and, probably, age in the Mongolian Altay are brought to mind [Novgorodova 1984].)

In north Asiatic petroglyphs one encounters representations of animal births. The most interesting is shown on the Tom' River petroglyph (fig. 28). The moose cow stands in profile with legs set wide apart and head thrust forward. Through her vagina, a little moose calf is being born.

In these ways, the first and basic idea laid out in the many Neolithic drawings of the Siberian forest zone was the multiplication of animals. These true-to-life scenes also provided elements of magical action, in which an anthropomorphic, protecting deity took part.

The idea of a successful hunt, the assurance of success in hunting, was the second activity important for survival and was expressed with clarity equal to that of the reproduction images in these drawings. Hunting scenes are displayed in a series of representations. The most significant among them is a realistic drawing of enclosure-hunting for moose. A surround of branches stretches in a semicircle (fig. 29, no. 3), at the edge of which are represented people with drawn bows shooting at a swiftly running moose. Inside the enclosure are drawn two figures consisting of vertical stripes with transverse short lines resembling crosses. Evidently, they symbolize protecting spirits. This is a lively scene of animal hunting with all its peculiarities, its own tale of the hunting occupation, of the hunter's joy in success and disappointment in failure. It should also be noted that the enclosure on this petroglyph is represented peculiarly, as though from a bird's-eye view. Such a pictorial view is found in no other petroglyph.

This is not the sole picture of enclosure hunting. The oldest magical drawings of surrounds are known from pictographs on the Angara and Lena. Here, they appear to be executed by vertical stripes of red paint. Not whole enclosures but symbolic drawings of them are shown which, one supposes, their authors believed to provide hunting luck. The ancient master was so economical and succinct that, in most cases, he limited himself to the vertical poles of a surround, without other details or even the game itself.

Other methods of hunting are shown in the petroglyphs. Among the mass of drawings, most remarkable are their concise nature and yet their powerful perceptions of the great suffering of the wounded animals. In them is communicated not only the image of the moose, but more—its pain. They depict, in a manner of speaking, the animal's inner world, its fear and its dying convulsions.

The drawings show two hunting methods. In one case, the beast is shown caught in a noose. With trembling legs, it bellows fearfully in quivering anticipation of death (fig. 29, nos. 1, 2). Another picture is especially graphic. Here the moose, with one leg caught in a noose, raises his head tragically, its big jaws in a unique, sickly grimace. One feels that he bellows with pain. Other drawings represent animals with darts imbedded in their backs by some unseen hand (fig. 30). The act of wounding an animal is usually shown very simply. A long dart is thrust into the back, the neck is drawn forward, the jaws are open. The animals are shown in dying agony. Though mortally wounded, they still have strength; they bellow, they fight death.

The petroglyphs in fact show all the individual and collective forms of hunting known in very ancient times and further developed in the Neolithic, for example, in Mongolia (fig. 31).

The Tom' River petroglyphs portray a unique scene of the ancient Neolithic river-crossing method of hunting (*pokol*) (fig. 32). A solid group of moose is leaving the water with heads raised, bellowing. The animals are moving straight toward a man standing before them. Here, as in other drawings, basic attention is given to the man's actions. This is a scene of killing animals. The man holds in his hand some long object, probably a spear, which deeply pierces the moose. The moose roars, its enormous jaw open, distorted with pain. Below, by the man's legs, is the figure of a lifeless animal.

Another subject draws attention, a man skiing. This theme is known, but not widely, on other Eurasian Neolithic petroglyphs, for example, from Zalavruga on the White Sea (Savvateyev 1970), and from Tjoma in Norway (Kühn 1962–63, 1). The man has skis on his feet (fig. 55); in one hand he holds a single pole, in the other is a circle, evidently a noose. A number of his traits are amazing, especially his animal head. The Norwegian petroglyph also shows an animal-headed skier. This too is evident in the Angara River petroglyph of a skier copulating with a moose (fig. 25, no. 2). It may be that all three represent not real but mythical "cosmic hunters" trailing "cosmic game," perhaps the sun. According to the mist-shrouded legends of the Yakut, Ostyak [Khanty], and certain other Siberian peoples, this "cosmic hunter" commands supernatural powers of transforming himself into a person or animal, most often a bear. Yet on his feet are fully real ancient details of hunting equipment, skis. The petroglyphs show the Siberian way of skiing with one pole, which is practiced by hunters to this day.

Sacred Birds

Bird representations are found among the Neolithic petroglyph drawings of Siberia (fig. 33). They are especially numerous in those of the Transbaykal in the Neolithic era. Nevertheless, birds scarcely had much of an economic role. Often, birds totally without use for subsistence are shown. Thus, the Transbaykal petroglyphs show eagles and falcons in abundance.

In general, bird images are not new in primitive art. Drawings and sculptures representing birds appeared in the Siberian Paleolithic. Owls of Paleolithic age are known, for example, from the cave vaults of Trois Frères in France (Bogayevskiy 1934). In this way, birds in Eurasian Neolithic art may be judged part of a Paleolithic tradition. Moreover, it may be stated that birds are represented not only in petroglyphs but in Neolithic cemeteries and settlements, for example, the cemeteries of Bazaikha, Yaysk, and Vas'kovo (Matyushchenko 1963:97–103). But it happens that the most common birds in eastern Siberian petroglyphs are eagles and falcons in flight, with characteristic tails and predatory beaks (fig. 21), and proudly strutting geese, for example, at Sagan Zaba on Lake Baykal (Okladnikov 1974: pl. 16). These are not vignettes of real life but examples of Siberian or world mythology.

It is worth pausing to consider representations of ducks, geese, and swans, with some of whom an egg is commonly shown. Let us turn to this in view of facts from world mythology. It is enough, for example, to recall the image of the sacred goose of Egyptian myths (Mat'ye 1940) or the sacred geese in the burial chambers of Egyptian notables as evidence of the rather wide veneration of geese in agricultural Egypt. The Egyptians associated the origins of the sun god Ra and the whole universe with a bird image. On the hillock which emerged from the sea of the initial chaos was a nest with a goose egg from which Ra emerged (Book of the Dead, Mat'ye 1940). In later times in Egypt, the goose was thought to be an incarnation of the earth god Geb.

At the same time, the falcon or hawk symbolized Ra, who was shown with the head of a hawk. The goddesses Mut and Isis were symbolized by the vulture, which represented protectiveness and was therefore displayed above the statues of Egyptian pharaohs. Other sacred birds were the heron and ibis, which had the power to find the road to the home of the dead, and which were sometimes personifications of the human soul. Human souls were also personified by falcons or swallows.

A part of these myths continued in later times and other places, for example, in Rome. In general, historical and ethnographic data show that birds, especially predators and wading birds, were recognized by many peoples as divine beings or, in any case, as symbols of relationships with the world of spirits and shades in distant celestial or post-funerary regions. Swift running, high flying, arriving in the spring from somewhere in the distant south and departing thither in the fall, all these traits permitted people to perceive birds as something mysterious and puzzling, to recognize their special capacities as intermediaries between man and spirits.

In this way, sacred birds are rather widely known in the mythology of the world's ancient peoples. These are basically the same birds seen in the drawings of the Siberian petroglyphs. Clearly, not all birds were equally valued by ancient peoples. Economically rational concepts were associated only with water birds, which as game were basic sources of subsistence for many peoples. In other cases, the attraction must have been the early perception of birds' special capacities, such as the ability of owls and great horned owls (filin) to see at night. Generally, there is the characteristic concept in primitive thought of the triple division of the world into middle, lower, and upper horizons, hence, of birds as representatives of the upper world and its inhabitants.

It is quite possible that birds represented with eggs in the petroglyphs are examples of the Siberian variant of the creation myth widely known among the native peoples of Scandinavia, northern Asia, and North America (Longfellow 1956). According to the ancient Kalevala epic, the universe arose from an egg laid by a wondrous duck on the knees of the Air Maiden Il'matar, on an island in the midst of the sea. The Earth came from the lower part of this mythical egg, while its upper part became the celestial vault (Lennrod 1956:77). Myths associating birds with creation of the world are found, for example, among such Siberian people as the Buryat. They believed that, initially, there was no land, but the bird Angata swam on the surface of the world ocean with her twelve young. Angata dived into the water and brought up land from its bottom. She brought black earth on her nose and clay in her feet. Thus the land was formed, and grasses and trees grew on it (Khangalov 1960:III, 7).

The images of cranes and herons in mythology are no less interesting. Wading birds are not shown just accidentally on the petroglyphs; in world mythology they are commonly the bearers of good news. The beginning of life stems from a gigantic crane striding a primeval world, according to some peoples. In Finnish, Germanic, and Slavic mythology, wading birds had a visible role and a sacred nature. Who does not know that a loving, kind attitude toward storks, for example, persists to this day? Legends of wise birds are distributed across continents. We meet them among the North American Iroquois, among whom the heron Shuh-shuh-ga is the guardian of wisdom. He proclaims the end of the day, brings good news, and anxiously communicates threatening dangers (Longfellow 1956:89–100).

Many peoples, including the ancient dwellers of the western Siberian forests, associated quite different ideas and concepts with images of night birds—the owls and great horned owls. In agricultural Egypt, owls were judged to be unclean birds, while the Greeks saw in them evil messages of death. According to Anuchin (1982:III, 143), nineteenth-century Yakuts nourished fearful superstitions regarding owls. It must be assumed that representations of the owl or horned owl on the Tom' River petroglyph had a similar character. The malevolent representations of these birds poised over the moose most likely were symbols of their death.

Cast metallic figurines of horned owls of the first millennium A.D. in

Siberia and the Urals have most likely the same kind of magical character. Although individual finds of these figurines have been made virtually everywhere in western Siberia, the largest collection of such idols was discovered in Glyadenovo cemetery [on the Kama River, ca. 59°N, 56°15′E]. There, among over a thousand bronze representations of people, animals, snakes, and birds, the most notable birds were great horned owls and eagles. These were represented *enface* with spread wings, sharp beaks, and round eyes. It is absolutely clear that these figures were not merely offerings. Each representation had a definite meaning. Evidently, here also the image of the great horned owl was associated with death (Spytsin 1901).

But owls are not evil in all folklore. In the Buryat epic, the great horned owl is sometimes a protector of children and the domestic hearth (Khangalov 1960:III, 39).

Great interest attaches to the series of representations of predatory birds (eagles, falcons) on Transbaykal petroglyphs (Okladnikov and Zaporozhskaya 1969–70). Images of the all-powerful eagle are widely known in world ethnography, including that of Siberian peoples.

The costumes of the nineteenth-century Siberian shamans bore images of the birds mentioned, as well as others, such as loons. (These images played important roles in shamanizing, including the purported recovery of stolen human souls.)

Boats, Snakes, and Images of the Underworld

Representations of boats are noteworthy in the Siberian petroglyphs. They are always associated with other drawings on the Tom' River, the Yenisey, the Angara valley cliffs, and the banks of the Lena (fig. 34). However, the number of boat drawings is significantly less than those of animals. Evidently, they appeared only at the end of the Neolithic, becoming characteristic in the Bronze Age.

These drawings are executed very schematically, only distantly resembling boats with people sitting in them. The boats are always represented by a horizontal line, sometimes with raised stern and bow. The passengers are also drafted in a primitive manner, in the form of vertical lines with small thickenings on the end, slightly reminiscent of human heads. Sometimes these lines terminate in bifurcated "horns" resembling, in a lively way, arms lifted in prayer. They may also represent horned headdresses. Perhaps in their drawings the artists were uninterested in the verity with which boats, their characteristics, and the persons sitting in them could be represented. Not form but content was basic. For ancient man it was sufficient in this case to depict the schema, the symbol of the boat. Sketched hurriedly and carelessly, these pictures nevertheless carried meaning, and were closely tied with other magical subjects, which we will discuss below.

Boats are characteristic, in general, of the drawings of the northern Neolithic of Eurasia. They are found on the petroglyphs of Lake Onega, the White Sea, Karelia, and Scandinavia. Three types of boats are encountered. Most are the typical Siberian representation of the boat by a horizontal line. Along with these are boats with moose heads on the prow. These are very rare in Siberia, but more characteristic of northern Europe. Finally, there are boats with huge extended ovals at the stern. These are, evidently, stylized moose muzzles. These details indicate that the boats in European and Asiatic petroglyphs, often thousands of kilometers apart and made by different peoples, do not vary randomly. They correspond to concepts common to this vast area.

It is more difficult, as always, to guess the semantic content of boat representations on the petroglyphs. But possibilities exist here also. At least two sources can be seen for boat representations: realistic and mythological. The first is associated with the meaning that boats had in the real life of north Asiatic hunters and fishermen. In the Siberian *taiga*, the boat was the basic, indispensable means of summer transportation. Economic and cultural ties came into being during the Neolithic within the basins of each of the great Siberian rivers, the Ob', Yenisey, Lena, and Amur. Corresponding cultural commonalities (*obshchnosti*) emerged.

Mythology reveals that, in many people's ethnographies, the interment of dead kin and the complex concepts of souls floating to the otherworld are associated with boats. According to the tenth-century traveler and colonizer of the Volga, Ibn Fadhlan, the Rus buried their warrior dead in boats. The roots of this ancient custom go even further into the depth of centuries, to dynastic Egypt, where there arose and splendidly flourished an agricultural religion of dying and reviving nature. One of its attributes was the "floating" of the dead, by river, to the underworld kingdom of Osiris. Following this concept, the Egyptians placed mummies on funerary boats and brought them to their burial sites. Such a funerary procession is shown, for example, on the Ani papyrus of the fourteenth century B.C.

It is fully probable that representations of boats on river banks in Siberia, Scandinavia, and Karelia also were associated with ancient concepts of souls floating toward the place of ancestral origins, the world beyond, following the setting sun. In Siberian shamanistic folklore a well-known image is that of the moose or reindeer accompanying the boat of the deceased in its journey by way of the river of death. These appear to be images of buck deer diving into the waters of death. Thus, the ideas and myths of the native Siberian population which appear at first glance to be local, arose in reality during ancient times from concepts existing in a wide area of northern Europe and northern Asia. They were parts of an ancient world outlook.

More than this, similar concepts are expressed in North America, notably in the Song of Hiawatha, an Iroquois myth restated by Henry Wadsworth Longfellow. Chibiabos, Hiawatha's brother, was summoned from death and honored:

> Ruler o'er the dead, they made him,
> Telling him a fire to kindle,
> For all those that died thereafter,
> Campfires for the night encampments
> On their solitary journey
> To the kingdom of Ponemah,
> To the dead of the Hereafter . . .

As he traveled, Chibiabos

> Crossed the melancholy river,
> On the swinging log he crossed it,
> Came unto the Lake of Silver,
> In the Stone Canoe was carried
> To the islands of the Blessed,
> To the land of ghosts and shadows.

> (Longfellow n.d.: 221; Russian trans.,
> Longfellow 1956, 5:130–31)

Apparitions on Siberian petroglyphs are interesting because they are commonly parts of a meaningful composition. Next to the boats on the Tom' River petroglyph is placed the drawing of a fantastic animal combining features of a bear and those of a crocodile or dragon (fig. 35). It has great gaping jaws, a huge body with a humped back, and short, heavy legs. The animal very distantly resembles a bear with an unusually long, even hypertrophied snout, one more like a crocodile's than a bear's. The drawing is purposefully placed among boats and other representations signifying the idea of death and the underworld. The general subject is clearly mythological. The monster on Shishkino cliff represents a close analogy, although it is a much clearer example (Okladnikov 1959:98).

A monster of this type with the features of a crocodile or dragon with gaping jaw is well known in the mythology of the Turkic and Mongolian peoples of northern and inner Asia, among whom the monster personifies the underworld. It is usually represented as a dragon or snake and is called *mantys* or *mangatkhay*. According to some legends, it swallows the sun, which dies at night to be reborn the next morning, to people's joy. Among other groups, it is the moon or stars that are swallowed.

These ancient myths, illustrations of which appear in the petroglyphs, were found equally among both forest-dwelling hunters and early agriculturalists. Similar myths, explaining the succession of day and night, sunrise and sunset, were known in Egypt (Mat'ye 1940:8–15). According to these myths, Ra, the sun, floats on the celestial Nile, on the vessel Mandzhet in the day. At night he transfers to the vessel Mesket. During his night travels, the god passes through twelve gates (corresponding to the twelve nighttime hours) which are guarded by snakes. But the god overcomes the snakes and, emerging from the underworld, continues his travels, now on the daytime vessel. In some variants, the sun is blocked by a crocodile swallowing him.

It is not accidental, evidently, that the monster is repeatedly shown next to boats of the dead and beside reindeer with reversed heads. The images are clearly tied to each other and to funerary rituals which, in turn, are related to the concepts among ancient peoples of "underworld dwellers"—the land of the dead, the transmigration of the souls of the dead, and of river-boat travel to another world, that of the ancestors. In this way, Siberian petroglyphic drawings, combining compositions of boats and monsters, are examples of the world outlook of ancient peoples.

Man, Anthropomorphic Beings, and Masks

Man appears constantly on the petroglyphs of northern Asia. But more accurately, it is an anthropomorphic being with a human body and animal or bird features which is shown. Sometimes, such beings are tied to activities with other representations; for example, in hunting scenes. The artistic execution of these figures is characteristically more conventionalized than that of animals.

Several stylistic groups of representations can be distinguished. There are anthropomorphic figures shown in hunting activities with drawn bows, nooses, or harpoons in hand, chasing moose or wild goats (ibex), holding reindeer, or impregnating animals (fig. 36). Characteristic for these human figures is the presence of various animal or bird features: pointed ears, narrowed snouts rather than human faces, triple-clawed bird feet. The second group consists of a very small group of female figures, often with sex organs designated, squatting with parted legs and extended arms. The basic aspect of these figures is the desire to emphasize the feminine essence of childbirth. The third group comprises well-known representations that only distantly resemble anthropomorphic figures. In fact, these schemas are very traditional and of one type. A figure is represented by a thin, vertical line, which stands for the body; above this, there is a thickening recalling the head; and, on the sides, huge circles connect with the body (fig. 37). Sometimes it is evident that these circles are arms placed on the hips. In any case, the style of these drawings is definite, strongly executed, and stable. Moreover, it is sharply different from the style of all other anthropomorphic representations. A fourth group is made up of small, stylized anthropomorphic figurines found in eastern Siberian petroglyphs. Commonly, these are chains of human figures apparently holding hands.

Two birdlike incised figures on the Tom' River petroglyph are unique. Before us are man-birds shown in ecstasy, bird beaks open, as though in motion, arms bent at the elbow, at least one hand like a three-clawed bird foot, and slightly bent legs with spurs at the heels, providing a dynamic whole (fig. 38). The figures bear a clearly expressed phallic nature. Another pair of figures, also from the Tom' River petroglyph, is generally similar, but even more conventionalized. Here the bodies are trapezoidal and appear to be dancing. Other details vary, with one figure multiply phallic (fig. 39). All these representations are in outline and turned to the right. They belong to the very beginning of the Bronze Age, well dated by comparison with birdlike representations from Tas-Khaza in the Minusinsk Basin that belong to the Okunevo culture of the late third and early second millennium B.C. (Vadetskaya et al. 1980:148; Leontyev 1978:88–118; Lipskiy 1961:271–78). They are distinctive in their conventionally expressive execution but share with drawings of the early Neolithic the basic idea of fertility.

The earlier figures, too, are shown in motion, dancing, excited, ready for sexual acts (figs. 40, 41). The roots of these figures are religious traditions that go back to deep Paleolithic antiquity, that inexhaustible wellspring of art. In 1912, M. Begouen discovered in the Cave of Three Brothers (*La grotte des trois frères*) in southern France a drawing of a dancing wizard with slightly bent legs. Here, among typical Paleolithic drawings of woolly rhinoceri, mammoths, cave bears, bison, and reindeer was represented, in a barely accessible place, a person with reindeer antlers on his head, a long beard, wolf ears, a tail, and owlish eyes (Begouen 1925, 1929; Bogayevskiy 1924). Other details are no less interesting: the wizard is shown in profile, and his body is bent far forward. The most important features of the Tom' phallic figures and the Paleolithic wizard coincide, as it were. Here is an illustration of how an idea, an image, a tradition born in the Paleolithic, can persist thousands of years later among north Asiatic hunters.

At the end of the Neolithic and in the transition to metal, which lasted longer in the forest than on the steppes, a general tendency toward symbolism can be observed. New subjects appear in art which indicate a growing complexity of worldview and changes in social life among primitive hunters. Of special interest for the history of art in this period are the distinctive guises [*lichiny*] or, more exactly, masks represented on stone. Masks are known on many petroglyphs in northern Asia, being especially numerous on the cliffs along the Amur, Angara, and upper Yenisey rivers and in the Transbaykal. They differ in detail, with each art region having characteristic masks of a defined style.

The masks of the Sakachi-Alyan petroglyphs are numerous and distinctive (figs. 42–46). They are softly polished on basaltic boulders. They are of varied types: some skull-like, others with enormous eyes, still others with transverse stripes, or with ears.

Heart-shaped mask representations are also known in the Tom' River petroglyph. One is particularly expressive (fig. 47). It is the sole drawing on the surface of the stone. Its wide, oval face ends in a sharp chin. Large circles with dots in their centers designate eyes. Below is one stripe, the mouth, and another crossing the whole face—a moustache or facial tattoo. A highly conventionalized mask also found on the Tom' River petroglyph consists of three spots, eyes and mouth, on the flank of a schematic moose figure (fig. 48).

Much more complex and detailed masks occur on the petroglyphs of the upper Yenisey (fig. 49) and eastern Siberia. No two glyphs are alike. Each is filled with various small details: transverse and vertical lines, circles, spiral figures, or hammer shapes. Yet these details form definite parts of a human face, an enormous toothy mouth, nose, eyes. But all this is combined in a special way in each case and not at all like a normal human face. These masks are augmented by various external elements such as wavy lines, ears, and triangles (Okladnikov 1966:176, pl. 32).

Petroglyphs as Ritual Places

The petroglyphs of northern Asiatic forests display with great power and clarity the thoughts and hopes associated with a hunter's life, the concern for luck among primitive hunters of the *taiga*. In them, vignettes of real life are accompanied by magical representations. Among these drawings, moose images predominate. This is explainable, first, by the exceptionally important role of this animal in the daily life of *taiga* dwellers. It was simply impossible to survive without them. The hunt for moose penetrated all lifeways, thoughts, and hopes.

The moose is the largest of the deer family. The body length of a grown male reaches over three meters; his height, over two meters. His antlers, shovel-shaped and spiked on the edges, have enormous power; all forest predators fear them. V. I. Iokhel'son [Jochelson] (1898:94) has written: "When a moose roams the forest, barriers do not exist for him. Throwing back his wide, shovel-shaped antlers, he breaks a path for himself everywhere. With his powerful chest he breaks tree trunks in his way. Seizing young trees with his antlers, the moose tears them out of the ground and throws them aside." For these reasons the forest hunters on the Lena, Yenisey, and Ob' called this forest giant by the honorific term "Great Beast."

Naturally, this attitude of respect for the moose, which evolved over centuries, developed because of not only his strength but his real significance. In ancient times, hunting this animal was the main basis of survival.

People ate its flesh, dressed in its skins, which were sewn together with its strong sinews, and used its bones for tools and utilitarian objects such as arrows, harpoons, awls, and ornaments. A moose carcass would yield up to six hundred kilos of meat. Here indeed are reasons for man's affection toward the moose. Moose therefore stood first in the beliefs and rituals of these ancient hunters. The image of the moose often assumed supernatural traits and magnitudes along with real ones.

Among the Evenki [Tungus], there were cliffs [*bugady*] that served as clan sanctuaries at which the most important social activities and public clan-worship were conducted. On such a site "depended the good fortune of the kindred" (Anisimov 1958:29). It was believed that the zoomorphic clan ancestor was hidden in the cliff (Anisimov 1958:29). A similar sacred character, inherited evidently from earlier hunters, was attributed to certain cliffs by herdsmen of the Altay and Khakasia. In Siberian ethnography generally, cliffs are held to be the dwellings of totemic divinities (Okladnikov 1959:54).

Unquestionably, certain cliffs were revered on this same basis in the past. Turned toward the south, illuminated by the sun, protected against the "evil eye," and difficult to reach, these were religious centers for nearby tribes. The Tom' River petroglyph was particularly significant in this regard. Below the levels with drawings was a wide stone ledge (figs. 50, 51). In former times, this platform was the very place where primitive mysteries honoring ancestors were played out, and where ceremonies and clan festivals were conducted. It is most probable that the large moose with clumsy stumps in place of legs, on whose flank a person's eyes and mouth are represented (fig. 48), is a portrait of that mythical ancestor to whom the rites were dedicated. The southern orientation of this and other petroglyphic sites is associated with solar signs, often in conjunction with figures of animals and birds. Correspondingly, rituals at petroglyphic sites commonly took place on the spring equinox.

In general, as indicated by ethnographic data, these festivals were not strictly religious. They were also tied to daily life, bearing a festive character. This is borne out by the description of one such ceremonial among a phratry (or group of associated clans) of nineteenth-century Ob' Ugrians [Ostyak or Khanty]. The first week, and sometimes a second, at the time of the winter solstice, was dedicated to the Old Man with Claws, the bear, the totemic ancestor of the phratry. During this part of the festival, songs were sung and sayings about the bear and the origin of people were recited. The Clan Ancestors appeared and performed their dances. Each ancestor had his own particular costume, song, and dance. After two weeks, a long pause ensued, during which there were dances from time to time, whenever people gathered together. The final and most interesting part of the festival took place during the spring equinox. At that time, in addition to "Bear Songs," "Bird Songs" were performed.

These celebrated how totemic ancestral birds flew north, built nests, and raised young, some of whom were part bird and part human. One of the concluding acts of the festival was a mock moose-hunt. One man dressed like a moose, while two others were hunters. The moose sought to escape, but the hunters overtook it and killed it (Chernetsov 1964:29; Ivanov 1934).

The *girkumki* ceremonies which the Evenki [Tungus] formerly conducted before the mating season of moose and deer (*Artiodactyla*) are of no less interest. The central figure of the ceremonies was the shaman (fig. 52). At first, in his mind, he "flew" over the entire *taiga* where animals were located. Later he "lured" the animals into the clan hunting areas. For this he supposedly assumed the appearance of a moose cow and led the bucks to the hunting areas. At the end of the ceremony, stuffed animal images (*chuchelo*) in reproductive poses were placed near the shaman's tent. Near these images, the magical *girku* dance was performed. It symbolized animal fertilization. In fact, it was a pantomime imitating the call of the bucks by the females during the mating season (Anisimov 1958:56).

This provides a basis on which to identify places with petroglyphs as primitive clan and tribal sanctuaries, as religious centers. Here, in ancient times, life pulsated and festivals took place. They included three component parts: ritual dances and pantomimes, songs and recitals, and the marking of drawings on sacred cliffs. From the recitals arose the basis of epic tales. From the petroglyphs emerged narrative and mythological scenes bringing down to our day the mysteries of these remote times.

Three-eyed Idols
and Enigmatic Masks 3

In the Steppes and Forests

In order to understand what happened in north Asian art during the "paleometallic epoch" (the Eneolithic and Bronze ages), we must turn first to the fundamental historical changes which took place during that time.

At the end of the fourth millennium B.C., the steppes of Eurasia, which stretch many thousands of kilometers from central Europe in the west to inner Asia in the east, were the scene of important historical changes. Here, a new economy of food production based on agriculture and animal husbandry was formed. It was, in fact, a revolution in economics and tribal histories comparable to the Neolithic revolution in other parts of the globe. Many factors facilitated this change, notably the geography of the steppes. Such ecological peculiarities of the steppes as grassy vegetation, the absence of extensive forests, a relatively dry climate, and negligible winter snow-cover promoted livestock raising as the basic form of productive economy. Primitive rationality and environmental adaptation led to the development here of seminomadic herding, with the predominance of sheep and goats in the herds, year-round maintenance on pasture, and seasonal migrations of limited scale. Both sedentary and seminomadic economies and lifeways were combined. (Flood-plain hoe agriculture developed in suitable areas.) Moreover, coincident with the dissemination of a food-producing economy in this region of Eurasia came the beginning of metallurgy.

Concurrently, fundamentally different culture-historical and economic ties arose in the Eneolithic as compared to the Neolithic. These crossed the steppes. The rivers, which had played a significant role in the Neolithic, ceased to have this function in the new epoch. All the main rivers, the Dnepr, Volga, Irtysh, Ob', and Yenisey, cut across the Eurasian steppe zone. In consequence, new means of transportation which were more suitable for the steppes—first carts and later mounted travel—now became primary.

In all, the Bronze Age, from the second half of the third millennium B.C. throughout the second millennium B.C., was marked by great increases in material production and cultural complexity. Two developmental trends are to be found. On the one hand, adaptation to local environments and resource patterns brought about the rise of numerous archaeological cultures and their variants. On the other, the new trade routes facilitated the extensive distribution of new artifacts such as bronze implements (including two types of sickles, socketed celts, Seyma-Turbino bronzes). Associated with this was the ascendancy of new metallurgical centers and the formation of cultural provinces on their base. These processes culminated in the formation of large culture-historical commonalities, the Catacomb, Timber Grave, and Andronovo cultures. As a characteristic historical phenomenon, cultures of the steppe influenced those of the forest, leading to the dissemination there of progressive economic activities: metallurgy, forest-type animal husbandry, and river flood-plain agriculture.

In the Bronze Age, a basically common ideology and religion formed among the ancient steppe tribes. In ways reflecting steppe-cultural peculiarities, this ideology embodied three worldwide dimensions of primitive materialistic philosophy: the cults of the sun, sacred animals (figs. 53, 54, 55), and nature (the Tree of Life, the restoration of life). These cults already are clearly evident in the early period of the steppes, for example, in Okunovo representations in Siberia and in the "solar" badges and plant ornamentations of the Catacomb and Andronovo cultures. In its turn, the development of a common ideological base facilitated a culture-genetic leveling and consolidation of tribes in the Eurasian steppe zone.

It is essential to mention another aspect of Bronze Age steppe cultures. The steppe world entered at this time into contact with the great ancient civilizations. These as yet weak ties were evidently with three areas, the Balkans, Caucasus, and central Asia.

But these abrupt changes in economics and world outlook took place essentially in the southern steppe part of northern Asia. In the depths of the Siberian forests and on the arctic shores of Asia, the foraging, hunting economies that had developed in the Neolithic still persisted. In this way, a partition of great scale and historical consequence took place at this time in northern Asia between southern herding peoples and the hunters and fishermen of the Siberian *taiga*.

Bronze Age art is represented by several genres: (1) rich decorative art, which survives, unfortunately, only on pottery and bronze artifacts; (2) petroglyphic art, which differs in subject matter and, in some places, technique from that of the preceding period; and (3) religious representations on gravestones and artistic metal castings. The last genre is new. (See map 3.)

Bronze Age Ornamentation

Here, we shall deal only with decoration on pottery and on metal objects. The differences in motifs between forest and steppe areas must be noted. Evidently, differences in lifeways were reflected in differences in art.

The Steppe

Siberian steppe pottery of the Andronovo and Karasuk periods (the second and early first millennia B.C.) was characterized by clearly geometric ornamentation with sharp zonal divisions (fig. 56). In Andronovo culture, different patterns characterized the shouldered bowl (*gorshok*) and the semicylindrical bowl (*banka*) (Maksimenkov 1978). The former has clearly profiled walls expanding from a narrow base to the wide shoulder, and then curving smoothly, via an indented neck, to an everted lip (fig. 57). The latter is more variable in shape but commonly widens from base to lip, which is not everted. An intermediate shoulder is weakly expressed or may be totally lacking (see fig. 58).

Ornamentation on shouldered bowls is sharply defined, clear, handsome, finished. The lip of the vessel is usually decorated with slanting or upright hatched triangles. The neck is predominantly decorated with horizontal grooves or lines of indentations. The shoulder and main part of the body are covered by an excellent textile pattern, a clear interweaving of broken lines, meanders, and triangles. The excellent regularity and saturation of this pattern suggest that it was applied with the aid of some device. All the decorative figures and interweavings were made by imprints of a small combed stamp, laid on in parallel three to six times. This was done so elegantly and precisely that it is hard to determine the beginning or end of a particular pattern.

The semicylindrical bowls are found in the same cultural contexts as the shouldered bowls, but they are decorated quite differently, by a toothed stamp or a slanting incision tool. The herringbone, an ornamentation characteristic of earlier periods, predominates. The entire surface is decorated; zoning is absent. Unquestionably, these vessels and their ornamentation have a local Siberian origin.

Here are two contrasting plans, designs, and means of ornamentation; two forms of pottery; two traditions. This is no accident. This reflects two lines of genetic and economic development. Ethnogenetically, it would be appropriate to connect the tapestrylike meanders with the most ancient Indo-Iranians of northern Asia. It is not surprising that on the bottoms of certain vessels, swastikas and solar circles are represented. The semicylindrical bowls with their plain ornamentation reflect a completely different genetic line. This is a local tradition. It is possible that these two kinds of wares and ornamentation reflected two types of economies, by now blended: agriculture and herding.

In the Karasuk period at the end of the second and beginning of the first millennium B.C., pottery decoration in the steppe became somewhat simpler (fig. 59). Meander patterns disappeared. There were fewer bands of decoration, and the execution of the decoration became simpler. At the same time, the initial decorative components—hatched triangles and diamonds—remained. Also, the designs were still executed with the drag-and-stab method, or else incised with a sharp instrument, probably a knife blade. Only the top of the vessel was now customarily decorated. [Figure 60 summarizes Andronovo-Karasuk continuities and changes in steppe pottery shapes and ornamentation.]

The Forests

Ornamentation in the Siberian forest zone presents a more complex picture (Kosarev 1981). In the deep interior regions of this zone, ornamental art developed on the basis of attainments in the previous Neolithic era. As a rule, ornamentation covered the entire vessel. It was quite varied. It consisted of stamp impressions generating slanting lines, little crosses, nets, and wavy lines, all encircling the vessel. Also noteworthy were zigzag "duck" figures closely resembling stylized representations of water birds. The ornamentation, in the Bronze Age, of the contact zone of forest and steppe was most complex. Both northern and southern elements were present here, as is particularly characteristic of the Yelovo culture. There, along with forest elements, triangles, diamonds, and even meanders were typical (Kiryushin and Maloletko 1979).

The drawings on vessels of the Samus' culture (fig. 61) were truly exceptional. The ornamentation proper consisted of vertical notches, and of quasi-geometric figures such as elongated diamonds and triangles. But this was not the basic artistic element characterizing this culture. Present on Samus' vessels were anthropomorphic representations—stylized heads with mouths and eyes indicated, and with long antenna-like projections. These figures were executed in a quasi-geometrical style, with heads in the form of triangles or circles, and bodies indicated by a pair of parallel lines, very abstractly. Isolated details were of the same style. They included bodies with transverse or vertical hatchings (Matyushchenko 1973:20–22).

The bronze artifacts of the Siberian forest zone are artistically interesting. They belong to the Seyma-Turbino type, distributed over an extensive area from eastern Europe to western Siberia, in the forests and forest-steppes (Bader 1964; Chernykh 1966, 1970). In this territory, lanceolate socketed arrowheads and knives occurred. Especially characteristic were bronze socketed celts with and without side "ears" [loops]. The typical ornamentation of these artifacts can be related in its components to the steppe. Its basis was rows of triangles or diamonds. Probably, this steppe influence in decoration was associated with the absence of local sources of metal in the forest. Raw materials had to be imported from the southerly, mountainous areas of Siberia, although the castings were local. This factor probably played a decisive role.

Okunevo Statuary

Stone statuary occurs on the steppes of Khakasia and the Minusinsk Basin, on the Yenisey (map 3), and in the valleys of the Altay. The pieces vary in dimensions and outline, resembling cigars, sabers, or columns, and are triangular or quadrangular in cross section. Thin slabs with extensive flat surfaces and even formless boulders are also known. They run from one to four meters high, and are of granite or sandstone. Beginning in the nineteenth century, many investigators studied these enigmatic monuments. It is clear now that the oldest of these monuments relate to the Eneolithic, the initial dissemination of animal husbandry, agriculture, and metallurgy to the south Siberian steppes; the later objects can be linked to the Turkic period of the first millennium A.D. These two groups differ in both artistic purpose and execution.

The earlier stone statues convey the images of manlike beings; the later are those of ordinary human figures. They will be dealt with at the end of this work (see chapter 6). Here, we will dwell only on the stelae and depictions of the so-called Okunevo culture of the third and early second millennium B.C. in south Siberia.

The Okunevo monuments have been classified on the basis of key markers—the "eyes" or circles, nose, headdress, stripes, and other accessories—into three categories of representation: simple, realistic, and complex (Vadetskaya et al. 1980:48–49) (figs. 62, 63, 64). Representations of the first group are few. Typical are face masks with two eyes, with a transverse stripe over the eyes, but without a defined nose (fig. 63, no. 2). Sometimes lines radiate from the head; sometimes dots indicate nostrils. On some stelae three eyes are shown. The "realistic" group is likewise not numerous. These masks have two large eyes and a nose in low relief. However, they lack transverse stripes and rays (figs. 62, no. 3; 63, no. 1). The masks in these two groups may be the earliest. They have a limited loading of decorative elements and bear only a general resemblance to those of the basic third group.

This large, third group consists of complex representations full of fantasy and enigmatic thought (figs. 63, no. 3; 64). It appears that they are not truly anthropomorphic but iconographic images related to solar, vegetative, and snake cults. While they appear to have faces and even bodies, these features seem secondary semantically to other attributes: transverse lines usually partitioning images into three parts; circles, often concentric, and in threes or fives; and "headdresses" of a varied and often fantastic nature.

48

(The transverse lines across the facial images can be viewed both as markings and cosmic divisions, e.g., daylight/night, above ground/below ground [figs. 63, no. 3; 64; 65, nos. 6–8; 67].)

Common on Okunevo statues are multiple circles that look like eyes, often in threes (fig. 62, no. 1) or fours (figs. 65, no. 7; 67). A widespread opinion is that such supplementary "eyes" are facial markings. A more probable thought, expressed by I. T. Savenkov early in this century, is that they are astronomical features. In his view, a group of three circles would represent the movement of the sun. To the right would be the eastern, rising sun; the center, the midday sun; and the left, the western, setting sun (Vadetskaya et al. 1980:58).

Solar symbolism is widely evident on other parts of these stelae. Several types are known: concentric circles, nucleated circles, circles enclosed in a square, circles with radiating shoots, and, most basic, circles with four external triangles (fig. 63, no. 3). Commonly, one solar mark is shown on the front of the stela, and several on the sides and back (figs. 63, no. 3; 64). It is important to stress that all statues have solar symbols.

The "headdresses" or "crowns" above the heads of the mask images particularly deserve attention. These include straight, radiating lines (figs. 62, no. 1; 63, no. 3; 65, nos. 6–8; 67), but most of these figures show more complex designs. Only remotely resembling ears or horns, the designs can best be seen as shoots breaking through the ground (figs. 63, no. 3; 64; 66). Unquestionably, we have before us complex, graphic transmissions of attributes of a vegetative cult.

The following facts demonstrate this. The shoots resemble horns or ears only by their placement on the mask faces. But they come in threes, fives, sevens, and they resemble ears neither by their position on the heads nor by their shapes (e.g., fig. 64). There are food grains of several different species shown in characteristic forms (contrast figs. 63, no. 3; 64; 66). In particular, statues found near the village of Uybat and on the left bank of the Bira River opposite Tazmin *ulus* [both in the Minusinsk Basin] show leafy, triangle-topped shoots.

The long wavy lines which go upward from some masks also need discussion. These details appear to have more than one meaning. We have accepted the branches growing from heads as vegetative, elements of the Tree of Life. Yet some are serpentine, with snakelike heads. These cases are not accidental, for snake cults are widespread among Siberian and Far Eastern peoples. Numerous snake images are found on shamanistic drums and costumes among the Negidal and Tuvinians (Ivanov 1954:161, 187–89, 212, 301–8; Zelenin 1936). More than this, reverence for snakes occurs in other parts of Asia, in the Pacific islands, and in North America (Kharuzin 1905)—in a word, very widely.

In the Okunevo context, most significant snake representations are found on slabs from the Askyz, Malaya Yesi, and Chernovaya rivers. The

Askyz River slab (fig. 67) shows a deity with rays emanating from his head and with snakes in his hands and on his body. The slab on the Chernovaya River shows snakes with a predatory animal. Evidently, here is a peculiar variant of a well-known Near Eastern motif: the image of a fertility goddess with snakes in her hands (Vadetskaya et al. 1980:126, pl. 35).

The equivalence of ideas of fertility, the radiating sun, and snakes is expressed among many north Asian peoples (Khlobystina 1971:168–80). Although many differences separate them, vegetation and snakes share two specificities: biological cyclicity—the extinguishing and revival of life processes—and the tie of this cyclicity with broader natural cycles of the sun and the earth, more specifically, the underworld. There is, moreover, frequently an external resemblance of snakes to vegetation.

In these ways, the Okunevo stelae with their representations were religious monuments, sanctuaries in the steppes of the cults of a solar deity and the vegetative forms of nature. They were places of worship and offering. Even in the eighteenth century, travelers repeatedly observed Khakas worship and offerings to these "stone peasant women" (kamen-nyye baby). As Radlov (1895:17) wrote, "Each of them [worshippers] rode thrice around it . . . and placed some of his provisions at its base, so that the statue might be fed." Later, in the nineteenth century, this "stone old woman" was no longer openly worshipped, but her face was smeared with fat and sour cream.

In the stelae reviewed, we see two types of monuments. One, which we have described as "simple," embodies purely solar symbolism. This is a simplified and personified image of the sun, a solar deity with a radiant head from which come beams or tongues of flame. The image is clear and simple in execution, giving evidence of the development of a solar cult.

A different, more complex character is expressed by sanctuaries where there are figures of more complicated design, with masks divided into three spheres, complex shoots on the head, and circles and other solar marks on the body. These correspond to more complicated world outlooks, including the following basic cosmogenic and vegetative elements: the sun as a divine source of growth and reanimation; a cult of the vegetative powers of nature, the reawakening of life (grain, shoots); and the Tree of Life (half tree, half snake). Many stelae express the idea of an animal rebirth, e.g., stelae in the shape of a ram's horns, and shoots very similar to horns.

[The great transformations of culture in the third millennium B.C. involved complex processes which are still only partially understood. In the Yenisey valley particularly, population successions as well as internal evolutionary processes can be identified. The initial food-producing, metal-using culture, Afanasyevo had its roots in the west, in the Eurasian steppe. It was succeeded by Okunevo with a more Mongoloid population, paddle-and-anvil rather than coil-made pottery (Semenov 1982), new burial rites, new art, and a distinctive cult of vegetative deities celebrated in specialized stelae (Maksimenkov and Martynov 1968; Vadetskaya 1967). Okunevo in turn was succeeded by Andronovo culture, once more related to the west, and characterized by new pottery types and burial customs.

At the same time, significant continuities can be traced, for example, those between Afanasyevo and Okunevo in specialized censers, and in votive statuettes (Ivanova 1968). Moreover, Samus' culture in the western Siberian *taiga* maintained in pottery decoration many Okunevo artistic traditions. More generally, roots of the Scytho-Siberian animal style, particularly the image of the man-wolf, can be traced to Okunevo (Sher 1988). Particularly intriguing are the analogies, noted long ago by Kiselev (1951:164–72) but misdated by him to Karasuk, between Okunevo and Shang Chinese art. These include nucleated, four-pointed stars, and especially "geometricized faces" identified in Chinese art as *tao-t'ieh* beings (Cheng II: pls. 11, 13).]

The Golden Reindeer
Flying to the Sun
4

Steppe Culture and Scytho-Siberian Art

In the sixth century B.C., cultures of the Scytho-Siberian world formed in a vast area of two continents, Europe and Asia. The Scytho-Siberian was a steppe world, stretching from the Danube in central Europe on the west to the Transbaykal and inner Asia in the east. It had a common base of centuries of experience in herding, flood-plain agriculture, and economic and cultural linkages across the steppes. The common base was expressed, first of all, in art. Animal images constituted that characteristic artistic trait of the extensive Scytho-Siberian world which permitted, long ago, the establishment of the shared features of the period over an enormous territory of Eurasia (Chlenova 1967:110–13; Artamanov 1973:218–36, 253–55; Rudenko and Rudenko 1949).

Let us state briefly only the basic theories on the origins of the Scytho-Siberian Animal Style.

In the nineteenth century, A. Furtwängler (1883) advanced the theory of a Greek origin for Scytho-Siberian art. This theory was developed by other investigators, who, however, recognized the influence of Near Eastern art but permitted the local development of only a few themes (Lapo-Danilovskiy 1887; Formakovskiy 1914). The unsoundness of this theory was repeatedly brought out (Pogrebova 1950). In competition with these ideas, G. O. Borovka and, following him, D. N. Eding and E. Minns revived a theory of the local origins of the Scytho-Siberian Animal Style and its ties with the Neolithic art of eastern Europe and Siberia (Borovka 1928). E. Minns thought that Siberia was the homeland of the reindeer image, and that from there the image penetrated more westerly art. Moreover, he judged that the basis of Scytho-Siberian art was in the Bronze Age of Siberia—the Karasuk culture (Minns 1944). This hypothesis was reflected, to varying degrees, in the work of K. Hentze, A. Tallgren (1934), and other investigators. But the theory of a Near Eastern origin of the Animal Style achieved widest acceptance, because of the close resemblance of Siberian representations to Near Eastern ones. M. Rostovtsev formulated the basic statement of this theory, which emphasized an ultimate center in the Near East albeit with relative independence in the development of the western Siberian Animal Style (Rostovtsev 1922, 1925, 1929).

A considerable number of studies have appeared since the 1920s on the Animal Style as a whole. In addition to the authors already cited, the following are among those who have made definite contributions: M. I. Artamanov (1966, 1968, 1971:24–38), S. S. Chernikov (1965), K. F. Smirnov (1964:216–46), B. B. Piotrovskiy (1962), O. M. Dalton (1926), K. Jettmar (1964), T. Talbot-Rice (1957), J. Potratz (1963), and N. L. Chlenova (1967:110–65; 1971:194–95).

In examining the origins of the Animal Style, two considerations must be kept in mind. First, the dissemination of the Scytho-Siberian Animal Style was promoted by the progressive evolution of animal husbandry and with it a highly mobile population, and by the development of contacts on a large scale across the breadth of the steppes. An underlying element was the common ethnic origin of the carriers of Scytho-Siberian homogeneity. The Eurasian steppes were basically populated by ancient Indo-Iranians.

Second, notwithstanding the common artistic forms of the Animal Style, i.e., figures of the reindeer, ram, and a curled-up feline predator, several large, developmental regions can be distinguished. They differ considerably in both subject matter and the manner of artistic communication. These regions include: (1) the northern Black Sea and adjoining territories (Scythian Style), (2) the Volga and southern Urals (Sarmatian), (3) central Asia (Saka), (4) the Altay and forest-steppe regions of western Siberia (Altayan), (5) the central parts of south Siberia (Tagar), (6) the Transbaykal and Mongolia (inner Asiatic), and (7) the Ordos of Inner Mongolia, the easternmost province of Scytho-Siberian art. [In this review, only the Altay and Tagar regions will be considered.]

Today the most correct viewpoint appears to be that, in each of these regions, the Animal Style arose and developed substantially independently, yet was affected by external contacts. It appears proper to divide the formation of this art into three chronological parts.

First came the formulation of the earliest examples of the Animal Style, evidently under the influences of Hittite-Assyrian and Irano-Achaemenid art (in the second millennium B.C.). It may be conjectured that the diffusion of these earliest examples took place near the end of the Bronze Age, and was associated with the migration of peoples practicing the cult of the sacred ram. This displaced the sacred bull and solar-deity cults extant there heretofore.

In the second period, c. 1000 B.C., the reworking of the most ancient Animal Style motifs in south Siberia took place. It comprised the incorporation of local peculiarities, including artistic expressions of reindeer cults, the creation of new artistic images, and the recasting of local animals in new styles. These processes can be attributed to the Karasuk period.

Finally, in the fifth to third centuries B.C., the flowering of the Animal Style in the Eurasian steppes took place.

Altay Art

A distinctive body of art came into being among the nomads of the Gornyy Altay (High Altay) during the second half of the first millennium B.C. The gathering of artistic materials from the territory began in the middle of the nineteenth century.

In 1865, the academician V. V. Radlov conducted excavations of large *kurgans* (burial mounds) with loose stone overburdens at Katanda and Berel'. In them were the rich interments of early nomads (Radloff 1884; Gavrilova 1957). (See map 4.) In these *kurgans*, for the first time, various excellently preserved wooden implements and skillfully sewn fur garments were found. Most remarkable in these collections was a series of horse figurines sewn on a silk band. In 1927, a new series of artistic manufactures of wood, leather, and metal was taken from the Shibe landmark (*urochishche*) excavated by M. P. Gryaznov (1928a, 1928b). The same person investigated Kurgan 1 in the Pazyryk valley in 1929 (Gryaznov 1950b). Then in 1947–48, S. I. Rudenko investigated four other large stone-covered *kurgans* at the same site. Later, Rudenko's excavations of two stone-covered *kurgans* in the Bashadar canyon and two others near the Tuekta village produced a considerable quantity of art materials. Similar results were attained in V. N. Kubarov's excavations, beginning in the 1970s, of stone-covered *kurgans* on the lofty Kosh Agach plateau of the Altay. To this day, art materials continue to be accumulated from the *kurgans* of the High Altay, although many of them were robbed in antiquity. However, even those that were plundered have yielded much material that aids our understanding of nomadic cultures of the Scythic period (Rudenko 1960; Gryaznov 1962).

Spacious burial chambers of logs were built under the huge stone covers of the *kurgans*. These chambers consisted of double frameworks with a wooden floor and a double ceiling. For example, in *Kurgan* 2 of Bashadar, the burial pit had an area of 5.2 by 6.3 meters and a depth of over 6 meters. It had a floor of wooden blocks on which a log framework had been constructed. Horses and horsegear were interred next to this structure. In *Kurgan* 5 at Pazyryk, pieces of a disassembled chariot and the bodies of four draft horses, as well as riding horses, were buried. Here also were found parts of a tent and a freight cart. The interred lords had been embalmed and then placed in heavy, hollow-log sarcophagi.

The art materials found in these *kurgans* basically consisted of decorated horsegear and clothing (figs. 68, 69, 70). Household utensils and cult objects also displayed artistic merit. Altay art was predominantly decorative. At Pazyryk, in particular, extraordinary preservation in the permafrost maintained a fullness of forms and materials all but unknown in archaeology. It included wooden sculpture in the round, bas relief, linear silhouette drawings, carpets, artistic embroideries and colored cloth appliqués, and objects of leather, felt, and metal. The ancient Altay nomads produced an art of many forms and materials; it incorporated mythological themes yet was ornamental and decorative in execution. It was fundamentally applied.

Sculptured objects, basically of wood, predominated. These included table legs in the form of a stylized tiger; bridle cheek pieces (*psaliya*) in the form of unnaturally lengthened, tormented rams and reindeer; and buckles for horse trappings in the forms of reindeer and wolves. Triumphs of artistic technique were attained in the frequent combination of bas relief and full sculpture. For example, an animal body would be represented in bas relief while its head, made from a separate piece of wood, would be fully sculpted. The ancient artists knew how to represent animal figures only in profile or full face, but they still achieved amazing dynamism and expressiveness in their work. Bas relief representations yielded unnatural, contorted animal figures with heads turned backward and hind legs turned up (fig. 69, no. 5). This was a device characteristic of Altay art. Yet these profile representations transmitted fully dynamic images in such a lively way that the artificiality of their poses is hardly noticeable.

Dynamism was characteristic for this group of artistic works even where it would appear impossible to attain. Thus, in fully static animal figures, impressions of readiness to move, run, or jump were achieved by wavy, curled ears, twists of the body, and distortions of eyebrows and bristles. Rhythmic repetitions and alternations in accompanying decoration also gave the impression of movement, even impetuosity. Dynamism, the feeling of movement, was excellently gained by simple devices, too, as when an animal was indicated to be swiftly running or jumping, with head stretched forward, antlers thrown back, and hind legs extended (fig. 69).

The ancient Altayans often made bas-relief representations and small sculptures from thick hide, a material widely used among herdsmen. Figurines of moose with antlers thrust back, bas-relief bird figures, antelope and horse heads, and griffin and tiger figures were executed in leather. In general, the combination of two or three different materials (wood, leather, felt, fur, dyed horsehair) was characteristic of sculptures. Often, with a wooden base, small details such as wings, antlers, or ears were executed in thick, hard, rawhide (figs. 75, 76). Sculptures in felt (fig. 69, no. 5) were truly unique. Most interesting among them are four convex swan figures sewn from soft, colored felt.

A peculiarity of Altay art was the production of silhouetted animal figures by the appliqué method. Representations were cut out of monochromatic or multicolored felt and leather, then sewn or glued onto a base of another color. Most interesting is the scene of a tiger attacking a moose, which was made by this method (fig. 70). The leather moose figure was partially covered by an oval of beautiful silvery color; the tiger was orange. All this was sewn onto a saddle cover. Predators (griffins, mythical lions, tigers) attacking herbivores were favorite themes of this genre (fig. 71). Most remarkable is a dynamic scene of a mythical eagle attacking a moose (fig. 71, nos. 1, 6). The composition was glued onto a red saddle cover, and covered with tinfoil (Rudenko 1952: 276–77). Another scene on a felt coverlet showing a ram attacked by a tiger is exceptionally expressive. The dying animal's tongue is thrust forward, his forelegs have collapsed, while his hindquarters are inverted and inert (Rudenko 1952:274–75). The ram had a red head, a golden eye, and blue antlers.

A few works are linear, graphlike drawings. The drawings of predators and herbivores on a log coffin at Bashadar, and the tattoos on the body of the lord buried in *Kurgan* 2 at Pazyryk are examples. The tattoos include pictures of tigers, mountain sheep, fish, *saiga* antelope, and griffins and other mythical beings (fig. 72).

The clipped pile carpets found in the *kurgans* of the Altay are particularly precious. They are the oldest in the world. One such pile carpet was found in *Kurgan* 5 at Pazyryk, another at Bashadar *Kurgan* 2. The large Pazyryk carpet is rectangular (1.9 × 2 m). Its field consists of separate zones of rhythmically repeated drawings. Its central part is made up of small squares decorated with eight-rayed rosettes of wings and flowers. The rest of the carpet is taken up by rows of repeated drawings. First comes a row of griffins with heads turned back, then a row of spotted deer, also in single file, and a border of star-shaped rosettes. The edge of the carpet is a frame of depictions of horsemen (fig. 73) and griffins. The carpet is multicolored, with a predominance of soft shades. Its artistic formulation is within the stylistic canons of Iranian decorative art of the Achaemenid period.

Unique artistic textiles were found in the same *kurgan* (Pazyryk *Kurgan* 5): two saddle pads and a horse breastpiece embroidered with the finest of wool in three Near Eastern designs. One pad was covered by a dark-violet cloth with white squares, inside of which was a pattern of rows of multicolored triangles and "tongues of flame." On the other pad was a cloth with rosettes and depictions of censers, on both sides of which crowned women were standing in a posture of prayer. On the third piece of cloth, a procession of lions was represented (Gryaznov 1962). The colored border of the felt wall-hanging from Pazyryk *Kurgan* 1 with representations of tiger heads also belongs to this group of artistic treasures.

The artistic images on the felt panels of the large tent from Pazyryk

Kurgan 5 were executed in the style of appliqué works. One rather large piece of felt which has been preserved bore the picture of a phoenix, an anthropomorphic monster, and a goddess sitting on a throne. She holds a sacred tree in her hands (fig. 132). Before her is a mounted warrior (fig. 74).

The art of the ancient Altay nomads was both distinctive and closely similar in themes and style to that of other Scytho-Siberian peoples. This was art of the Animal Style, full of images of hoofed grass-eaters and predators. Among the former, reindeer, moose, ibex, and mountain sheep were most common; among the latter, wolves and tigers. Roosters and eagles were the most common birds, while the burbot was the most frequently represented fish. There were also representations of wild boars, *saiga* antelopes, horses, swans, and geese. There were splendid examples of fantastic, zoomorphic creatures, such as the mythical eagle with animal ears and a toothed mane (figs. 75, 76), and anthropomorphic monsters (Rudenko 1960:32–34).

Altay art was enriched by techniques and designs from inner Asia and the Near East, and by artistic inheritances from Assyro-Babylonian and ancient Iranian sources. The pile carpet and a series of textiles from Pazyryk *Kurgan* 5 were probably Iranian rather than locally made. The depiction of offerings by crowned women in long brocade dresses is particularly close to Near Eastern representations. Yet the borrowed images and artistic techniques entered organically into Altayan art. The reworking of some images is interesting and distinctive. Thus, for example, the Iranian griffin was interpreted in the Altay as a tiger with wings, a mane, long ears, antelope horns, and, sometimes, an eagle's head (fig. 71, no. 4).

A significant place in ancient Altay art was held by geometric figures and vegetative motifs, the latter commonly on horsegear and household objects. Round badges that hung on the horse's forehead and were evidently solar symbols were common. [See also, below, the discussion of cults of solar animals.] Similar badges also decorated the cheek pieces of horses' bits (*psaliya*) and bridle reins. Globular and half-moon decorations were fairly common. Figures in the shapes of diamonds, triangles, crosses, and commas were used for decoration (fig. 77). The last were a basic form of saddle and bridle decoration. However, most common were vegetative patterns and entire garlands of hanging plants. Leaf-shaped forms often were transformed into round, quadrangular, or diamond-shaped rosettes.

Somewhat extraordinary yet often repeated in ancient Altay art was a representation distant indeed from the Altay mountains, the lotus, the sacred flower of the Indus valley and the Nile (fig. 78). This graceful blossom was carved from leather on horsegear emblems, on felt carpet-bordering, on a leather flask, and on a woman's purse from Pazyryk

Kurgan 2. These examples have many analogues in the Near Eastern art of Assyria and Achaemenid Iran (Loud and Altman 1938). [Other exotic elements require brief mention. Particularly important is a Chinese silk saddle-cloth from Pazyryk *Kurgan* 5 (fig. 79). As Rudenko has noted (1953:357–58) the quality of thread and embroidery is so high that it must be regarded as royal, a gift for a princess wed to a foreign lord. Its theme of pheasants, i.e., phoenixes, in trees corresponds to courtly communications. Another almost certainly exotic but puzzling type of object is the Europoid face with animal ears and bushy hair and beard found on several wooden saddle ornaments (fig. 80). Such a representation, very unlike Scytho-Siberian or Iranian art, is typically early classical Greek.]

In these ways, a distinctive, original art style which may be termed Altayan was created in the Scythic period. Its peculiarity was an exaggerated representation of heads and antlers. The latter were often hypertrophied and shown with special care. Evidently, they were the basic carriers of ideas. In representing predators, the artists paid special attention to the transmission of images of jaws, beaks, claws, and paws. In representing animal bodies, separate sections would be sharply divided: the shoulders, pelvis, limbs. [Note figure 85, bottom, for this convention in Tagar art.] This was achieved through strongly emphasized lines and protrusions conventionally stressing muscular prominence and body form. Semicircles, points, and ovals made up such protrusions.

Altay art was characterized by animals in an amazing variety of positions: standing, lying down in various ways, in motion, running, galloping, and fighting. Fighting scenes were typical, especially attacks on and torments of hoofed grass-eaters by predators. Prominent in these were depictions of the agony and bodily collapse of prey on the point of death, and the flexibility and power of the predator.

Most remarkable in this art was another trait, the capacity to place, to incorporate, any image into a prescribed form. This was a kind of practicality, a utilitarian dimension of this artistic style. The art of the High Altay was distinguished by its remarkable feel for its subject matter, its high mastery in execution, its inherent artistic manner. This art was alive, succulent, filled with the immediate influence of the surrounding world. It still brings to us artistic images of ancient nomadic mythology from the mountain valleys of the Altay.

Altay art was subjected to external influences. But these only enriched it. It remained at its root part of the Scytho-Siberian world.

Tagar Art, Sixth to Third Centuries B.C.

East of the zone of Altay art, in the upper reaches of the Yenisey and the adjoining steppes, Tagar Animal Style art arose in Scythic times. This art is best known for its large number of bronze badges or emblems (*blyashka*) representing reindeer in a traditional way, resting with legs bent under the body. Also noteworthy in this art are convex and high-relief representations of standing rams (which are cult objects); stylized snake figures with moose heads; and other stylized animal figures, primarily predators, on dagger and knife hilts (fig. 81).

In general, five characteristics distinguish Tagar art. First, in its images, herbivores (reindeer and rams) predominate, in contrast to Altay and especially Sarmatian art, where images of carnivores take a significant place. Second, the animals shown in sculpture and high relief are typically in quiet poses, and shown without excessive detail. Heraldic accessories are lacking. This contrasts especially with Scythian art. Third, a tendency toward "monumental" effects is particularly felt in battle- standard finials surmounted by animals. Fourth, Tagar art lacks a narrative orientation. Neither group scenes nor battles between predators and herbivores occur. [Petroglyphs provide a partial exception.] Finally, Tagar art, like all art of the Scytho-Siberian world, was primarily applied, used for the decoration of household artifacts, weapons, and religious objects. But these decorations also carried a high level of symbolic meaning.

Let us now examine basic genres of Tagar art: reindeer images, representations of rams and goats (ibex), geometric ornaments, and petroglyphs.

Reindeer Images

Representations of reindeer in specific, strictly maintained poses appear in the fifth century B.C. and disappear in the second century B.C. (Chlenova 1971:105). They are shown in cast bronze badges and may be divided into two groups on the basis of technique. The first group consists of bent-convex and flat-convex relief representations with musculature marked. The second group is flat and stamped or cut from a sheet 1.2 to 2.5 millimeters thick. Moreover, bas-relief figures are provided with one or two loops, which the stamped ones lack.

Stylistically, reindeer images differ from each other in shape—the treatment of antlers, legs, muzzles, jaws, eyes, and tails—and in relief. While even individual variations between these badges are significant, they can be grouped into six general types, with several subtypes.

Type 1 is comprised of reindeer with S-shaped [sinuous] antlers (fig. 82). Two subtypes are known, convex-relief and flat with rod-shaped antlers that have S-shaped tines or prongs. Representations of this type are close to the Scythian ones of the Black Sea in the degree of relief, overall handling of antlers, and pose. However, they also exhibit significant differences: the first prong never makes a loop, the base of the antlers is not prominent, while the legs, in contrast to the Early Scythian, form a loop. Nevertheless, this group is typologically close to the Black Sea Scythian (Loehr 1955:64–65; Rostovtsev 1922; Schefold 1938; Chlenova

1971:169), to Sakkyz in Iran (Ghirshman 1950), and to Chilikta in Kazakhstan (Chernikov 1965). It may be considered the earliest of the Tagar Animal Style.

Type 2 includes reindeer with comblike antlers (figs. 83–85). Its typical stylistic traits are rod-shaped antlers with tines in the form of upward-directed hooks. Figures of this group are flat or slightly convex. Several subtypes may be distinguished in antler form. Type 2A (fig. 83) is the basic Type 2 variant. In Type 2B (fig. 84), the antlers are curved and the prongs are often joined. In Type 2C, the antlers twist while the prongs form loops or commas. Type 2D has straight antlers joined to the back, and prongs shaped like open hooks (fig. 85, top). In Type 2E (fig. 85, bottom), the body is partitioned into segments in the Altay manner. Type 2F has flat wide antlers with many small prongs. It appears to be a purely local type without analogues in the Scytho-Siberian world.

Type 3 reindeer are characterized by joined tines, forming rings in rodlike antlers (figs. 86–88). Type 3A (fig. 86, bottom) has a massive mooselike muzzle; Type 3B, a disproportionately massive neck and enormous ears; Type 3C (fig. 87, top), open, toothed jaws and circles cut through the haunches. Type 3D has a narrow body, equal in length to the neck and head, and open jaws. For Type 3E (fig. 87, bottom) the criterion is a humped, mooselike muzzle. This subtype is found only in the forest-steppe, being absent in Minusinsk Basin collections.

Type 3F (fig. 86, top) is a very schematic figure, similar to those represented on the Mongolian and Altay-Sayan "Deer Stones" (fig. 104). Type 3G (fig. 88) is distinguished by enormous semicircular antlers with three superimposed, semicircular loops. Type 3H has a thin, elongated muzzle with cutouts, and antlers with small rings. Type 3I has a thin, extended muzzle with perforations, and antlers with small rings.

[Types 4, 5, and 6 (fig. 89) are very conventionalized.] Type 4 represents deer with bowlike antlers. It is varied, including Type 4A (fig. 89, no. 1), a unique, schematic figure wrapped with gold foil; Type 4B, a massive figure with thick, tine-less antlers; and Type 4C (fig. 89, no. 2), a stylized representation distantly resembling a reindeer or a moose.

We have termed Type 5 "degraded figures." These are unique, very stylized representations, which combine moose and bird traits with rodlike antlers that have sharp, straight tines (fig. 89, no. 3).

Type 6 emblems are flat figures with small or even missing antlers, unclearly delineated (fig. 89, nos. 3, 4). Subtype 6A has flat antlers with oval tines; Subtype 6B is an outline figure with thickened trapezoidal antlers.

The types described show that there was a significant center of artistic development in southern Siberia during the Scythic period. Most prominent were characteristic modifications of reindeer emblems. Many unique, inimitable reindeer designs arose, for example, figures of Type

2A, with straight antlers, and Type 2C, in which twisted antlers and looped tines combined to form a wide, perforated plate. Equally distinctive were the reindeer with comblike antlers of Type 2F. Type 2E, however, was executed in Altay style. Distinctive features can also be noted in Type 3. These included, first of all, reindeer figures (Type 3I) with huge, flat antlers surmounted by semicircular prongs; reindeer with toothed jaws and concentric circles on their haunches (Type 3D); and those with mooselike muzzles (Type 3E). The last are truly typical for northern Asian art, and are encountered basically in the forest-steppe zone. Finally, the mooselike figures of Type 4, with rodlike flat antlers, are unique.

These data confirm that stylistic variations in reindeer emblems were associated with specific geographical areas, hence, with local concepts and traditions of art. At the same time, a general chronological succession for the emergence and disappearance of particular types can also be noted. Thus, highly convex and flattish convex emblems occurred, basically, in assemblages of the fifth to third centuries B.C., while flat emblems were associated solely with assemblages related to the late fourth and third centuries B.C. The two shapes co-existed in part.

Speaking generally of the origin and development of this genre of art, it may be conjectured that Type 1, with S-shaped (sinuous) antlers, diffused first, and then persisted and developed throughout Tagar culture. It in turn derived from earlier prototypes. Once Type 1 arose, local forms of this artistic pattern began to form and develop. Stylization took place, with the infusion of traits of the moose into the reindeer figure. This was definitely expressed in the artistic treatment of the neck and head, especially the lips, and even in the representation of the typical moose antlers on a series of figures. These changes reflect complex conceptual interactions among Siberia's inhabitants during the Scythic period, the transfer to a new genre of elements of petroglyphic art dominated by the moose.

Ram and Goat (Ibex) Representations

Artistically stylized images of rams are also widely known in Siberian Tagar art. Reindeer emblems constituted relatively independent figures although their function was applied: They were sewn on clothing or fastened to various objects. Freestanding ram figures were very rare in Tagar art, since figures of rams were exclusively applied. They augmented and decorated various religious objects, household goods, and weapons (fig. 90). Specifically, ram figures were shown on the following: (1) battle-pick butts (fig. 91); (2) altars [for burnt offerings] (fig. 92); (3) bell-shaped finials on battle standards (figs. 93, 94); (4) badges of two or four connected ram heads; (5) the tips of dagger hilts (fig. 81); and (6) side handles for bronze mirrors.

In contrast to reindeer images, those of rams and goats were widely known in the Siberian Altay and central Asiatic arts of earlier periods. In Siberia, they were known primarily in Karasuk art. Also, they were prominent in the petroglyphic art of the Altay, Transbaykal, Mongolia, and central Asia. There are few petroglyphs of these animals in the Eurasian forest belt. Evidently, this image and its religious formulation were associated mostly with central Asiatic regions where wild sheep and ibex had been objects of the hunt from earliest times. There too arose one of the world's oldest centers for their domestication. All this created historical and esthetic conditions for the rise of such an artistic image and for a ram cult. Starting in the Pamir region and the Altay-Sayan uplands, this cult later (primarily in the Bronze Age) diffused through the north Asiatic steppes and neighboring regions along with sheep-and-goat animal husbandry.

Ram images were widespread in Asia (Kiselev 1951:145, 156–57), including Kazakhstan (Gryaznov 1956:14) and the Pamirs (Litvinskiy 1972:144–49). Ram and goat images were found among the Sauromatians (Smirnov 1964:240–41, 355–59) and, in the west, on several Black Sea objects (Rostovtsev 1929:pl. 17; Salmony 1933:pl. 9; Borovka 1928:pl. 29). These animals were equally prominent in Altay and Tuva art of the Scytho-Sarmatian period (Late Tagar) (Rudenko 1960:pls. 50–54; Rudenko 1952:166, 170, 172, 222; Gryaznov 1958:pl. 21; Mannay-Ool 1970:67, 72). These figures range from the conventionally realistic—proudly standing animals with well-modeled heads and horns (fig. 94)—to those that give the image of the ram only in gross form (fig. 91).

All these images have, however, a number of stylistic features in common. These include a schematic way of depicting the body: hooves connected or placed closely together; small modeled head with eyes and nostrils shown as two circles (depressions or convexities); and massive, semicircular horns connected to the body. Full-relief [three-dimensional] figures are encountered in Tagar art only on the finials of bell-shaped standards (figs. 93, 94). These show stout, well-muscled rams with two tightly curved horns standing on four strong legs (Martynov 1979:123, pl. 45). All other examples are executed either in a simplified-flattened manner or in one we may term "conventional full-relief."

Figures executed conventionally may be classified into two types. One type is that of convex-flattish or full-relief figures on altar tops (fig. 92). Weakly detailed bodies are characteristic for these. They are, in general, executed most schematically, with lean bodies and pairs of legs joined together. Yet the knees of the front legs and the annual growth rings on the horns are always shown. The other type is the flat, highly stylized representation found on pickax butts (fig. 91) and some altars (Martynov 1979:123, pl. 54). In most cases, their schematicism is ugly. The legs pass directly into the butt of the pickax, while the figures are very generalized. Often they are in pairs. Yet here too, all attention is focused on the horns, on which the annual growth rings are always shown. Obviously, this detail was basic, tied to the semantic loading of the image.

Ornamentation

In Tagar art, decoration and ornamentation had less of a role than in the Animal Style. In accord with rules of ornamentation, decoration beautified objects and helped define their form and construction. It formed objects. It made them showier, more noticeable, and more finished.

There are several classifications of ornamentation. Most often it is divided into animal, plant, and geometric, depending on the underlying model figures (Petri 1923:16). V. Vanelov (1956:184) separated ornamentation into four groups: geometric, plant, animal, and mixed. A. Haddon (1895) used two groups, the first including patterns and constructions using the sky and celestial phenomena, and the second, living beings, including man. However, it would be scarcely correct to apply one of these classifications to Tagar ornamentation, since they all relate not to formal and graphic aspects but to meaning. That meaning can be determined in only two circumstances: when an ornament more or less clearly transmits an arbitrary form of a real object, or when the people using this ornament explain it.

For the origins of ornamentation there exist several theories: the magical (Shternberg 1936), zoological (Balfour 1893), interwoven multi-causal (Haddon 1895), and anthropomorphic (von den Steinen 1894; Putnam 1887; Maslova 1951). But it would be incorrect to encompass the origins of ornamental art within any of these theories. Obviously, in each concrete situation the process involves multiple factors. In some cases, zoomorphic origins prevail; in others, the simplest geometric figures. In seeking these origins, one must reason that ornamentation has never been a goal in itself. On the contrary, it has, more than other forms of art, always been tied to the object decorated.

Tagar ornamentation was associated only with a defined, small group of objects; these were basically bronze artifacts, i.e., ornamental figures, decorated knife and dagger handles, and pickax butts (fig. 95). Most Tagar bronze objects were undecorated. This situation emphasizes the semantic significance of ornamentation, its immediate tie to designated objects only.

Tagar ornamentation was graphic in its execution, and geometric in form of drawing. It had two initial elements, lines and circles. Their combinations yield several basic ornamental motifs:

Vertical-line Ornamentation. The simplest and most widespread, it was executed as an indentation going down the length of a dagger handle or pickax butt. In view of its simplicity and organic connection with the form of the artifact it is doubtful whether it had any semantic significance. However, this ornament does not lack artistic significance, for such lines were placed in a set order, forming a drawing. Here is an example where practical needs organically combined with the artistic tastes of the Tagar population.

Slanted-line Ornamentation. This ornament consisted of incisions of thin, slanted lines inscribed transversely on knife and dagger handles. Sometimes the drawing was arranged in two columns separated by vertical lines. Combinations with small zigzags and triangles along the edge of a handle also occurred. Earlier, this pattern was known on Karasuk (Bronze Age) knives. This appears to be its origin in Tagar art.

Angular Lines. These occurred on pickax butts. They made up a column of V's the length of the butt. They were derived from Karasuk prototypes. Often, they were used as a border as well as a main ornament (Grishin 1976:pl. 16). In late materials, they were known as an Ob'-Ugrian [Khanty-Mansi] ornamentation (Ivanov 1963:152, pl. 96).

Wavy Broken Lines. These were often placed on knife handles, more rarely on pickax butts. Wavy or broken lines were placed lengthwise on objects and commonly framed on two sides by lines. Their use could also be horizontal and transverse. This ornament was long known in Siberia, beginning with the Early Bronze Age. As an element separating ornamental zones it was used on Karasuk knives and vessels, and on Bronze Age pottery in the forest zone (Matyushchenko and Igol'nikova 1966). In historic times, this ornament was used as a border and zone-separating pattern among the Ob'-Ugrians [Khanty-Mansi], Nenets (Yurak Samoyed), Sel'kup, Ket, Dolgan, Evenki [Tungus], Yakut, Altayans, Shori, Buryat, Tuva, and Khakas (Ivanov 1963, fig. 306).

Vertical and Slanted Crosshatching. Knife handles were sometimes decorated with thin transverse lines which cut across one or two longitudinal lines, forming a hatching. The initial elements of the ornament have been known in Siberia since the Paleolithic. But its direct origin in Tagar art must be related to Karasuk culture. In late materials, it was further developed; evidently, on the basis of this, showy square ornamentation arose among Siberian peoples (Ivanov 1963:86–87, pls. 39, 40).

Triangles and Diamonds. These were the favorite geometric linear figures of the Scythic period in Siberia. They commonly decorated knife handles in various combinations. Columns of connected diamonds usually were placed lengthwise on handles. This ornament was known prior to Tagar times, in much of Siberia. First, hatched triangles and diamonds were the most common ornamental elements on Karasuk bronze wares and vessels (Chlenova 1972:pls. 2, 3, 6). Second, these designs were widely known earlier on Seyma-Turbino bronzes, and on western Siberian pottery vessels of the Bronze Age (Bader 1964:fig. 64; Chernykh 1970: figs. 42–56; Tikhonov 1960; Kosarev 1970:116–72, fig. 1). Probably, their sources were related to these Seyma-Turbino bronzes. In late centuries, they were very widely known among Turkic peoples of the Altay-Sayan uplands: Tuva, Khakas, Altayans, Yakut, and Chulym Tatar. They were found in the western Siberian forests among the Ket, Sel'kup, Nenets [Yurak Samoyed], and Ob'-Ugrians. Beyond Siberia, they occurred among the Mountain Tadzhik, Turkmen, Uzbek, Karakalpak, and Kazakh, as well as among the people of the Caucasus and Volga. Such a wide distribution is apparently to be explained by a wide ancient basis for the ornament. There is an opinion that diamonds and crosshatched squares may be stylized representations of the sun.

Circles. These were known only on Tagar bone artifacts and knife handles. Usually, they were unsystematic combinations of five, seven, or nine circles or apertures. There is scarcely a basis for considering them as ornaments. The circles appear more appropriate as property marks (*tamga*) or magical number markings. They were known among Siberians and peoples worldwide since the Paleolithic (Frolov 1973:19–20). Evidently, this ornamental symbolism was connected with a sky cult and representation of the sun. But as the Tagar people had other solar symbols, such as round bronze disks and "mirrors," circular ornamentation did not develop as widely as among other peoples.

The types of ornamentation which we have brought together display genetic connections with those of the forest-steppe and forest cultures of the late Bronze Age in western Siberia. And an introductory historical analysis has shown their wide development subsequently, especially among the Turkic-speaking population of south Siberia and the inhabitants of the western Siberian forests (Ivanov 1963:464–73).

Petroglyphs (D. B. Shimkin)

Rock art in the Tagar period encompassed two genres. One was the well-known Deer Stones, stelae elaborately decorated with assemblies of flying reindeer, solar symbols, and various other signs (fig. 104). The other was petroglyphs on boulders and cliffs.

Although petroglyphs of Tagar age appear to have been abundant, they have not been systematically described and analyzed. Here, only one site of exceptional significance will be considered.

On the Boyar ridge, which runs east-west on the right (north) bank of the Sukhaya Tes' River, near the river's junction with the Yenisey are two petroglyphs, a quarter-mile apart, the Lesser and the Great Boyar Mountain pictographs. These were discovered by A. B. Adrianov in 1904, repeatedly visited but not accurately copied until the 1970s (Devlet 1976a:14). The Lesser pictograph is on a relatively smooth sandstone surface; the Great one is pecked into a somewhat eroded, partly lichen-covered rock wall, which has made its perception difficult except in favorable lighting near sunrise.

According to Devlet's analysis, the Lesser pictograph is the older. It represents a hamlet of both log structures and *yurts* (fig. 96). In it are numerous large cauldrons, a human figure in a tunic, a phallic anthropomorphic being, reindeer, and dogs (Devlet 1976:pls. 7–10). The Great pictograph, which has been carefully recorded by Devlet (1976:pls. 5,6), is likewise the depiction of a hamlet of perhaps twenty structures. It has a content similar to the Lesser pictograph, with the addition of herds of cattle, a mounted reindeer (and a herd of domesticated reindeer), sheep and goats, and an enigmatic figure (in the right-hand corner) possibly representing the underworld (figs. 97, 98).

Both these pictographs were evidently drawn as units, with the Lesser one probably the older. Devlet (1976:16) dates the Great pictograph to the terminal Tagar, the first century B.C. This may be too conservative. At the same time, her interpretation that these were not representations of real settlements but ideal ones serving magico-religious purposes is most probable.

Cults of Solar Animals, Vegetative Forces, and the Sacred Fire

The representative art of south Siberia in the Scythic period was the symbolization of a complex system of worldview and religion. It included the cults of animals, especially the reindeer and the ram, the personification of the sun, as well as plant cults and cults related to the sacred fire. These cults contributed significantly to the conceptual basis of Zoroastrianism in the Iranian world, and were in turn influenced by that religion. Let us examine each of these cults in turn.

Cults of Solar Animals

The domination of a zoomorphic image (reindeer and ram) in art permits a more exact judgment of its semantics, in particular, its ties with a solar cult. The sacred reindeer, to which various supernatural traits were attributed, was the basic zoomorphic being among all Tagar groups. It was connected with the totemic concepts of the Indo-Iranians of Siberia and the Black Sea.

But the image of the reindeer had considerably more meaning than merely being the ancestor of a group of people. Its semantics were many sided, in several categories of meaning. Basic among them was the association of this animal deity with the sun. Evidence of such a canonization comes from reindeer emblems with semicircular antlers and round apertures on the body (figs. 85, bottom; 86; 87). Moreover, special interest attaches to a flat reindeer figurine from the Tisul' cemetery with arc-shaped antlers wrapped in gold foil (fig. 89, no. 1; Martynov 1979:130–46). The figurine lay in a buried vault, close to the chest of the interred. It had been sewn to his clothing. The deer's head was small, narrow, and extended. The entire figure was made schematically. The main element of the figurine was evidently the antlers, so affectionately wrapped in gold foil. The gold strips were wound around the muzzle and then passed over the antlers and body. This unique representation discloses its identity better than others. It is "The Golden-Antlered Reindeer," the cosmic model of the sun as Luminary. Its conceptual predecessors were solar cults and myths widely distributed in the Neolithic in Europe and Asia, as indicated by solar circles on petroglyphs.

This gold-decorated reindeer was a unique creation. Among a great many bronze figurines, none other equalled its treatment. Rather dissimilar reindeer figurines wrapped in gold foil have come from the great Salbyk *kurgan* in Khakasia, and from the Chilikta *kurgan* in Kazakhstan. These too appear to be "golden reindeer" related to a solar cult.

Let us turn now to reindeer emblems with semicircular antlers and round apertures on the body. They are flat, and they have narrow, elongated muzzles, projecting sharp ears, long necks, and lean bodies. A peculiarity of this group of representations is that on the front shoulder blade is an elongated cutout remarkably like a wing. The rump may be denoted by a strongly marked circle. Moreover, the tines from the main stem of the antler repeat this circular emphasis. In addition, figures of Type 3F (fig. 86, top) express a dynamic tension very similar to the sky-climbing deer on the Deer Stones (figs. 88, 103, 104). They have extended, thin necks and small heads. They are tensely set to fly.

The semantics of these bronze reindeer emblems have long concerned scholars, and there is much that still remains enigmatic. Considering the facts cited above, we propose that the images we have examined were objects of a solar cult which, as is known, finds some type of concrete embodiment among almost all peoples. The form of the sun was rendered here by the semicircular antlers, connected in one whole with the animal's body, and by the circular cutouts. In this art as in mythology, there was not a full displacement of the sun by an animal but a syncretism. Brilliance and radiance were transmitted in one instance with the help of gold. In another, the decoration of the "solar" antler by small semicircular tines emphasized its repeated rise and movement. And many emblems were provided with oval, wing-shaped apertures at the shoulder to emphasize such celestial movement.

Concepts of the sun in the form of an animal (reindeer or moose) can be identified in northern Asia from the Paleolithic onward (figs. 99, 100). In the Scythic period, these concepts became enriched and more complex, integrated with the mythology and worldview of the entire Scytho-Siberian world. These ideas, with changes in detail, have persisted among later Siberian peoples. The myths of the Lapps, Dolgan, Orochi, and other peoples have retained the image of the cosmic moose or reindeer and its hunt by a mythical hero—Aroma-telle or Khollan-uola among the Yakut, Kogutay among the Altayans, and Tunka-pokha among the Mansi [Vogul] (Okladnikov 1964b; Formozov 1966:42). At the same time, the moose or reindeer have been concrete materializations not only of the sun and its movement, but of the entire universe, the heavens, and other luminaries.

The origin myth of the Lapps is fullest in suggestive details. In this context, the cosmic reindeer is represented as a living monster, a huge animal with black head and golden antlers traversing the heavenly vault. At night it is found in the world ocean or the underworld, the habitation of the spirits of the dead. This origin myth retains complex totemic ideas on the origin of people from reindeer, the ties of the old sorceress (noyda) with the reindeer progenitor (Khirvus) (Charnoluskiy 1965:25). Lapp tales are full of examples of women-reindeer (myandash-dev) and men-reindeer (myandash-parney) (fig. 142) (Charnoluskiy 1965:74, 80; Kharuzin 1890; Okladnikov 1964:61). In this way, reindeer relate not only to the cosmos (upper world) but to terrestrial life as well, through the direct ties of animals and people. This is a kind of primitive understanding of the unity of human society and nature.

Let us return to the cosmogenic theme. For example, a legend is known of the fearful cosmic hunt, by the thunder god Termes, of the golden-antlered sun-reindeer. That animal is described as sparkling white with raised head and antlers thrown back, flying with invisible wings and half-closed eyes. Certain details in this description coincide remarkably with those on Tagar bronze and gold reindeer images. In these figurines, the heads are also raised high. The animals have enormous antlers and appear to "fly with invisible wings." The eyes are shown only by slight convexities. Comparing the legend and the figurines suggests that these figurines represent cosmic reindeer, images of the solar deity of the ancient Indo-Iranians of the Eurasian steppes.

We find solar reindeer on north Asiatic petroglyphs and on special so-called "Deer Stones." Among these, very likely, the oldest is the sun-reindeer represented in the Tom' River petroglyph (fig. 101). This representation is unique. In the middle of the cliff is a huge, stylized depiction of a reindeer with radiant head. Basic attention in this picture is focused on the unusually large head from which rays emerge. The body is shown schematically, and the legs are disproportionately thin. It is as though the reindeer is swimming in the celestial element (Martynov 1966:16–20, 28;

Okladnikov and Martynov 1972:221–28). Among other petroglyphic representations of solar reindeer, one should note the drawing of a hunt for solar reindeer (fig. 102), and of reindeer virtually flying (fig. 103). Both are from the Gornyy Altay.

A somewhat different artistic treatment of solar reindeer is on the Deer Stones of Tuva, the Transbaykal, and Mongolia (Dikov 1958:pls. 15, 17; Volkov 1967:135–42, figs. 22–29). On these stones, reindeer are shown with extended heads and unnaturally luxuriant antlers. They have short legs. They are flying upward to disks shown on the stone (fig. 104). All these stones reflect one mythology, one semantic content, marks of the ancient solar cult of the herdsmen of the Eurasian steppes.

"Mirrors," Solar Badges, and Plant Cults

Apart from animal figures, other solar signs were widespread in Tagar culture. Specifically, bronze disks placed in graves along with reindeer figurines were common (fig. 100). To interpret them, one must recall that, beginning in the Bronze Age, a tendency developed to render images in the form of arbitrary signs or symbols. These often united different semantic contexts, which resulted in multiple meanings. Let us examine these disks from this standpoint.

In the past, these disks have often been called "mirrors," although they lack handles, unlike the Scythian and Sarmatian mirrors. They were cult objects, grave goods. They were found equally with male and female interments, usually by the chest or stomach. More rarely, they were found near the arm or shoulder. In that case, they were customarily with some other object, such as a reindeer emblem or a knife. The placement of these disks with burials indicates that they were basically carried on the chest, hung from a cord around the neck.

Solar signs were known to all cultures of the Scytho-Siberian world: the Scythians (Melyukova 1958:44, fig. 8; Smirnov 1966:77, 91; Rostovtsev 1918; Minns 1913; Borovka 1928); the Sarmatians (Smirnov 1964:301, 306, 307, 309, 327, 329; Shilov 1959:517, figs. 71–79; Sinitsyn 1959:156); the inhabitants of the High Altay (Rudenko 1952:119; 1960:pl. 23; Gryaznov 1947:11, fig. 4); the Saka of central Asia (Bernshtam 1952:39, fig. 17); and, to the east, the peoples of the Transbaykal (Dikov 1958:pls. 9–12, 16) and Mongolia (Volkov 1967:129, fig. 16). The earliest examples of solar signs are known from the ancient Mediterranean civilizations (Egyptians, Etruscans, Greeks) and the Near East (Calmayer 1964:20, pl. 2; Bossert 1923). Round disks to which the name "mirror" has been attached were used everywhere not only for personal adornment but also as magical objects. In temples, they increased light; in dwellings, they drove off evil spirits.

Mirrors probably symbolized light and, in many cases, the sun itself. This was true among most of the ancient peoples of Eurasia, for whom mirrors were associated with various religious and magical concepts (Khazanov 1964:89–104; Litvinskiy 1964). The shining surfaces of mirrors, sometimes covered with gold or silver, possessed the marvelous power of reflecting a person—"his soul" (Frazer 1935). A mirror could therefore be viewed as an object favorably influencing human fates—as a talisman. Evidently, it was because of this function that the wide distribution of bronze disks and the custom of carrying them on the chest took place in Tagar culture.

The concept of mirrors as talismans was found among most inhabitants of the Eurasian steppes in the first millennium A.D. Reflections of this concept occur in later ethnographic materials. For example, the Taoist monks believed that mirrors would protect them from unclean and evil spirits, reflecting the spirits from a person and guarding him, bringing him luck (Watson 1962:90). It is therefore no accident that mirrors were later an important ritual possession in Buddhism and Siberian shamanism. For example, the Buryat shamans had holy mirrors which supposedly "descended from the sky as a gift of the benevolent celestial deities" (Okladnikov 1950:170). A. M. Khazanov (1964:89–104) has shown that the same concept was found among the Sarmatian and other Iranian peoples.

Our observations show that the basic functions of the Tagar "mirrors" were as symbols of the sun and fertility. In connection with this, it must be remembered that one of the attributes of the Great Mother Goddess, whose cult was widespread in the Near East, was a mirror which she held in her hand. From this arose the proposition, which we share, that mirrors symbolized fertility (Khazanov 1964:33). Yet it must also be noted that the circle as a symbol of the sun and a mark of fertility was known widely in Eurasia even in the Neolithic. Supporting evidence comes from the Neolithic and Bronze Age pictographs of northern Asia and the Urals. These show circles basically in association with pictures of female moose (Okladnikov and Martynov 1972:221–29).

Another solar image of the Bronze Age is that of the sun's disk in a boat. This is known from Siberia, Kazakhstan, the Urals, Caucasus, Karelia, and Scandinavia (Okladnikov 1966:258, pl. 114; Martynov 1966:27; 1970:31, 33; Okladnikov and Martynov 1972:219, 223; Okladnikov and Zaporozhskaya 1972:219, 223; 1969–70:I, pls. 18, 27, 33; and II, pls. 21, 30; Chernetsov 1964: fig. 42). In addition, the solar chariot, also associated with circles on Asian pictographs, represented the solar deity (Sher 1980:277–85).

In northern Asia, amulets related to the sun cult are widely known (Gryaznov 1950a:133–34; Vadetskaya 1967: figs. 3–20; Khlobystina 1971: 173). Late Neolithic and Bronze Age sites in the Cis-Baykal area are sources of white nephrite disks and rings, which also pertain to sun worship. Thus the oldest representations of the sun as a circle are found equally among the ancient agriculturalists of Egypt and the ancient herders of Europe and Asia. In all cases, the sign seems to be related to fertility for animals as well as plant growth. This sign is not likely to have had a single historical center but rather had been an expression of a common human philosophy and worldview.

The sun deity Ra was represented by the ancient Egyptians as a disk with snakes on each side or as a disk with life-giving arms protruding. Such a representation is found on the throne from Tutankhamen's tomb. In ancient agricultural civilizations the sun cult was always associated with fertility, with the deity personifying nature. Such, for example, was the Isis cult in ancient and Hellenistic Egypt (Kinzhalov 1958; Mat'ye 1956:32, 34, 40; Zelinskiy 1922; Formozov 1966:40–43, fig. 15).

We have introduced these materials in order to show the deep genetic ties between Tagar bronze disks and world solar symbolization. The following iconographic and ideological features identify this relationship, notwithstanding variations in materials or manner of execution: (1) The circle is the generally accepted world symbol for the sun; (2) there is a semantic association of the circle with animals (bull, reindeer, steed), boats, or chariots; (3) there is a semantic association with man or an anthropomorphic being (Tagar burials and anthropomorphic figures on petroglyphs); and (4) there are associations with the idea of resuscitation or reincarnation. These general features indicate that Tagar symbols of the solar cult and the cult itself arose from a wide Eurasian religious base.

The solar cult or deity did not exist isolated from a fertility cult. This idea is expressed very clearly on "mirror" disks in a number of cases. The solar disks from burials of the third century b.c. from the Siberian Stepanovo collection (fig. 105) are marked with concentric circles and small oval indentations resembling wheat seeds. Moreover, in the Shesta-kovo and Serebryakovo cemeteries piles of millet and wheat seeds were placed under bronze disks. In two cases, remains of charred plants lay under such disks (Martynov 1971:205; Martynov and Bobrov 1971; pl. 7). These offerings may be interpreted as follows: Those sending the deceased to the "land of the dead" provided them with solar symbols to light the way, and with seeds, in which secrets of the mystic power of awakening and growth were hidden, as a symbol of reincarnation. It would, furthermore, be incorrect to assume that these cults were associated only with funerary ritual.

The Cult of the Sacred Fire

In Tagar culture, the solar cult was closely related to the worship of the divine power of the sacred fire. Evidence for this comes from two sources: first, the presence of traces of burning in Tagar graves; and second, the special devices which archaeologists have termed "standards." The latter represent cast bronze artifacts reminiscent of Scythic cauldrons with pierced walls, below which is a socket. Above is a rim, surmounting which are figures, normally of rams with raised heads (fig. 92). In burials, the standards are found near the head of the deceased. But often they may be separate from a particular burial, lying by the wall or in a corner of a collective sepulcher. Their function was long enigmatic. Customarily, they were judged to be signs of social power or marks of an especially noted warrior. But research has shown them to be devices for lighting fires, altars of a particular type.

The traditional artistic form of the Tagar altars deserves special attention. Rams in a standing pose alone are represented on them. As mentioned earlier, in Tagar art the image of the ram is encountered only on specific types of artifacts, i.e., altars, bell-shaped finials (figs. 93, 94), and battle pickaxes (fig. 91). Images of this animal fulfilled the same conceptual and mythological role in Tagar culture as the central Asiatic-Sarmatian deity, *farn* [*khvarenah*] (Rosenfield 1967:198–99), who had various concrete manifestations: as a ram, carnivorous bird, gazelle, or fire; in late representations, as a person or even an abstraction such as diffused light, the companion of victory, the symbol of greatness, fame, luck, or fate (de Menasce 1973:191–92). In later times, the Kushan rulers of India associated *farn* with royalty, especially by means of the metaphor of flaming shoulders (Stein 1887; Wood 1959:10, 17, 29–32; Rosenfield 1967:198–99).

In archaeological materials this religious and mythological image is most commonly fixed in the shape of a ram (Chlenova 1972:71, pl. 9). This was the case in the Scythic era among the Asiatic Saka, the inhabitants of the Altay mountain valleys, the Sayan, the Pamir, and people of the Tagar culture. In addition to ram representations on altars and weapons, pottery with zoomorphic handles is known from southern Tadzhikistan, southern Uzbekistan, the Fergana valley, and the valley of the Chu River. Such pottery was also known among the Sarmatians of the Volga and the Kuban, found even in the Alanic period of the first centuries A.D. in the latter area (Skalon 1941:214; Smirnov 1951:263–67; Abramova 1959:59; Vinogradov 1961:32–46; Kuznetsov 1962:60).

The worldview basis of this cult is understandable. It arose from a materialistic understanding of happiness and blessings among herders and farmers holding property in common. For this reason, the more common, traditional etymology of the word *farn* is "sun" or "divine fire." Note the wide array of concepts associated with *farn* in Persian and Pontic onomastics of the northern Black Sea region: "bearer of a good *farn*," "bearer of an Aryan *farn*," as in Farnak, son of Mithradates Eupator (Miller 1886; Abayev 1949:70–72, 156, 196; 1958:421–22).

The evidence reviewed, especially the ram as an icon of *farn*, and its ties with divine fire and sunlight, all widely distributed among ancient Iranians, permits one to assert that this cult was strongly developed in the population of Tagar culture. In Tagar sites, as among Pamir Tadzhik of later times, it was customary to bury a ram under the foundations of a dwelling. This was in reverence for the *farn* as the protector of the household. (See also fig. 90, nos. 45, 46.)

In the past, the Ossetians (another Iranian people) believed in the *farn* of a household and that of a people (Henning 1945). Often, the *farn* appears as an enlivening force. Henning exemplifies this through the tale of Caesar and the thieves. A thief had broken into Caesar's tomb, put on his royal raiment, taken the signs of power, and said: "Caesar, awake! Awake! Do not fear, I am your *farn*." It is interesting to note in this connection that finials with rams were part of the mortuary rite in Tagar sepulchers (fig. 93). They are not common in burials. Possibly, they signified leading community members who were "possessors of *farn*."

In connection with the question examined, it is necessary to review still another manifestation of the worldview closely associated with the cult of the ram, *farn*, and burnt sacrifice on altars. In later materials, still associated with this cult, the image of a deity manifesting the Old Iranian *farn* is known on Kushan coins. These display several variants with differing attributes, including a vessel emitting fire in one hand and tongues of flame arising from the shoulders (Stein 1887; Wood 1959:10, 17, 29–32; Rosenfield 1967:69, 198–200).

Finally, the influence of Zoroastrianism, already found in the fifth century B.C. in Iran and Bactria, can be perceived in Tagar altars and, more generally, in the fire cult. It is most likely that the basic ideas of Zoroastrianism, the deification of natural forces (land, water, fire), found a favorable cultural environment among the agricultural and herding peoples of northern Asia. The concept of a battle of two origins preached by Zarathustra was very old, having its basis in the simplest concepts of the Tagar people even before the diffusion of the Zoroastrian religion. In the same way, a concept of the purifying power of fire was well known among Siberian peoples long before the Scythic period. Thus there was potential syncretism.

At the same time, it is necessary to consider that Zoroastrianism was a religion of settled agriculturalists and herdsmen. In it, concepts of life and death, including life after death, were widely developed. And in Zoroastrianism, along with concepts of the abstract divinity and the cult of fire, a more personalized worship centered on the sun and the solar divinity. All this indicates that the basic ideas of Zoroastrianism were close to those of south Siberian people in the Scythic period and were diffused accordingly.

The Steed Bears the Sun in Its Hooves

5

The Consequences of the Great Migration of Peoples in Northern Asia

After the tempestuous events of the Great Migration of Peoples, which encompassed the second and first centuries B.C., the course of historical development changed significantly in northern Asia, particularly in its southern parts. That economic equilibrium, that type of mature, complex, yet primitive economy which had been created over centuries in southern Siberia from the early Bronze Age onward was destroyed. Its basis had been a rational animal husbandry, with seasonal herd movements, combined with floodplain agriculture. It was directed toward a maximum use of natural geographic conditions. But now economic development and an accumulation of surplus value in the steppe came through the simple reproduction of livestock, through increases in the numbers of animals, which led finally to the strengthening of nomadism. Its beginning had been a type of animal husbandry that was characteristic for this area and, as stated earlier, more rational environmentally.

With this, the pattern of life changed. It became mobile, as lifeways characterizing nomads unfolded. In fact, the economics and lifeways of the contemporary native populations of south Siberia developed. An important event of this time was, moreover, a change in the ethnic composition of the native populations. The former dominance in the south Siberian steppes of a Europoid population, which was true for the Scythic period, became a thing of the past. The population of the north Asiatic steppes became mixed, complex in ethnic composition. It included within it both traces of the Europoid local population of the earlier period and the Mongoloid population type of the Hunnic epoch, that of the Great Migration of Peoples. Historically known peoples appeared during this period. They included numerous Turkic tribes (Türki, Kimak, Karluk, and others) and others in the Far East (I-lou, Mohe, and others). These new processes embraced not only the steppe but included an enormous part of northern Asia. There was a general process of tribal and national formation which generated the direct ancestry of the contemporary native peoples of northern Asia.

It is essential to mention still another trait of this new historical epoch. Characteristic phenomena included incessant migrations, conflicts and wars (especially over pastures and trade routes), and internecine struggles. The peoples of Siberia, especially in its southern part, and of the Far East lived through an heroic period with all its peculiarities during the first millennium A.D. As a consequence of these events, the first states were formed in inner and northern Asia. In the middle of the sixth century A.D., a feudal nomadic state arose among the Türki of the Altay and inner Asia. Under the *kagan* [great lord] Bumyn, their dominion extended westward to the Amu Darya. Later, under *kagan* Dizabul, it reached the north Caucasus and the northern Black Sea steppes on the west, and the steppes of Mongolia and Manchuria to the east.

But the history of the Türki kaganate was one of unceasing wars and internecine struggles. Successful wars led to an extension of state boundaries and to internal strengthening. However, in 742 A.D. the Türki were defeated by the united forces of the Uygur, Karluk, and Basmil. The Türki kaganate fell, and its place was taken up by the Uygur kaganate, which lasted from 745 to 840 A.D., when it was shattered by the ancient Khakas. This people created a state, the Kyrgyz kaganate, which dominated the territory from the Irtysh on the west to the Transbaykal to the east. Then the Kimak union formed on the Irtysh. It influenced the Kipchak, another Turkic people, who wandered as nomads between the Irtysh and the southern Urals, and eastward to the Ob' and the Altay mountains. In the Transbaykal, on the eastern fringe of the Eurasian belt of the steppe, can be noted the emergence of the Kurykan tribe, who were reported in Chinese chronicles and evidently were ancestral to the Yakut.

During this period, the ancestors to later Tunguso-Manchurian tribes arose. They included the I-lou of the Chinese chronicles, and the numerous and powerful Mohe (Derevyanko 1975:247). In the mid-first millennium A.D., tribal consolidation took place in the southern parts of the Far East (the Amur, Maritime region, and adjoining areas of Korea). It culminated in the formation of the Pohai state of 698–926 A.D. (Derevyanko 1981:331). By the early twelfth century A.D., it was succeeded by the Jurchen empire which ultimately conquered north China (Shavkunov 1968:127; Medvedev 1977:222), only to be destroyed by the Mongols.

Clearly, basic historical events unfolded in this period in the steppes of inner and northern Asia, and in the southern parts of the Far East. Here nomadism arose and disseminated swiftly as the leading economy and lifeway. Here indeed was formed a nomadic civilization in the form of the first feudal, nomadic states. (See map 5.)

This development embraced other dimensions as well. Crafts developed further in the early Turkic nomadic states. This embraced the mining and smelting of iron, and the production of steel. The blacksmith's craft basically supplied military equipment, a few household objects (knives, strike-a-lights), and horse gear. The jeweler's craft also developed, providing costly gold and silver vessels for the feudal herding elite (dishes, bowls, goblets), horse-gear decorations, and the belts of mounted warriors. Plow agriculture arose along with statehood in former stone-age areas of the Amur and Maritime regions.

Despite these cultural developments, nomadism remained basic, influencing and changing lifeways for a considerable portion of the population of the north Asiatic steppes. Nomadism forced people to get along with a minimum of household goods, and to standardize the inventories of domestic artifacts. The basic dwelling became the frame-mounted felt *yurt*, so functional and convenient for nomadic wandering. Other necessities included carpets and bedding, leather cases and trunks to hold household baggage, an iron cauldron, and several vessels. All this and the dwelling could be packed on a carriage.

The mounted warrior, too, carried everything with him. He held his horse's reins in hand, while everything essential hung from his belt, or was otherwise fastened to him. This included his arms, quiver with bow and arrows, sword or saber; a strike-a-light and small sack with punk for lighting a fire; a knife; and other objects. Fastened to his saddle were a leather flask and a purse with dried meat and smoked cheese.

Throughout the first millennium A.D., the nomadic system developed and expanded continuously. It moved its frontiers forward, conquering neighboring peoples and redrawing the ethnic maps of Asia and eastern Europe. This progressive, step-by-step development continued until this system bore its own destroying force in the form of the Mongol-Tatar conquests (Sbornik 1970:473). In the twelfth century, the power of the various Mongol-Tatar tribes—Kereit, Merkit, Naiman, Mongol—increased. A period of consolidation passed rapidly; in 1206 A.D., Temujin was declared Chingis Khan at an assembly of Mongol feudal nomadic leaders. With this, the Mongol people were transformed into warriors, their land into a military camp. Then began a hitherto unknown policy of conquest.

This effort was directed initially against neighboring Asiatic peoples, then the Caucasus, Iran, and Eastern Europe. It led to the destruction of states and the annihilation of entire peoples. It stopped the development of economic capacity and culture. In northern Asia, these events led immediately to a regression in historical evolution lasting many centuries. Evidence to this effect was the intensifying loss of many attainments in material and spiritual culture by the peoples of northern Asia. These losses included writing, advanced architectural techniques, and many crafts. Agricultural techniques stagnated or even regressed. All culture declined.

The art of the pre-Mongol period in northern Asia was an art of nomadic herdsmen creating their own nomadic civilizations and forms of government. In its development, two periods are well marked: one extended from the Hunnic conquests and the fall of the Scytho-Siberian world to the formation of an Old Turkic ethnos in Siberia (second century B.C. to fourth century A.D.); and the other lasted from the sixth century A.D. to the Mongol conquest [i.e., the centuries of Turkic domination].

Art in the Hunnic (Tashtyk) Period: The Second and First Centuries B.C.

A gradual extinction of the classical Scytho-Siberian Animal Style of art took place after the Great Migration of Peoples ensued in northern Asia. Yet some examples of this still persisted. Strongly stylized "bifigured" representations of reindeer with joined bodies and legs, but with two heads looking in opposite directions, appeared at this time. Moreover, along with the customary images of reindeer and rams, there were now found representations of wild asses and horses, evidence of a considerable departure from the customary, traditional canons of Scytho-Siberian art. This departure was expressed by the appearance of subject matter and forms not according with the antecedent art. Along with images of horses and wild asses, there was a wide distribution of rectangular, open-work bronze belt-buckles and of bird representations. A widespread application of incised and molded ornaments, primarily on pottery, and new ornamental motifs uncharacteristic of the antecedent period became typical.

Evidently, these changes in art, as in all other archaeological materials, reflected major general changes coincident with the beginning of a new historical epoch in the Asiatic steppes, the basic elements of which were sketched earlier in this chapter. [Let us now consider in detail three aspects of artistic change: the Animal Style, rectangular open-work belt buckles, and ornamentation on vessels.]

The Animal Style

Judging by the materials from the basic sites of the first and second centuries B.C., the Animal Style in Siberia was then represented by a considerable range of subject matter. From the esthetic side, there are observable in this art greater conventionality than in the previous period, more static figures, and less artistry in the means of image portrayal. At the same time, it is necessary to note the heraldic embellishment of basic images by various details. Let us also draw attention to several basic subjects of this late Animal Style: antlerless deer, wild asses, antlered

77

"bifigured" reindeer, animals within circles, and bird representations (fig. 106).

Antlerless deer and wild asses were executed in traditional poses; the deer's legs were bent under the belly. Either young deer or roe deer with small muzzles were pictured (Stepanovo collection, Lysaya gora). The second variety of figures depicted were recumbent wild asses with massive heads. They were images which have become known as "animals of downcast mien." These representations continued the traditions of Scytho-Siberian art, albeit under different historical conditions. As a whole, they were less graceful than figures of the earlier period (Kyzlasov 1960, fig. 33).

Antlered "bifigured" reindeer are a second subject of post-Scythic art, a development of the reindeer badges of the fifth to third centuries B.C. These reindeer figures were cast in pairs and then joined. "Bifigured" ram images also appeared (Lysaya gora), and were characteristic elements of the transitional period of the second to first centuries B.C. By the end of the first millennium B.C. they were also encountered in other cultures. Probably, the origins of the Izykh plates so crudely representing animals are linked with these. Near to these also are the schematic votive animal figures known from the Kama culture of the sixth to ninth centuries A.D. (Smirnov 1956:175, pl. 38), as well as the so-called "equine" (kon'kovyye) pendants from the Upper Kama cemeteries of the seventh to ninth centuries A.D. (Gening et al. 1970:pl. 41).

Among the products of the second and first centuries B.C. are representations of animals placed within a circle. Commonly, standing rams are shown with ringlike thickenings at the end of the muzzle and with apertures on the breast and haunches; horses are similarly portrayed. The encompassing circles have notchings very similar to the annual accretions on ram horns. Such animal figures within circles are found mostly in hoards or cult sites (Martynov 1973). Sometimes this image is presented in reiterated form: three circles are connected together, with the figure of a standing ram in each.

In their design and meaning, such figures were probably close to the bronze, circular partitioned wheels which were widespread at this time. They are known from materials of the Kosogol hoard (Nashchekin 1967) and from casual finds in Siberia. In other areas, they relate to a later time. They have been found in catacombs of the Dmitrovskiy cemetery (seventh and first half of the eighth century A.D.) (Pletneva 1978:14, fig. 36; Gening et al. 1970: Appendix to pl. 47; pls. 55, 56). Earlier finds in Bashkiria are among the materials of the Birsk cemetery of the Bakhmutichinskiy culture (Mazhitov 1968: pl. 1). In Siberia, as is known, they appear regularly in the last centuries of the first millennium A.D.

In the post-Tagar period of the second and first centuries B.C., stylized bird figures become rather characteristic. Commonly, they are paired, with bent-beaked heads turned in opposite directions. Their feathers are carefully shown. In certain cases, figures resembling bird wings are segmented by lines, the result giving an impression of feathers. However, two types of bird representations are most widespread. Neither is connected with art of the Scythic period. One is of large, short-legged birds with short necks and bent, predatory beaks. They are shown lying down, their legs folded under, while their heads are turned back so that the bill connects with the back. Incisions on the surface of these figures imitate feathering. The figures are bent-convex in shape. In their feathering, pose, distinctive neck, and back they resemble cormorants. The second type constitutes full-relief figures with long necks, outstretched wings, and large beaks. They are like geese or cormorants. Hilts or handles of punches in the form of birds appear in post-Scythic times.

Rectangular Artistic Belt-Buckles

These appear as a characteristic trait and artistic creation of the new epoch. They were distributed in south Siberia, Mongolia, and the Ordos. M. K. Devlet (1973:56–58) has classified them by subject matter and style into four groups: (1) representations of a pair of quietly standing animals (fig. 107); (2) representations of two animals, fighting within a rectangular frame; (3) representations of intertwined snakes within a frame; and (4) open-work, with zigzag-shaped cuts and representations of stylized heads, eyes, and elongated oval indentations.

Buckles of the first type are the most numerous and varied. A pair of animals (bulls, camels, horses) standing quietly is represented on them. The bodies are shown in profile, while the heads are full face. In one, the tails are bent over the back and end in extended oval depressions. The wool dangling over the bellies is represented by similar depressions. The hooves, ears, and sharp horns of the animals are also portrayed. Not cows and bulls but yaks are represented here. The figures resemble each other in detail as mirror images.

Another subject of these rectangular bronze buckles is a scene of fighting animals (figs. 107, 108). A series of such buckles shows the battle of two wild asses. They are known in the Khakas-Minusinsk region, in the Hunnic sites of the Transbaykal, and among the Ordos artifacts (Rudenko 1962a:74–75, pl. 38). The animals are shown as though squeezed into a rectangular space. Their bodies are twisted unnaturally in battle. They bite each other. Attacking each other, they are intertwined. In the execution of these images a definite artistic manner is felt. This is a sort of school of bronze-casting creativity. In the east (Transbaykal, Ordos) these depictions of herbivores are accompanied by depictions of snakes or dragons.

A third subject shown on the bronze belt-buckles is represented by four intertwined snakes within a quadrangular frame (fig. 108). The heads of the snakes are broadened and adjoin one of the narrow walls of the frame, while their tails are connected with its opposite side. In some cases, neither the heads nor the tails are specially marked. The snakes are placed so that their sinuous bodies unite at some points and form free spaces, a kind of lattice, at others.

In addition, rectangular buckles with open-work geometric ornamentation may be noted (fig. 108). They are represented in three basic variations. Several buckle plates, convex on the face and flat on the back, have been found. They are decorated with zigzag-shaped partitions forming designs of iterated apertures. On the corners and the partition joints, buckles of this type are decorated with stylized griffin heads with extended-oval ears and round eyes. These buckles may also be distinguished by a distinct geometric design.

We regard the artistic rectangular bronze buckles to be products of Hunnic art. Their distribution in southern Siberia may be explained by the Hunnic expansion, which began between the third and second centuries B.C. Earlier than this time such buckles are unknown.

Other artistic objects were associated with the Hunnic expansion, e.g., spoon-shaped belt ends, known from burials of the second and first centuries B.C. and from casual finds in the forest-steppe region and the Transbaykal. The origin of buckles decorated with ram heads in a pseudo-Animal Style is also attributed to the early Hiung Nu.

Pottery Ornamentation

In south Siberian post-Scythic art, the ornamental motifs decorating most vessels became very diversified (fig. 109). Such ornamentation became a specialty of artistic creativity in the new era. The decoration is also an excellent indicator of the complexity of ethnohistorical processes taking place in south Siberia in the last two centuries B.C. Four lines of development can be clearly defined: (1) Scytho-Siberian (Tagar) continuities; (2) local (Tashtyk) developments typifying the new epoch; (3) introduced Hunnic patterns; and (4) motifs characterizing neighboring forest-steppe regions of western Siberia (Mogil'nikov 1970:174–75).

A territorial grouping of motifs may be distinguished as unique. This includes ornamentation depicting stylized birds and plants. Seemingly very similar in intent are "grain" ornaments reminiscent of individual grains and indeed entire ears of grain. But most motifs in this art have rather definite and stable ties with ornamental traditions in other territories. Moreover, certain patterns such as round pits and circles are encountered equally often in both the steppe and forest-steppe zones of Siberia, so that it is difficult to associate their origin with any specific part of northern Asia. Circles are known from the Tashtyk period of the Khakas-

Minusinsk area and in Tuva. Yet they had an equivalent distribution in the north Asiatic forest zone.

The "duck" ornament definitely had a forest origin. We must emphasize that this pattern is not encountered in the previous period in the steppe. It, as well as the form of the vessel it decorated, was typical of the forest region of the Ob'. It had been known among the western Siberian forest tribes since the beginning of the Bronze Age. Its basis was assuredly the splendid meander pattern of comb-impressions on the Neolithic and Bronze Age pottery of the Trans-Urals. In the first millennium A.D. the "duck" pattern was particularly widespread in the Siberian forests (Chindina 1977).

It is interesting to note that certain motifs—"broken line" (fig. 109, no. 10), "wavy" (fig. 109, no. 11), and "linear" (fig. 109, no. 12)—have direct analogies with ornaments on Hiung Nu pottery from Transbaykal settlements and cemeteries. They are known from Ivolga *gorodishche* (fortified town) and are basic in the royal Noin Ula *kurgans* of Mongolia (Rudenko 1962a: pl. 17; Devlet 1964:209, fig. 2).

Thus, analysis of works has shown that the art of the second and first centuries B.C. was distinctive. Its characteristic was syncretism, a joining of traditions from different sources. These included, on one side, those of the old Scytho-Siberian art, and on the other, new subjects associated with the cultures of the Hiung Nu and western Siberian forest tribes. In addition, along with changes in the nature and content of this art, its conceptual and mythological associations were transformed. But, as before, the sun and sacred animals remained in the center of the mythological system.

The ideas and images that were close to the inhabitants of northern Asia in Scythic times were evidenced as well in the Siberian materials of the middle and second half of the first millennium A.D. Slightly convex solar disks with concentric circles on the face are widespread in Siberia (the Yelikayevskiy and Ishim hoards, and materials from Kulayka) (figs. 110, 111). The prototypes of these religious objects were unquestionably the Tagar solar badges. In the opinion of I. I. Meshchaninov, solar symbolism was also expressed in the sanctuaries of Mongolia, the Altay, and the Transbaykal. Their composition included radiating paths paved with stones that surrounded the *kurgans*.

Solar themes can be uncovered in still later ethnographic materials in which ancient religious-mythological traditions were embodied. For example, among the Altayans, the sun and moon are represented on shamanistic drums in the form of circles with intersecting lines, as they are on petroglyphs. Badges representing the sun are typical for the shaman's costumes of northern Asiatic peoples (Anokhin 1924; V. I. Anuchin 1914). Representations of the sun are known among the Buryat and Yakut in the form of shamanistic *ongon* (fetishes) and on household objects (Zelenin 1936). Solar symbolism is also known among northern peoples of western Siberia. For example, among the nineteenth-century Yukagir, silver mirrors termed "chest suns" were found (Ivanov 1954).

Here, too, in the first millennium A.D. are found concepts joining the sun with mythological animals. An interesting example is a round badge of this age. In its center is represented a reindeer with luxuriant antlers ending in a solar disk. Another badge from Siberia, published in a volume by V. V. Radlov (1888:16), is equally interesting. A circle of six reindeer with branching antlers is incised upon its round surface. Again, a mirror in the Loo collection was decorated on its borders by two pairs of animals (Salmony 1933). Yet the specific association of the reindeer with the sun gradually faded. Other animals, especially the horse, replaced it.

This concept is clearly personified in badges from the Ishim collection and from Aydashinskaya *peshchera* [cave]. In both cases, a horse is represented with legs squeezed together and holding a round solar disk. Such an evolution of the image is, of course, explicable by historical events: the dissemination of seminomadic and nomadic lifeways, and the increasing economic role of the horse, beginning early in our era. Moreover, in the period of nomadic dominance in south Siberia the epic image of the celestial steed unfolded, in particular, in the Altay poem "Temir Sanaa" (Temir Sanaa 1940; Gryaznov 1961). It is easy to note that the description of this steed coincides in detail with that of the "celestial reindeer."

The fabulous heroes (*bogatyri*) of early Russia galloped on such steeds. Their hunt is represented, for example, on a goblet from Krasnoyarsk relating to the seventh to tenth centuries A.D. On it is shown a mounted warrior firing from his galloping horse at birds and beasts. [This is a favorite theme, incidentally, of the contemporary Sassanian art of central Asia]. However, the Siberians show not an ordinary warrior, nor is his an ordinary steed. He gallops not on the earth but in the sky, between clouds, high above mountains and forests. Evidently, among the sources of this scene are Tagar images of the cosmic reindeer galloping in the celestial element. Images of the zoomorphic deity associated with the solar cult are found in Siberian ethnographic materials. Not only was the imagery preserved, but reindeer representations as hunting and herding fetishes (*ongon*) persisted even into the nineteenth century among the Tuva, Dolgan, and Nenets [Yurak Samoyed].

In this way, in the representations of Siberian peoples, the image of the cosmic reindeer widely known in northern Asia beginning with the Scythic period was preserved in art, tales, and heroic epics. Among the Turkic peoples, the derivative cult of the horse was associated with fertility and with spring and autumnal festivals.

On the basis of the data presented we may conclude that a fundamentally new religious and festive ritual unfolded in the Tagar period. It was called forth by the rise of a new dualistic mythology, a new pattern, for which a strictly ordered deistic hierarchy was characteristic. Its head was a zoomorphic deity manifested in the image of a reindeer. [Its relation to Iranian religious evolution needs further study].

Petroglyphs and Representations on Wooden Planks

In the Türki period of the first millennium A.D., petroglyphs were numerous in south Siberia. They are known in the Altay, Khakasia, Tuva, and the Transbaykal. As a rule, their locations are not isolated. They are on the same cliff surfaces on which earlier drawings had been made, or else they are close to such earlier designs. In contrast to these earlier materials, those of the Türki period have been poorly studied, a fact arising from their technical peculiarities. They were engraved on cliff surfaces by means of quite thin lines forming outline representations. Only in recent years has their copying on cellophane begun.

Türki [and, more generally, Old Turkic] rock art differs from that of earlier periods not only in technique of execution of the basic mass of representations but also in style and subject matter. Its basic subject is the horseman riding on his steed, shooting from a bow, casting a noose (lasso) on animals, or throwing a spear. In this art, massive battle and hunting scenes predominate.

Narration is characteristic of these depictions. They are entire panels on which are represented scenes of real events or perhaps those of an epic. This is why warriors are shown, armed, clothed, with quiver at belt, riding steeds. They are shooting at enemies with characteristic three-surfaced arrows. They bear marks: property marks (*tamga*), lattices, or mere assemblages of lines. The figures may be crossed out or crossed over, perhaps as a symbol of those fallen to enemies. The mandatory persona of all these scenes is the steed which, along with the warrior, is the basic actor of the new period.

The stylistic manner of this era is typified by dynamism, by constant motion. The horses are shown running, straining forward, with tails and muzzles extended. Their manes are clipped in toothed patterns. Such are the Türki pictographs at Sulek in Khakasia, the Shalobolino, and other petroglyphs on the Yenisey, and the Karakol River representations of the High Altay. The medieval representations known in the Baykal region from Mankhay *gorodishche* [fortified town] are closely similar in subject matter. There, on twelve sandstone slabs, are engraved warriors with weapons and banners, as well as Bactrian camels, goats, and individual figures of horses (Okladnikov and Zaporozhskaya 1959:109–12). (See figs. 112–18.)

The artistic manner of these drawings displays certain carelessness. The figures were sketched in outline and then incised with a sharp stone or iron knife on the rock surface. Certain drawings are simply schematic, unproportioned. It is felt that their artistry did not predominate as a goal, which was rather the assembly of personae, and the representation of activities. They seemed to have been made in a hurry, as quick records of narrated scenes.

However, the techniques of pecking and broaching representations did not disappear completely in the first millennium A.D. Pecked drawings are especially numerous in the Transbaykal sites of the medieval Kurykan (Okladnikov and Zaporozhskaya 1959:109–44; Okladnikov 1959:110–55). Kurykan petroglyphs constitute the most numerous parts of the pictures of the Shishkino cliffs of the Upper Lena.

An absolute predominance of representations of horses and horsemen can be noted in these petroglyphs. The artists portrayed the particular traits of a special breed of horse: long-legged, with a long, narrow body, long arched neck with a small humped head, and with a strongly muscled chest. These are horses of a southern type, "hot-blooded." They are closest to the Akhal-Tekinskiye steeds of central Asia. It is also interesting to note that horses and dogs participating in mounted hunting are shown, but no other domestic animals. Typical scenes are hunts of reindeer and Siberian stags with nooses (lassos). The horsemen in these pictures are shown dressed in belted tunics (*kaftan*), some in chain mail or armor, characteristic of medieval protective gear. But it was not the horsemen but the horse that was drawn with loving care. On its head would be a splendid plume of hair or feathers; under its neck, a tassel; on its back, a blanket. Its mane was clipped in a toothed pattern. The horses themselves were graceful and showy.

Banners, quadrangular cloths fastened to long poles, were typically shown in Kurykan representations. Banners are also represented in the ancient Khakas drawings of the Sulek pictograph. According to A. P. Okladnikov such banners enjoyed among Asiatic peoples a special religious reverence as distinctive talismans in which the tribal protecting spirit resided, and which safeguarded that powerful force on which the military success and even the survival of the tribe in battle "depended."

But let us return to the steed and his trappings. The significance of the horse in the real lives of steppe nomads was so great that, evidently, in this time of formation of heroic epic and shamanism the steed was transformed into the personification of divine powers. In the heroic epic of the Altayans, there were steeds on which heroes leaped between high mountains.

In addition, representations of *yurt*-type dwellings, carts, and felt tents on wheels drawn by horses or camels became typical in this time. Also evident are enormous figures of shamans in traditional dress, with tambourine drums and drumsticks in their hands (fig. 52). Representations of this kind are found on petroglyphs of the Karakol river valley in the Altay.

Unique monuments of representative art close in their execution to the petroglyphs were discovered in a burial complex of the Tepsey III site. In Crypt I, along with fragments of a burial mask, pottery vessels, animal bones, ash, and charred fragments of wooden dishes, there were found eight wooded planks with incised figures and some fragments of other charred planks (Gryaznov et al. 1979) (fig. 119). Their essence may be summarized:

Plank 1: On one side of a three-sided wooden plank were depicted animals (Siberian stags) and a person; on the second, mounted horsemen; on the third, foot warriors in long tunics.

Plank 2: A forty-four-centimeter fragment of a plank was preserved. On one side were shown animals (moose and a bear); on the other, a warrior and other figures.

Plank 3: Two fragments totaling forty-two centimeters were preserved. On one side of the plank, figures of a Siberian stag and a moose were shown; on the other, a warrior, bear, and other figures.

Plank 4: A sixty-three-centimeter fragment of a plank shows horsemen on one side; on the other, foot warriors and people in boats.

Plank 5: This was fully preserved, with a length of one-hundred and ten centimeters and a handle. On one side were represented a Siberian stag, wolf, and bird; on the other, poorly preserved images of warriors and horsemen.

Plank 6: Four cut fragments totaling sixty-eight centimeters in length were preserved. Siberian stags and a moose were portrayed on one side; on the other, a warrior in slat armor, Siberian stags, a bear, and a horse.

Plank 7 and others: Several small fragments from two planks were preserved. On one, representations of animals could be noted; on the other, warriors in slat armor, wounded and dead.

The discovery of the charred wooden planks with engraved drawings manifested a truly new finding in the art of the Türki (Old Turkic) period. Evidently, the planks were about one meter long and six to twelve centimeters wide. The drawings were made with fine knife-cuts. On one side, we are convinced, reindeer, moose, bears, and other northern Asian animals were commonly represented; on the other, battle scenes, more likely, extracts from heroic epics. As a whole, these drawings play on themes of war and hunting.

The quality of this art should be emphasized. The horsemen and foot soldiers are shown expressively, with special feeling. Horsemen and foot warriors are dressed in characteristic clothing, belted, armed, and sometimes in armor. They dash about on restive steeds, run, fire from bows. Here also are dead and wounded. Pictures of defeat and victory, the driving off of looted stock, chases—all are shown. The representations on charred planks are only the incised outlines of originally poly-chromatic work. They were a kind of miniature of the third and fourth centuries A.D.

It is interesting to note that these "miniatures" on heroic themes were composed before the advent of Old Turkic writing. Evidently the narrative scenes on the petroglyphs and the wooden plaques fulfilled the same roles as the records of heroic epics in later times. They celebrated their subjects by artistic means, by pictures of epic scenes.

As has been mentioned, the decorated planks were found in a crypt of Tashtyk age. They were part of an extensive artistic inventory. According to the calculations of the excavator, M. P. Gryaznov, the site included over twenty burial masks, bronze horsehead figures, buckles with fixed tongues, numerous sheep astraguli (dice for gambling and divination), pottery, and the charred remains of wooden and birchbark utensils. Among the latter were a small barrel with a tube in the middle, and boxes with ornamented covers. Most significant were two life-size dolls sewn from leather and stuffed with grass. In each were small sacks with the ashes of the cremated person who was represented by the doll. Excavations of Tashtyk cemeteries at Barsuchikha II and on Oglakhta mountain, conducted by L. P. Kyzlasov in 1969, had previously uncovered similar dolls.

Tashtyk Burial Masks

Clay masks appear in Yenisey burials from the second century A.D. (figs. 120–23), after the collapse of the Scytho-Siberian world and the advent of the Hunno-Sarmatian period. At this time, burial rituals in general became more complex. The placement of bodies in crypts and the placement of cremated remains in the burial chamber were concurrent practices. As noted above, sacks with ashes of the deceased were sometimes sewn (as at Oglakhta cemetery) into life-sized dolls stuffed with straw; the figures were provided with clay-masked heads, and clad in fur coats.

These masks have aroused considerable scientific interest but they remain insufficiently studied from both their physical anthropological and art historical aspects. The first reports of these objects appeared at the end of the nineteenth century and early in the twentieth. They have been most fully studied by S. V. Kiselev (1951) and L. P. Kyzlasov (1960). Five types of burial masks have been delineated: (1) face masks; (2) masks of the front part of the head, including the ears; (3) masks of the front part of the head, including the neck; (4) mask-busts; and (5) fully sculptured heads (Gryaznov et al. 1979: 90–105).

The burial masks were made of good clay or a mixture of white gypsum-like terra cotta, brown (kaslinovyye) clays, and kaolin with traces of limestone. In addition, spectral analysis has uncovered traces of copper, manganese, and strontium in their composition.

The manufacturing techniques and the functions of these masks are of interest. The earliest masks and allied sculptures are from *kurgans* of the second century B.C. to second century A.D. They were then made either from "fatty" yellow clay or else in layers of clay covered by a white plaster mass. How they were prepared has been established. Since, in graves of this period, pieces of burnt clay with prints of hair, teeth, ears, and skin folds have been found, it appears that raw clay was placed upon the face of the entire head of the deceased. Evidently the skull was trepanned beforehand to remove the brain. The skull was smeared with moist clay which ran through the nasal passages and the orbits into the skull. In consequence, prints of the soft tissues, neck folds, ear forms, and hair remained on the reverse sides of the masks (and on fragments). Not rarely, red hairs stuck to the clay have been preserved. Sharp images of eye sockets, lips, noses—even moustaches—have remained. On the obverse side, the facial outlines were rendered artificially; the noses lacked nostrils (Kiselev 1951:446–59; Kyzlasov 1960:147–51).

Evidently, these masks were not prepared mechanically in a cast which took the facial imprint of the deceased, in the manner of contemporary death masks. Rather they were artistic creations of sculpture and painting. The masks were painted with patterns in red and black paint. It is believed that these patterns represented tattooing on the deceased person's face.

The basic function of the burial masks becomes evident through comparison with Khanty [Ostyak] burial masks. Among the Khanty, whenever a person died, an old woman left with the deceased would wrap his head in a fragment of reindeer hide or in a cloth, or else sew it within a sack. Then she would sew a copper button or coin opposite those places where the mouth, nose, eyes, and ears of the deceased would be. According to Khanty beliefs, once the deceased had lost the capacity to see, hear, smell, or speak, he would definitely lose contact with this world. The same measures would bar his exit into the world as an evil spirit who might hurt the living (Barzhenov 1895:488). This same striving to be freed of the deceased who is "entering a new life" explains the obligation for all those attending a Khanty funeral to be purified by leaping over a burning fire and by being sprayed with beaver musk.

Such an "isolation" of the deceased from the living was the function of masks with Tashtyk earthen graves. These were directly placed on the faces of men, women, and children. This isolation was essential since, in the burial ritual then taking place, the mummified corpse would lie unburied until the living could carry out all rituals connected with the ancestral cult.

At the same time, another function of the masks was transmitted by artistic means. With the help of molding and painting, the masks became individual portraits which captured the image of each deceased person, thanks to the high mastery of Tashtyk sculptors. Such tendencies can be explained only by a desire to preserve permanently the image of the deceased.

The masks found in crypts of the first centuries A.D. differ significantly from those just described. On the reverse side of these later masks impressions of a face or hair are lacking, but there are always traces of impressions of an untanned sheepskin [shagreen] with a rough surface. Very often there are sewing marks. Evidently, the pieces of hide were sewn together into a sphere stuffed, perhaps, with packed grass. These masks were made on a soft base, i.e., the sphere, or perhaps a cast was made of the face and then the sphere was used to press plaster against it. All parts of these masks were made separately—the neck, chest, chin, nose, and ears. Moreover, many of these parts were often made very schematically, e.g., noses without nostrils, or ears without conventional configurations [lobes] (Martynov 1974). It also is probable that the masks were made after the deceased person had been cremated. As a whole, the masks are associated both with cremation and the desire to preserve the image of the deceased. Their ashes and painted face masks remained in the crypts.

The painting of the masks is also interesting. The procedure was as follows: Spirals in two colors, red and blue-black, were painted on the forehead, temples, and cheeks. Patterns were painted in the same colors on the neck and chest of the busts. Light blue and green paints were used, in addition, for painting cheeks. It is assumed that the spirals and other patterns represented tattoos, which were later used by the ancient Khakas as well. Painting not only restored tattoos but other ancient details also. Eyelashes were marked, lips were colored. Even the nostrils were drawn in whenever they were not specially pressed in. The drawn lids of the closed eyes were painted light blue. The masks were true portraits, with no two alike.

On female masks, representations of necklaces, beads, and pendants were painted orange. Necklaces were also represented by pasting on oval beads made from the same mass as the masks. Again, in certain masks, holes were drilled into earlobes, clearly for hanging real earrings.

These facts indicate that the masks found in Tashtyk crypts were created primarily for rituals associated with a cult of the dead, and executed after the body of the deceased had been cremated and when the ashes were being buried. It must be supposed that between these two acts there was a period, perhaps significantly long, when the masks were evidently found in the dwellings of kinsmen performing needed rites. For these, portrait representations of the deceased were indeed necessary. For this reason too, women's masks were decorated with the bead necklaces and earrings they previously had worn. The final products were not merely masks but busts which could stand freely; some had widenings at the bottom, evidently as stands.

The number of masks in the crypts is less than the number of persons interred in each. This means that the complex rituals associated with masks were not performed for some of those interred. Because masks were found for children as well as men and women, this deficit cannot be ascribed to the effects of age or sex. Evidently, it reflected something else; that is, this epoch was characterized by differences in the social status of individuals or even entire groups of the population, by social ranking, or even by social stratification.

Special anthropological studies of the masks have shown that most of them represent a mixture of Europoid and Mongoloid traits, reminiscent most of all of contemporary Shori and Khakas [both being northeastern Turkic peoples]. This conclusion by physical anthropologists fully coincides with archaeological and historical information. It confirms the penetration of new Mongoloid and mixed types into the Europoid population which had been dominant in south Siberia in the Scythic period.

The clay sculptured heads from the early crypts of the second and first centuries B.C. provide a lively impression of the Europoid type that was later replaced. In comparison with later figures, these Europoid faces are narrower and longer, with weakly marked chins, and miniature, slightly snub noses (Kiselev 1951:450).

Among such masks, a head from the Shestakovo *kurgan* on the Kiya River is the best preserved (fig. 120). It was found in a crypt of the first century B.C. in a mass of charred bones. The head was shaped from pulverized clay with minute quartzite inclusions. In its interior, as x-rays showed, cranial bones were preserved; there was also a hollow space. The neck part was of insignificant dimensions. The chin was slightly raised and thrust forward. The facial part and the occiput had been molded separately; seams connecting them were noticeable near the ears. There is a basis for supposing that the facial part of the sculpture was made as a negative of a death mold. For this reason an actual face with deeply individual peculiarities is recorded: a somewhat snub nose, thin lips, large forehead, a handsome cast of the eyes. It is the image of a young person. But many facial details were poorly worked up. The surface of the facial part was thickened by smearing with a layer of dilute clay. Some unclear traces of paint remain, the cheeks in particular having a rosy color.

The head was secured to three rectangular pintles, prints of which have remained inside the sewn opening of the head. On the occiput several openings can also be noted, with thin hair ropes coming out of them. They too supported the head. In this way, the head was apparently part of a funerary doll representing the deceased (Martynov 1974). The means of its attachment to the "body" shows that it was carried, placed first in the dwelling and then in the ritual center at the *kurgan* prior to being deposited in the interior of the crypt.

Kulay and Relka Bronze Castings: The Early Phase

Cast bronze art objects related to the Kulay culture of the first half of the first millennium A.D. in the forest zone of western Siberia have been collected over a period of years. They have come almost exclusively from offering places and hoards in this area. For this reason it seems that the Kulay complex comprises objects of basically religious function, the stylized figurines of animals, birds, and anthropomorphic beings cast in bronze.

Let us briefly examine the basic groups of Kulay artifacts (figs. 124, 125): (1) stylized moose representations; (2) tree-like zoomorphic figures; (3) anthropomorphic masks and idols; (4) bird figures; (5) other types of castings.

Stylized Moose Representations

These (fig. 124) came from Kulayka mountain and the Krivosheino hoard (Urayev 1956: fig. 44; Myagkov 1929: pls. 2, 3). They are so-called flat, one-sided castings with open-work designs. In them, the massive head and the distinctive front part of the moose muzzle are well transmitted. The eyes and nostrils are represented by apertures. In most cases, the mouth is open, while the neck is extended somewhat forward. In comparison with the animal's normal proportions, the legs are too small. In fact, the front limbs are deformed so peculiarly that they sometimes resemble carnivore paws. Sometimes the limbs end in three or four claws. Stylistic peculiarities of the Kulay images include their open-work nature, their outline character, and the detailed visible structuring of the animals' interior (the so-called "skeletal style"). Moose figurines with several heads positioned one above the other are typical. There are some shown with the heart or their young within their bodies.

Evidently, these peculiarities were of much importance. Perhaps basic to these figurines were their open-work design, conventionality, a purposeful carelessness of execution, and, often, a multiplicity of heads. All these features indicate the unreality of the images. These were not mere beasts but spirit animals only vaguely resembling live creatures. They are amorphous, all but invisible, uncatchable, with the legs of other animals.

Tree-like Zoomorphic Figurines

These come from Kulayka, Bochkar, and the Krivosheino hoard. They are carelessly conventional, [readily] apprehended as tree trunks capped by a bird or animal head from which, like tree branches, come the heads of moose or carnivores (fig. 136). This category of representations is quite varied, displaying different levels of stylization, from relative realism to the outer limits of schematicism. The figures exemplify an undoubtedly persistent striving by their creators to unify in one image varied zoomorphic beings, to show their identity, their unbreakable ties to one another.

Allied to this category of artifacts are those in the form of two symmetrically placed animal heads turned toward each other—moose, or moose and snakes (Kulayka). The poses of the snakes and animal heads, with characteristic curves, suggest the same idea of growth and rebirth as the woody images.

Note should be taken of a rather unusual horseshoe-shaped object, again from Kylayka mountain. The ends of the horseshoe are animal heads of uncertain species. Their muzzles are turned in opposite directions. In contrast to the zoomorphic figures just reviewed, these lack any expression. These heads, lifted high, denote magnificent quietude. The necks below are marked by pairs of relief lines, like those on certain Kulay zoomorphic figures, especially moose, but the meaning of the lines is unknown. On the interior of the horseshoe is the representation of a predatory bird with outstretched wings, its beak turned to one side.

Anthropomorphic Masks and Idols

These are known from the Krivosheyno hoard and among the finds on the Bundyur, Bokchar, Vasyugan, and Shaytanka rivers, and other places of the forest zone (Myagkov 1929:pl. 3; Kosarev 1974: fig. 46). The masks were made in a specific way: each featured an oval face, narrowed chin, flat forehead, and oval slits in relief for the eyes and mouth. Not rarely, a horizontal ornamental stripe decorated the upper part of the forehead. Like the animal images, the anthropomorphic figures were rendered in outline form. Only the head and torso appeared more or less distinct and finished. Most often, the arms and legs were barely indicated. Two and even three joined figures are found.

Among the masks, one found on the Shaytanka River is particularly interesting. This is a round disk with faintly marked facial features. Five elongated animal heads, possibly snakes with open jaws, radiate from the upper part of the disk. In general, a number of traits emphasizing the solar nature of this and allied Kulayka images should be stressed. These include horizontal ladderlike ornamental bands on the upper foreheads of some masks and anthropomorphic figures [note an allied version in fig. 126]. Sometimes, in place of a ladder, zigzag lines are shown. These are characteristic expressions of solar symbols.

Bird Figurines

These are rather numerous and most commonly represent predators— great horned owls and others. They are almost always shown full face.

The heads are executed in relief, with details brought out by incised lines. In all cases, the wings are extended and bent downward. The wings and tail feathers often are decorated with dotted lines, elongated grooves, wavy lines, or ladder patterns. On the chests of some figurines are human heads. Both small and a few large figurines have been found.

Other Types of Castings

These include sculptured finials done in a realistic style, in contrast to the Kulay artifacts. The following types are known: hollow finials in the shape of a predatory bird (L. M. Pletneva 1978:fig. 1); bear heads; fish heads decorated with incised lines and several quadrangular, open-work lattices; images of predatory birds with outspread wings and beaks turned to one side; and figures of animals with open jaws.

A poorly worked surface characterizes all Kulay flat castings; all are rough. Their technique of manufacture was primitive: they were cast in wooden molds without further processing. Accordingly, the Kulay images lack a special esthetic quality. Evidently, this is to be explained by their religious functions, some images being part of shaman's gear. The zoomorphic plaques were associated with a hunting cult. The places where these images were found may be considered as sacred.

Some images were connected with rites honoring spirits and probably represented them.

Kulay and Relka Bronze Castings: Late Phase

Kulay cast artifacts were widespread in the central Ob' region from the middle of the first millennium B.C. to the fourth and fifth centuries A.D. But this mythological-artistic style of metallurgy continued to develop later in the forest areas of western Siberia. A considerable number of zoomorphic and anthropomorphic cast images are known from as late as the eleventh to fifteenth centuries A.D. They are heterogeneous: flat, hollow, and full-relief. Engraving is applied rarely, and basically only to correct or emphasize particular details. Their subject matter comprises three large groups: (1) anthropomorphic representations; (2) complex representations; and (3) simple zoomorphic figures.

Anthropomorphic Representations

These may be subdivided into figures of people or anthropomorphic beings, and human masks or heads.

The figures are flat engraved images of human beings with disproportionately large heads. Their faces are oval with prominent cheekbones. Their eyebrows and noses are indicated by lines. Their lips are pursed. Their hair descends freely to the shoulders. They have three-clawed hands placed on their bellies, legs with heels together but toes apart. Either sleeve cuffs or bracelets are visible, marked by two transverse lines. On the sides and necks of the figures slight convexities indicate edgings on the clothing. These figures vary only in detail. A static pose, similar placement of the arms, the same leg position, hair flowing on the shoulders, and an emphasized belt occur in all of them.

Several types of human masks are known but all are unified by a single concept and, probably, function. Most typical are three bronze sculptured heads (fig. 126). The interiors are hollow, and lack an occiput. Each face is narrow; the nose, thin and straight. The eyes are open; the lips, thin and firmly compressed. The resolute chin intensifies the stern, even gloomy facial expression. The headgear is ribbed. Such a mask probably is essentially a concrete canonization of an ancestral spirit, a protector of the clan or tribe.

Complex Representations

These comprise a large group, within which may be distinguished convex figures of great horned owls with wings spread and masks on their chests. Their feathering is indicated by semilinear convexities, pits, and deepened or relief lines. Bird representations appeared in western Siberia in the first millennium B.C. and continued throughout the first millennium A.D. It is possible to include within this group the winged bears with masks on their chests (fig. 127, top) found on the Tara River and in the Vasyugan hoard. Also distinctive are pendants representing bears with human masks on their chests.

Scenes of battle between animals and predatory birds are widespread in medieval metallic castings. There are figures of moose, bears, or sables which are being attacked by an eagle, as well as figures of bears attacking moose. As a whole, the joining of bear, moose, and eagle into one image of semantic union, a composition of conflict, is most typical. Sometimes "swallowing" is suggested by masks shown within a bear; sometimes one figure "grows" out of another (fig. 127, bottom). Very complex figures embodying some type of mythological narrative are known. These include flat plates decorated with rows of heads and bear paws; another shows a human figure with bird legs and moose muzzle emerging from its head.

Simple Zoomorphic Representations

Hollow figurines of geese with open beaks are included in this group. The outlines of their folded wings and tails are rendered by deepened lines, the feathers by round or semicircular pits. Openings for a cord are found on their backs. These images were evidently hung from a shaman's costume. As mentioned earlier, goose figures appeared in Siberia at the beginning of our era, in the Hunno-Sarmatian period.

Horse figures constitute another zoomorphic image. They are realistic, and clearly transmit all details of the animal. These metallic figures are flat with convex edges on the mane and under the hooves.

The western Siberian metallic plates comprise part of a dominant sphere of first-millennium art, the Animal Style of northeast Europe, the Urals, and western Siberia (Chindina 1977). The distribution was not by happenstance since all of this territory was part of the developmental area of Finno-Ugrian peoples. Consequently, we may assess this art as being essentially Finno-Ugrian. It has two branches, the western, so-called Permian style, extending up to the White Sea in Europe (fig. 134), and the Siberian style.

In this art, the representation of local fauna—bears, moose, sables, horses, eagles, owls, cranes, wood grouse, and snakes—was typical (Gribova 1975). The figures were executed realistically or abstractly. Abstraction prevailed in composite imaginary animals ("newts" [yashcher] or winged bears) and in the execution of details, such as body parts or imaginary elements. The semantics of these artistic figures are complex and little investigated as yet.

Functionally, these objects are thought to be shamanistic pendants. Yet a complex religious-mythological basis is comprised within them. Many of the simple figures may be accepted as totemic. These would be reindeer in some areas, bears or birds elsewhere (depending upon the patrilineal clan dominant in a particular hunting and trapping area). But this cannot be a total explanation, certainly for complex images. We find the answer in the legends of the Siberian and European north.

At the base of these legends is the image of *myandash*, half animal, half human, the female *myandash-deva* and the male *myandash-paren* [Finno-Ugrian terms of Indo-Iranian origin]. (See fig. 145.) These mythological beings could change into a reindeer or a person, go hunting, marry ordinary maidens. They understood the "language" of the animals, and had mystic powers.

A Lapp legend states that an old couple had three daughters who were betrothed, respectively, to a raven, a seal, and a reindeer. When the suitors were outside, they appeared to be animals, but when they would enter the old people's house they would become humans. There are many other legends. In them, the *myandash* taught people to hunt, to associate themselves with animals, to keep the secrets of natural cycles.

The images cast in bronze and copper are evidently expressions of this mythological subject matter. These figures of bird-people and people with reindeer muzzles and antlers, these bear figures with human masks, are real *myandash*. But they are also totemic clan and phratry ancestors, and they magically embody the powers of human and animal reproduction.

Stone Statuary of the Old Turkic Period
in South Siberia

Among the most interesting historical and cultural monuments of south Siberia are the stone portrait statues of the Old Turkic period. These have come into the archaeological literature under the traditional but neither very apt nor accurate term of "old stone peasant women" (*kamennyye baby*). These figures drew the attention of early Siberian explorers. In the early eighteenth century, the famous traveler and investigator of Siberia, D. G. Messerschmidt, first described such a statue in the Abakan steppe: "I clambered up to the statue, called Kozen' Kesh, which stands in a nice valley covered with birches and pines. It was 5.5 feet high, rough-hewn from red stone and representing a man with his face turned south. In his right hand he held an urn similar to a teacup, while in his left hand he held the edge of his clothing. He was belted; a little bag hung from each side of his belt. His head was covered by a cap, from beneath which ears protruded. The local population when arriving here expresses great respect to it, never missing an opportunity to present it with some edible possession. For this reason, its mouth was smeared with fat or butter and shone in the sun as though lacquered" (Messerschmidt 1962, trans. Martynov).

Since that time, new finds have constantly expanded the data on these stone statues. It has been established that their distributional area included the entire Asiatic steppe zone from the southern Urals to eastern Mongolia, i.e., the mountain-steppe regions of the Altay, Tuva, Khakasia, Mongolia, Kazakhstan, and the Tyan Shan. More than five hundred Old Turkic portrait statues are known, with about two hundred coming from south Siberia. But it must be kept in mind that the materials we now know are naturally insignificant compared to the number, one supposes, that existed in the past.

The statues were prepared from large, specially selected, elongated stones which were more or less carefully dressed to a form roughly that of a human figure. Most often, men with Mongoloid facial features, with moustaches and small beards, were represented. Most of the south Siberian statues have headgear, while those from Tuva may also display hairstyles (Yevtukhina 1952:72–100; Grach 1961:192). On some figures, one or both ears bear earrings. Men's belts frequently carry an entire inventory of ornaments, buckles, and badges. A dagger or saber hangs from the belt. Finally, the overwhelming majority of the figures hold a vessel in the right hand or in both hands. Most often the typical vessels of the nomadic era have a spherical body and a high, rather narrow neck. Archaeologically, they date to the seventh and eighth centuries A.D.

A large part of the Old Turkic statues were associated with funerary enclosures. They were mounted on the eastern side of quadrangular enclosures, facing east. From them, rows of vertically set-in stones also stood to the east. There are often complex assemblies consisting of two or more adjoining enclosures situated north-south. No one today doubts the ritual role of these monuments, particularly as it has been confirmed by data from archaeological excavations (Kubarev 1978:86–98). Although stone statues are now associated with only some enclosures, it is clear that originally, warrior statues accompanied every enclosure. Subsequently, they may have been shattered by enemies, removed to other places, or destroyed by time. Evidently, the statutes were made not only of stone, but of wood, as was the case later in Polovetsian [Ghuzz] sculptures of the east European steppes (Pletneva 1974:29). Sometimes adjoining enclosures with their statues were also surrounded by a wall and trench. In a few cases, statues were placed within funerary enclosures or structures.

All Turkic stone sculptures in northern Asia comprise two basic groups, representations of human figures or those of heads or faces. In the representation of facial traits a certain conventionalization can be felt. Eyebrows are depicted as wavy lines, or else the eyebrows and nose constitute a T-shaped unit (figs. 128, 129, 130).

Study of peculiarities of dress, decoration, and ornament on the statues of south Siberia and Mongolia has permitted a fairly exact dating of many. Thus, a comparison of statuary "accessories" with archaeological data from medieval *kurgans* in Tuva and the Altay has shown that primitive representations of the form of stone slabs with flattish relief were the earliest, datable to the seventh century A.D. Most of the statues date to the seventh and eighth centuries A.D., a part to the ninth (Yevtukhina 1952:114–15). All may be divided into six basic types: (1) primitively dressed flat stone slabs with faces represented; (2) columns with distinct heads and some parts of the body, especially the arms (figs. 128, 129 left); (3) primitive, but already shaped, images with more or less delineated body features; (4) sculptured images of human figures with a vessel in one or both hands (fig. 129, right); (5) statues with belt and weapons; and (6) statues with headgear and specific hairstyles (fig. 130).

Almost no research on the origins of Old Turkic statuary has been done either for south Siberia or other regions. One can cite only the work of A. N. Bernshtam (1952:144), who judged that the place of origin of "old stone [peasant] women" was the land of the ancient Kyrgyz and Khakas, the Minusinsk region. It is here that the oldest forms of stelae arising in the Bronze Age are found, and where the tradition developed continuously. There is, in any case, no doubt that the Türki stone statues of the sixth to eighth centuries A.D. had their roots in pre-Turkic times, most likely in the Khakas-Minusinsk basin and the Altay (Kyzlasov 1960:160). One is convinced that these statues were associated with a wide, very ancient circle of cultural concepts and a clearly defined artistic canon. The oldest carriers of these concepts were probably pre-Scythic tribes (Sher 1966:26, no.1). [The relations of this statuary to central Asiatic mortuary statuary in Bactria also need to be investigated, particularly in view of the profound late Iranian (Sogdian) influence on Turkic cultures. (See Shimkin 1967).]

The semantics of this stone portrait statuary constitute an important problem. Two basic hypotheses currently exist.

One idea is that the statues, termed *balbal* [in Old Turkic], represent the most powerful enemies who were killed or defeated during the lives of noted Türki. Having placed an enemy's image at a Türki hero's grave or funerary construction, friends and relatives of the deceased would secure that enemy as a "servant" beyond the grave (Barthol'd 1897; Veselovskiy 1915). Developing and reinforcing this hypothesis, it appears most likely that the funerary ritual has a definite sociopolitical coloring. The placement of the statue, in addition to its ritual aspect, would be made in order to pursue a concrete political goal: "striving toward a maximum popularization of the idea of the solidarity and stability of the kaganate of the Central Asiatic Türki" (Grach 1961:80). Note of this act would disseminate quickly throughout the steppes.

The other theory is that most of the statues represented the Türki themselves and were placed on the graves where they were buried, or at places of their ritual cremation. If the first hypothesis excludes all but one significance for the statues, this second one permits a dual explanation: the statues could either be portrait representations of deceased Türki [and later Turkic] leaders or more crudely executed statues of those who would be his servants in life after death (Bernshtam 1952:143). Most investigators support this second hypothesis.

In resolving this problem, a significant role has been played by analysis of the poses of the figures. In particular, it has been proposed that the Old Turkic images were of sitting rather than [deferentially] standing people (Sher 1966:26, n.1). Examination of statuary from Mongolia, south Siberia, and the Semirech'ye (Kazakhstan) shows most figures to be sitting, or else carved with legs unfinished disappearing into undressed rock. New discoveries from Mongolia showing figures holding a vessel in one hand and a weapon in the other reveal that the legs were curled up. Unquestionably, these figures are those of important deceased Türki symbolically participating in complex funerary rituals and offerings. In connection with such a concept, S. H. Klyashtornyy's (1978:250–53) explanation of a series of *balbal* stones as "burial gifts" given to the main seated figures by participants in the funerary ceremonies seems most probable.

[S. V. Ivanov (1979:183–86) has noted the many stylistic correspondences between the medieval Turkic statuary and the cast portraits of shamanistic ancestors (Eezi) among the nineteenth-century Altayans. This particularly applies to the treatment of the eyebrows and the nose. A direct historical relationship appears probable.]

Summary: Patterns and Trends of the Medieval Epoch
(Demitri B. Shimkin)

More than a thousand years elapsed between the collapse of the Scytho-Siberian world under pressure from the Hiung Nu and other participants in the Great Migration of Peoples and the cataclysmic wars and conquests of the Mongols. This was a period of vast technical and socioeconomic changes. In the steppe and southern uplands, herd-oriented, year-round nomadic movement lent new efficiency to animal husbandry but also initiated constant, intensifying competition for pastures. This new mobility, the development of metallurgy on a substantial scale, trade, and influences from the Iranian world and China permitted the rise of the "barbaric" states. These were feudal, with an equestrian elite ["white people"], a great elite involvement in religion, a distinct lower class ["black people"], and an ethic of war and conquest that was purportedly divinely ordained.

Change also took place in the forest zone, where hitherto isolated peoples were increasingly linked to the south by trade networks through which furs and walrus tusks were exchanged for manufactured products, especially iron wares and jewelry. The rise of reindeer herding intensified these forces and extended their influence far to the north. To varying degrees, systematic warfare, social stratification, and the rise of larger, more complex social groupings accompanied these changes. These influences of change were particularly strong on the Pacific Coast, with the rise of the Mohe on the Amur; in the Lena Valley, where the Kurykan became dominant; and in western Siberia, where the founding of the Moslem trading city of Great Bulgar on the Volga led to extensive socioeconomic and sociopolitical consequences among the Finno-Ugrians.

These cultural events were accompanied by changes in art and ideology. Some were persistent, such as the new significance of horse and bird images. Others, such as the Turkic petroglyphs and statuary, glorified new values and new myths displacing the animal images of earlier times. Still others reflected elaborate concepts of man-animal and even man-animal-plant relationships, deeply rooted in the past, yet clothed in new elaborations. Art and shamanism became closely interwoven.

In general, the themes of this chapter of north Asian history, although discrete in detail, are aspects of a complex whole.

The Tree of Life  6

Near Eastern Origins and North Asian Expressions of the Complex

Having examined the ancient art of northern Asia in its major chronological stages, let us now trace the artistic handling through time of a major mythological theme, the Tree of Life. However, before doing so we must examine the origins and dissemination of vegetative cults, cults of dying and resurrecting nature.

Traditionally, these cults and their origins have been associated with the zones of early agriculture—the Near East, India, the Maya and Inca cultures [and their predecessors] in the Americas. Among these have been the well-known cults of Tammuz, Osiris, Mithra, Adonis, Attis, and other chthonic deities. Such nature deities were universally the guardians of the mysteries of rebirth and death in nature, of its cyclicity. They were associated on the one hand with a solar deity, and on the other with a mysterious underground world, the kingdom of the dead. In ancient Mesopotamia, Tammuz was a special god whose annual death occasioned ritual mourning (Witzel 1935; Oppenkheym [Oppenheim] 1980: 200). The origins of these rites unquestionably bear the imprint of very ancient ceremonies when each god was the representation of some natural force. And if a deity personified nature, which dies and revives, then this god too must die and revive. This idea was embodied in the narrative of the descent of Enlil into Hades, in the myth of Enlil and Ninlil, and in the legend of the departure of the god Ishkur for "the land without return." Unquestionably, the most interesting figure in this context was Inanna, the "queen of the heavens," spouse of the shepherd god Dummuzi. She was the symbol of abundant harvests. Here too was an associated cult of death and resurrection.

Rituals of this kind were most widely and festively celebrated in the eastern Mediterranean (Frezer [Frazer] 1980). The Egyptians saw in the resurrection of Osiris a guarantee of eternal life beyond the grave for themselves. A person could live in that otherworld forever if only his kinspeople and friends who might survive him would perform on his body all the operations carried out on Osiris's body.

From a perspective of world outlooks, it is interesting to note that Osiris was the god of grain. In one of his incarnations this god was a personification of bread, which re-animates from seed. At the same time, Osiris was the offspring of Heaven and Earth who taught the Egyptians agriculture and was the god of fertility in general. The ancient Egyptians saw in Osiris the god of life energy as a whole, disseminating his [creative] activities to animals [as well as plants]. People at this stage [of sociocultural evolution] saw no fundamental differences between the reproductive capacities of animals and those of plants. The Osiris cult was marked, as is known, by crude expressive symbolics, as is shown by hymns in his honor: "Thou art the father and mother of all people. Through thy breath, they live. Thy flesh gives them food." From him they expected the granting of offspring.

We must note that after Osiris was reincarnated, he was ruler and judge in the kingdom of the dead. Evidently, this function was no less important than fertilizing the earth. Both functions were associated as one in the Osiris cult, as is shown by grave figurines of Osiris stuffed with grain. These images were at once symbols and magical tools for the re-animation of the deity of nature. In the Egyptian texts, Isis figures as the One of Many Names, of a thousand names. The initial core of her entity was as goddess of grain, creator of everything earthly, mistress of plenty. She created the earth's green cover and was herself the greening field of grain.

The cult of Adonis (Tammuz) was widespread in the Near East, in Babylonia and Syria. Tammuz was represented as the youthful spouse or lover of Ishtar, the Great Mother Goddess, the personification of the productive powers of nature. Mating and the mysteries of the birth of new life among all animals were so closely tied to Ishtar that they were possible only with her beneficent influence.

Finally, let us devote special attention to the cult of Attis. Initially, Attis was a wood spirit. The tale of Attis's transformation into a pine led to a whole cult of trees. Pines decorated with violets and ribbons were taken from the forest. Attis, as a wood spirit, had power over hoards buried in the earth; correspondingly, he was identified with grain and given the epithet of "very fruitful" and "harvested ear of grain." The statue of this god in the Lateran Museum in Rome represents Attis with a sheaf of bread grains in his hand, a garland of pine cones, and grain shoots emerging from beneath his cap. The urn holding the ashes of Attis's high priest was similarly decorated with a relief of bread-grain shoots and crowned with an image of a rooster with a tail of bread-grain shoots. Cybele may likewise be seen as a goddess of fertility upon whom the grain harvest depended.

These cults, as is known, found their reflections in epic myths and literature that served as the basis for the Greek and Roman pantheons.

The materials now known concerning the ancient art of northern Asia and relating primarily to the period from the second millennium B.C. to the first millennium A.D. show that in this part of the globe, which is so different from the lands of ancient agriculture, symbols and images of reviving and dying nature were also widespread. Evidently, this basic, underlying worldview was common to all mankind. But the specific mythological narratives and symbolics naturally were different in different parts of the ancient world.

In the materials of the art of northern Asia three artistic and semantic images clearly appear as symbols of dying and reawakening nature, its circulation, and the cyclicity and mystery of its life-creating power. One of these we may term "The Tree of Life" (figs. 131–40). That tree with its branches is also a metaphor expressed equally well by branching antlers, hence its manifestation in animals (figs. 141–43). Finally, a woman giving birth provides still another expression of the Tree of Life [particularly when viewed, as in Mongolia, as a succession of births] (figs. 144–47). These different embodiments are not accidental, for they embrace three basic spheres of life, vegetative, animal, and human, in a religious and mythological understanding of life. Sometimes we do not perceive in north Asiatic art a clear separation of these images but, on the contrary, their union. (See map 6.)

Representations of the Tree of Life

[In northern Asia, artistic expressions of the image of a Tree of Life varied greatly. Among the Scytho-Siberians and in the medieval period of the steppe, the divine tree constituted a mythic category interacting with but distinct from human heroes and cosmic deities. It was seemingly a part of elaborate cosmologies and epic tales. In contrast, the Siberian forest tradition emphasized the continuity and unity of plant and animal life within which people were in a sense engulfed (fig. 131). This tradition included both late features related to Finno-Ugrian mythology and concepts of hunting cults and magic of at least Neolithic age. Finally, the Okunevo stelae already mentioned in chapter 4 appear to be reflections of complex solar and nature cults embodying concepts of reality far different from today's rationality.]

A most realistic representation of the goddess of fertility with the Tree of Life was placed in the 6.5 by 5.5-meter felt tent panel of *Kurgan* 5 at Pazyryk in the Gornyy Altay (fig. 132). The panel, which dates from the fourth to third centuries B.C., was completely preserved in the permafrost. On it the goddess of fertility is represented sitting majestically on a throne, dressed in long clothing resembling a robe of honor (*khalat*) decorated with marks resembling boots or footprints. On her head is a large headdress (Gryaznov 1958: fig. 56). The goddess is shown in profile, although her chest is turned slightly *enface*. She nearly touches her face with one hand, while in the other she holds a large branch with flowering shoots that end in five pairs of different flowers. Two blooms are cuplike in form; two are shaped like palmettes or unfolded horns; two are triangular; two have three thickenings at the end; and two are in the form of separated petals. They are purposeful combinations. These pairs symbolize male and female reproductive principles for five real plants at the moment of flowering. It also appears that the figures represented on the seat and headdress are meaningful. The legs of the throne are paired figures resembling plant seeds, while the throne back ends in a downward-hanging shoot with a thickening evidently symbolizing a root. The headdress, a large triangular cap, also deserves attention. Its lower part is black and jagged like cultivated fields.

Clearly, before us is a unique representation of the Siberian-Altay variant of the ancient Iranian nature deity of Anahita. The concrete attributes of the Earth Mother are narrative images of the arousal of nature in the spring: The long black clothing seems to be a symbol of this awakening earth, while the boots or footprints reflect the arrival of the new season. This image is reinforced by the symbol of cultivated land on the head, the root within the ground below her, the grain, and the bush flowering out of her legs.

Images on gold plaques from the Amur Darya hoard seem similar in meaning to the Altay depiction of a deity (fig. 133). The men are shown standing in typical nomadic Saka clothing, in short jackets, with hoods [*bashlyk*] on their heads. In one hand each man holds a bundle of twigs. [The men are probably priests of Ahura Mazda, the high Zoroastrian deity.] The indicated theme of plant growth is so important that it appears repeatedly on these plaques.

Another object dedicated to the tree cult is a gold belt-buckle from the Siberian collection of Peter I (Rudenko 1962b: pl. 7, no. 7). Probably of Tashtyk age, i.e., late Tagar-Early Hunnic, it has been interpreted as a scene from an epic poem narrating the death of a hero. But something more, a different level of meaning, attracts us when we examine the buckle. On it is represented an unquestionably cultic scene, the center of which is the Tree of Life (fig. 134), which is uncommon for its nine thick branches ending not in leaves but in thick, hypertrophied leaf buds. To one side stand two saddled horses. The lowest shoot of the tree is connected to the muzzle of one of the horses. A moustached man of Mongoloid type, pictured full face, holds the other horse by the reins.

Beside the tree trunk sits another man who is represented strictly in profile. With his long face and straight long nose, he is clearly Europoid. On his head is a tiara which changes as it extends upward into a long, curved shoot of the tree. Another shoot emerges from the man's neck. The two shoots unite and intertwine with others [and a quiver hung from the tree].

The two men hold a reclining third man, also moustached and of Mongoloid type. He is dressed in a short jacket barely reaching his hips. Most important is the fact that the tree grows out of the shoulders of this man, who is dead. This tree is the center of the entire composition. All the personae of the narrative mythological scene are united with the tree's branches. The tree is a sign of the revival of life, of new life, linked to the animals and the three men, above all the deceased who is probably the epic hero. [The leaf buds in particular carry this message.]

Another concept of the Tree of Life is evident in petroglyphs on Tepsey mountain near the Yenisey (fig. 135), also of Tashtyk age. Two are noteworthy. One is a pair of animals, most probably horses, tethered to a forked hitching post [a composition favored in protector-animal designs long traditional in the Near East] (fig. 146). The other is of a group of animals, including probable horses and an ibex, surrounding another forked pole. Sometimes dogs or colts are represented in this context. The central pole appears to represent the World Tree, the axis with which various world levels communicate, and along which spirits and sacrifices flow. This is an ancient Indic concept. In the Rig Veda, it symbolizes the pillar to which horses destined for sacrifice were tethered. That pillar was also the cosmic column on which rested the thrones of Mitra and Varuna, the dual world rulers. It was the site of human and, later, equine sacrifices (Ivanov 1974).

Even earlier than the Indic myths, the Sumerian epic of Gilgamesh conceived of the World Tree, a leafless plant with hornlike branches.

[The validity of this association of the Tepsey petroglyphs with remote and much earlier mythology can be supported by evidence of an elaborate World Tree concept among the historic Yakut. The great *olonkho* epic describes a leafless tree of life in the very center of the middle world. The tree extends from the depths of the lower world to the bright heavens, where it serves as a horse tether. Around it the high gods feast (Okladnikov 1955: 262–63). Earthly examples of the World Tree were leafless, many-branched, and used as ceremonial tethers and places for the suspension of offerings.]

The Kulay art of western Siberia has been reviewed in chapter 5. Let us re-examine it from the standpoint of the cult of a Tree of Life. As mentioned earlier, in that art of the late first millennium B.C. to the first millennium A.D. the most widespread images were cast bronze "woody" objects with branches in the form of horns, animal heads, bird wings and heads, and sometimes people (fig. 136). This calls to mind the wide distribution of a cult of the Tree of Life, the idea of the re-animation of life, in the depths of the north Asian forests. But it is possible to understand the meaning of this cult for the Kulay people only on the basis of later ethnographic materials.

Among contemporary Siberian peoples the tree cult bears no clear traces of totemism. Nevertheless, for Siberian hunters, trees were closely associated with beliefs in totemic ancestors. For example, the sacred birch played an important role in Sel'kup concepts of the post-funerary world. Among the Ob' Ugrians [Khanty and Mansi], the soul that continued to live could reside in a tree in the form of a bird.

In past rituals of many Siberian peoples, trees figured in the idea of rebirth (Kosarev 1978:94). In the *taiga*, the bones of sacrificed animals were, as a rule, placed in a sacred tree, while the skull was hung from a branch. The Ket of central Siberia would carry the bones of bears, moose, or reindeer into the forest and place them in a tree hollow or at the base of a tree, from the eastern side. They believed that these rites were essential for the revival of the slain animals. Holy birch groves were revered by the Nanay [Goldi] of the Amur.

The tree cult persists to this day among the Altayans. They particularly revere larches, especially those growing on mountaintops or near springs. According to their superstitions, larches are the guardians of the souls of trees, forests, nature. The trees' branches are decorated with multicolored ribbons. The choice of the larch was not accidental. The larch is the only coniferous tree which drops its needles in the fall and revives its greenery again in the spring.

The sources of the idea examined thus far go much deeper into antiquity. Particularly important in this regard are the numerous stelae of the Okunevo culture of the third and second millennia B.C. [These have been reviewed in chapter 3, but their interpretation should be developed further.]

The solar nature of south Siberian stone statuary of the Bronze Age has now been documented (Vadetskaya et al. 1980:76). Rays come out of the heads of many figures, which also bear circles and other solar symbols (figs. 65–67). At the same time, these are pillars of fertility, of the vernal awakening of nature. The huge, high stone columns stood in the steppes along the Yenisey. Many of them appear to have been distinctive anthropomorphic symbols of the Tree of Life of Eneolithic and Early Bronze Age herdsmen and agriculturalists.

At this stage, a complex artistic symbolics probably prevailed. It was based on a philosophical-mythological understanding of the world into which entered concepts of a sacred sun and its sacrificial power, a sacred cultivated land and its life-creating powers, and a sacred grain with its power of growth. Later these three vegetative origins merged into a unified concept of a World Tree (the Tree of Life).

The underlying processes of cognition and representation for these stelae cannot be approached from an Aristotelian logic, from "common sense" analysis. As Steblin-Kaminskiy (1976), Fraydenberg (1978), and others have shown, they need rather a metaphoric approach, based upon "semantic sequences." It must be initially assumed that, in these artistic works, "myth" and the "truth of life" were an indissoluble unity. In particular, it would be erroneous to create oppositions between the various functions—cognitive, esthetic, memorial, and other—of these productions. On the Okunevo columns we see a narrative symbolism which unites the reality of perceptions and religious-mythological images of the earth, grain, sun, and plants, an understanding of the mutual ties of natural events.

For our purposes we have selected several Okunevo representations which most significantly communicate this plant cult (figs. 137–40). They are disparate and may be divided into three groups.

The first group comprises stelae with pecked-out bas-relief faces. Young sprouts and shoots rise directly from their heads (fig. 137). A large number of solar signs, placed upon the front and side edges of the stone, are always present. This is one of the icons of the goddess of fertility.

The second group consists of representations that are only distantly like faces or masks. These are ovals usually marked with three solar circles and three furrowed, horizontal lines within the ovals (fig. 138). All are covered on the outer side with young, short branched shoots. Among the representations of this group, the so-called "deity with spear" (fig. 139) deserves special attention. In fact, if one examines this figure closely, it is possible to note easily that shoots emerge from the head in pairs and that the "arms" resemble arms only in shape. Rather, they are stalks with thin shoots; the "arms" hold not a spear but a thin stalk with four short shoots and a leaf-shaped thickening at the end.

The third group consists of facelike images with the Tree of Life emerging from their heads (fig. 140). This tree is made up of very long (relative to the head) wavy or straight lines with branching shoots on the sides.

These are the earliest Siberian reproductions of the Tree of Life, symbol of the cult of fertility and the renewal of life. They appeared in northern Asia with the diffusion of agriculture and animal husbandry. Later, they spread to the forests as well as the steppe zones of northern Asia.

The Tree of Life in the Guise of an Animal

Hunting and herding always had primary importance in the history of northern Asia. We have been convinced more than once how profoundly common, basic human ideas have been transformed by the influence of traditional types of economy. In particular, a cult of animal fertility, of equal significance to the Tree of Life in agricultural regions, was widely evidenced in the art of northern Asia. As a matter of fact, this cult of the World Tree in its animal manifestation had the same meaning, the same semantic load of the re-animation of life, and of natural cyclicity. Clearly, at its base also lay the seasonality of mating and the birth of new life, the direct connection of these phenomena with the time of year.

A syncretism of this kind can be observed not only in Siberia. It is also known in other regions. For example, animal incarnations are known for ancient vegetative deities. Dionysus is represented not only as a man with power over vegetation, but also as a bull or goat. Pan, the satyrs, and Silenus were represented as goats or else as anthropomorphic beings with goatlike muzzles and legs. The doubles of these goatlike spirits are widespread in the folklore of northern European peoples. According to Frazer (Frezer [Frazer] 1980:415), the grain spirit frequently was manifested in folk customs in the guise of a goat. Manifestations of Demeter in the image of a horse or even a sow are known. Osiris, an even older vegetative deity, was sometimes presented in the image of a bull or boar.

In Siberia, such a substitution of deities is even more characteristic. This is explicable in that hunting and animal husbandry were always more significant than agriculture in northern Asia. For this reason, the cult-worldview symbols of the World Tree as metaphor of natural revival were broken up and associated differently. They had a different graphic expression but one constructed on the same generally accepted philosophical-mythological basis.

Let us turn first to the most expressive materials of Altay art in the first millennium B.C. The carriers of the capacities of re-animation and growth were clearly horns (and antlers) which bore in themselves the idea of the Tree of Life.

In previous chapters, we have encountered the sun-horn. Now let us examine images on petroglyphs and animal sculptures in which horns (or antlers) are interpreted as living wood. In this connection, the sculptured head of a reindeer in the maw of a griffin from Pazyryk *Kurgan* 2 is unique (fig. 141). The griffin beak is carved from wood and framed by leather ears and symbolic feathering. The griffin is swallowing the reindeer's head, which is also carved from wood. However, the entire meaning of this scene lies elsewhere. The reindeer dying in the predator's maw has two enormous leather antlers, which are about seven times as large as its head. They are hypertrophied. They twist rhythmically in two strips. Each antler has nine identical curved tines ending in miniature griffin heads with beaks, eyes, and crests. In the whole picture, these appear to be ordinary wavy antlers similar to those represented on reindeer badges of the Scythic era [chapter 4]. However, the basic idea expressed in these antlers is clear. The antlers convey, as in the Tree of Life, the idea of reincarnation. One life is dying in a predator's jaws, but the life-giving forces embodied in the antlers provide repeated renewals of life.

This same idea, in which the horn (or antler) is the Tree of Life, is expressed in a whole series of petroglyphic drawings throughout the Altay-Sayan region. They are so numerous that we can examine only a few, summarizing their general stylistic features and semantic content. As a whole, a schematic, conventional execution of the animal's body and a relative hypertrophy of the horns are characteristic (fig. 142). A separate consideration of the horns (or antlers) as the basic feature of these drawings is needed. They are communicated by different means, yet, regardless of that, they are horns only by their position and ties to the animal's body. In fact, they are trees or tree symbols connected with an animal rather than a plant, a special kind of animal embodiment of the Tree of Life.

In this context, three basic groups of representations can be distinguished (fig. 143). The first group consists of animals with very small, schematic bodies shown in profile. They have one or two parallel straight antler rods with many short tines. Such antlers do not exist in nature. These are schematic representations of trees, with a trunk and straight branches emerging from it. The second group consists of reindeer with antlers shown in the form of luxuriant bunches of plants or twigs. The third group comprises grotesque images of animals with treelike antlers and diminutive legs. In these images all is unreal, unlifelike. All attention is focused on the enormous antler-trees, each represented in the form of two many-branched trunks. Thus the hunters and herdsmen of northern Asia widely employed a formulation of the Tree of Life as horns or antlers distinctive in artistry and meaning.

The Tree of Life in the Guise of a Woman

It is important to emphasize that in the earliest north Asian representations of the Tree of Life, in the Okunevo culture, the figures [insofar as they are human] are female. Moreover, these women are often shown with protruding or pendant abdomens, i.e., pregnant or soon after giving birth. Women's images in definitely erotic postures are repeatedly found in south Siberian petroglyphs. Such a representation is calculated. Women are shown with parted legs bent at the knee and with arms bent and raised overhead, together with drawings of bulls or fantastic beasts (Sher 1980:271, fig. 125) (fig. 144). The repetitiveness of these images shows that they were executed as a defined compositional unit—woman and animal—according to definite stylistic traditions.

Examining these images further, we conclude that they are associated with fertility, the re-animation of life and, in a primitive way, the World Tree. People, as well as pillars or rods, could symbolize the World Tree. The anthropomorphic icon of that World Tree can be traced not only in ancient texts but also in artistic representations. Moreover, such an anthropomorphic manifestation could be either male or female.

Two lines of development of this icon of the cult of fertility can be distinguished. There is either the image of a person or anthropomorphic being joined to a tree or branch, sometimes a being with a tree growing from its head, or else there is the image of a woman giving birth. [This may be, as it is in Mongolian petroglyphs, a ladder of successive generations giving birth, cf. Novgorodova 1984:40–46.]

[We have already touched upon the first image, which was quite typical for Siberia, e.g., on the Okunevo stelae (fig. 140) and also on the European petroglyphs. Let us now turn to the second.]

The eroticized image of a female deity giving birth appeared earliest in Anatolia and the Balkans. This motif is embodied in a terra-cotta statuette from Haçilar, in relief on a ceramic fragment from northern Yugoslavia, and on ceramic engravings from northeastern Hungary and Bohemia. All these finds date to the sixth millennium B.C. (Gimbutas 1974). But the icon of the Mother Goddess alone cannot serve as a serious basis for semantic interpretations since it reflects a human universal which might arise by the convergence of totally separate ancient societies. The case of the south Siberian petroglyphs is different, for the eroticized women are always shown with animals (fig. 144).

An amazing analogy to the Siberian pictures is a relief representation on the forward wall of the Temple of the Goddess of Fertility (Temple 10, layer 6) in the Early Neolithic city of Çatal Hüyük in central Anatolia. The clay figure, of almost life size, is located on the upper part of the wall; it is in virtually the same pose, with uplifted arms and widespread legs. From the lower part of her abdomen there descends a line in relief, connecting with three clay-molded bull heads, one on top of the other, located on the lower part of the wall (Mellaart 1967:125–27).

Analogies to the above type are widespread in northern and central Asia. Images of women in this pose are found repeatedly on the Kobustan cliffs of Azerbaydzhan. In a number of instances, the woman is shown with an animal, including a bull; in one case, she appears on the bull's body (Dzhafarzade 1973:151). Representations of women giving birth are known from the Tutal and other south Siberian petroglyphs.

A belief in the existence of a definite, ancient mythological subject relating an eroticized icon of a woman and a bull becomes understandable after turning to the text of the Rig Veda. A mythological element (*mifologem*) in a series of hymns (for example, VI.70) deals with the beginning of cosmic organization, that is, the creation of the world. In this myth, Heaven is a male principle personified as a bull, while Earth is a woman giving life. "They are spouses: Father Heaven and Mother Earth. The rain let down from Heaven to Earth [sometimes termed oil or honey in the hymns] is seed from which is born all that is living. . . ."

The deification of Father Heaven and Mother Earth, from which all beings in the universe arise, relates to a common Indo-European period of world mythological formation. It may be assumed that such ancient myths were distributed over a large area. There may thus be a remote tie with comparable (albeit much later) images on Lake Baykal petroglyphs. This motif was combined with the representations of moose and birds, the later being attributes of the World Tree. The same theme is embodied in the Tokka petroglyphs in Yakutia (Okladnikov 1974:pls. 15, 17; Okladnikov and Mazin 1976:4, 8, 84, pl. 31).

The theme of the Mother of Fertility is widespread in Siberian mythology. V. N. Toporov (1969:133–37) has isolated a typologically unified group of personae at one level of religious development. They are goddesses of the class of "mothers" who are mistresses of nature, and who guard fertility and the lives of its various manifestations. They include Totem among the Ket, D'ya menyu'u among the Yenets Samoyed, and Ya-nebya among the Nenets [Yurak Samoyeds]. For several of these deities, the functions are rather sharply defined. For example, Dy'a menyu'u of the Yenets and Ya-nebya among the Nenets are obliged to protect all births, especially those of human beings. Unfortunately, no evidence of the appearance of these mythological figures is available, nor are there indications of their associations with specific animals.

Closest to our subject is the image of the Yakut goddess Ayisyt, who bestowed fertility on women and guarded their children, and who was known as a widely dispensing benefactress. It is also interesting that three days after the birth of a child, images of a horse, reindeer, and moose carved from birchbark were employed in the ceremonies for Ayisyt (Okladnikov 1967:78).

The Finno-Ugrian *sul'de* figures of the first millennium A.D. [see also chapter 5] are relevant to tracing relations between people, the Tree of Life, animals, and, evidently, fertility. *Sul'de* were cast cultic plaques representing animals and people in a fantastic way. The most expressive were badges representing anthropomorphic figures with reindeer antlers. Sometimes, instead of antlers, branches ending in moose heads emerged from the heads of these figures. Sometimes the figures became animal heads or bird wings. The legs of these creatures might terminate in animal bodies (fig. 145). In these figures animals and people, as it were, grew out of each other.

These are *myandash* images, well represented in north Eurasian mythologies. Half people, half animals, born according to legend from the mating of women and reindeer, they appear to embody the idea of rebirth, the renewal of life.

Complex figures combining various features of natural cycles and fertility were widely known in ancient Eurasia. The Slavs had the cults of Yarilo and Veles/Volos, the former associated with the fertility of grain, the latter with that of animals (Gimbutas 1971:162–67). [The manifestation Veles is god of death and the underworld; Volos, god of cattle and wealth (Gimbutas 1987).] The oldest and most significant roots [of such ideas] were related to the god [sometimes goddess] Lada or Leli, known in southern, central, and eastern Europe. This deity personified the spring-summer flowering of nature, that chthonic power without which the spring arousal of nature could not take place (Rybakov 1982:420–23). [A relationship to weddings can also be noted (V. Miller, 1896).]

Complex Images of the Tree of Life

In conclusion, let us now consider two extremely interesting artistic works. I have in mind first the gold diadem from the Novocherkassk hoard relating to Sarmatian art of the second to third centuries B.C. (fig. 146), and second, the solar cart or chariot [from the Hallstadt culture] of Austria, dating to the sixth century B.C. (fig. 147) (Rybakov 1982:346–50).

The diadem is ascribed to a noted Sarmatian woman, the queen of the Roxolani [tribal union]. In its execution it remarkably combines opulence, the artistic grace of individual details, primitivism, and massiveness of the entire article. Cast golden pendants are attached to the bottom of the wide golden band. Large precious stones are set in the diadem surface. In the center is a small amethyst female bust of archaic style. The upper part of the diadem is crowned by gold representations of trees and animals. It is these that carry the basic meaning of the diadem: an artistic narration of the Tree of Life, the idea of rebirth in two hypostases.

In the center of the diadem, directly above the woman's head, is shown a branched, leafy tree. This placement is not accidental, for the tree seems to grow out of her head. There was a tree on each side, but only the right one has survived. Near each of the three trees was a pair of animals. Two reindeer with many-branched antlers turn toward the central tree. Moreover, their antlers are connected with the tree branches. On the sides are pairs of reindeer and large-horned rams [as though in procession]. This purposeful composition transmits a basic meaning for the diadem: the Tree of Life reflects an agricultural system of philosophy and mythology, and the antlers fulfill the same role in reflecting viewpoints toward herding. The diadem evidently belonged to the priestess of a nature cult.

Far to the west, in Strettweg (Graz, Austria), was found a complex, multifigured composition, a solar chariot mounted on a latticed platform (Schmid 1934). In the center of the composition is a large figure of a naked goddess holding a chalice. Two identical compositions confront the goddess. They comprise a reindeer with large antlers, with a naked youth at each side, holding the reindeer by the antlers. Before us is a cult scene and, simultaneously, an altar in honor of the god of the sun or fire. This composition unquestionably told of a sacrificial offering in honor of the supreme deity. But there is something more.

Let us turn to the semantics of the composition. The reindeer figures, when compared to the horse images in the same place, are conventionalized. Their antlers appear very unusual. They are large, much larger than the animals' bodies. They are thick, unnaturally straight, and pointing upward. They have tines that are short, thick, and round in cross-section. In fact, these are not antlers but trees. The men are thus holding onto the Tree of Life.

To sum up, thousands of kilometers distant from ancient agricultural lands, in the depths of the forests and steppes of northern Asia, the same ideas of philosophy and worldview are to be found. But they are embodied in distinctive ways, as the Tree of Life, and its analogues, reindeer with sacred tree-antlers.

Conclusion

Investigators have long been concerned with the essential characteristics of primitive and ancient art. But this domain as a whole has been studied unevenly. Some fields such as the art of classical antiquity or Paleolithic paintings have received much attention, but in other cases entire aspects of art and larger areas of the globe as yet remain poorly studied. Northern Asia is such a poorly known area.

From all that has been written in this book, it is clear that the primitive art of northern Asia did not emerge casually and independently of the broader history of mankind. Rather, it was the product of a long cultural development and much human thought. It underwent a prolonged and complex developmental course from the Paleolithic figurines of Mal'ta and the Siberian bone engravings, through the flowering of petroglyphic art in the Neolithic and Bronze ages, through the enigmatic rock art of the Eneolithic and the splendid artistic examples of the Scytho-Siberian Animal Style, to the medieval art of epics and forest spirits. And at each stage of development this ancient art reflected the peculiarities of historical processes operative in that region of the globe. But in the same way, the history of northern Asia cannot be conceived without art. In it has been not only an esthetic but a historical essence.

Primitive art is complex. It is quite obvious that reality was reflected in various forms in the consciousness of Neolithic people and the people of the Bronze Age. On the one hand, there were logical categories and concrete models that faithfully reflected reality, its determined aspects and phenomena. In the consciousness of past mankind there were, un-questionably, rudiments of real knowledge and true notions of the world, growing out of the continuous efforts of human work [and adaptation]. The existence of mankind and the development of human culture would be unthinkable without that. On the other hand, within the consciousness of ancient people were rooted distorted, fantastic impressions of the surrounding world, feeding their religious worldview. However, the ori-gins of these distortions too were directly associated with the practical life of ancient people. It is probable that primitive art reflected in itself the

113

conflict between these two opposing principles in the consciousness of early mankind.

Primitive art as a whole eschewed pessimism. It was an active, combative, even heroic art. With its help, man sought to understand the world and even to subordinate it to his wishes.

At the basis of spiritual life in antiquity lay a unity of several sources— poetic creativity (folklore), artistic creativity, ritual dances, and music. Naturally, they did not come into being separately but as an organic unity, as component parts of the religious and ritual aspects of archaic human behavior. We are convinced that the wealth of this cultic, esthetic worldview was embodied best and most fully in ancient art. Overwhelmingly, this art was realistic in form but mythological in content, marvelously combining the truths of primitive life and living reality with mythological images and magical impulses.

Maps and Illustrations

Map 1 Legend

No.	Name	Age Lowest Stratum*	Major River	°N	°E
				Location	
1.	Achinskaya	UP	E. Chulym	56°20'	90°20'
2.	Afontova Gora	UP	Yenisey	56°00'	92°50'
3.	Berelëkh	UP	Berelëkh	71°	146°
4.	Bogorodskoye	L	L. Amur	52°05'	140°30'
5.	Buret' and Mal'ta	UP	Angara	52°55'	103°40'
6.	Dyuktay	UP	Aldan	59°20'	132°30'
7.	Filimoshki	L	Zeya	53°50'	127°30'
8.	Irkutsk	UP	Angara	52°16'	104°00'
9.	Kokorevo	UP	Yenisey	55°05'	91°10'
10.	Krasnyy Yar	T	Angara	53°40'	103°30'
11.	Malaya Syya	M	Chulym	55°	90°
12.	Mandel Gobi	L	(desert)	45°20'	106°20'
13.	Mayna	UP	Yenisey	52°40'	91°30'
14.	Oshurkovo	UP	Selenga	51°50'	107°20'
15.	Sayan Shanda	L	(desert)	44°50'	110°10'
16.	Shishkino	UP	Lena	54°00'	105°40'
17.	Sokhatino	M	Barguzin	54°20'	111°
18.	Strashnaya Peshchera	M	Inya	51°40'	83°
19.	Tomsk	UP	Tom'	56°30'	85°
20.	Ulalinka	L	Katun	51°55'	85°58'
21.	Ushki I	UP	Kamchatka	56°15'	159°20'
22.	Ust' Kanskaya	M	Katun	50°40'	86°10'
23.	Ust' Tu	L	Zeya	52°40'	127°40'

* L. Lower Paleolithic; M. Mousterian; T. Transitional; UP. Upper Paleolithic

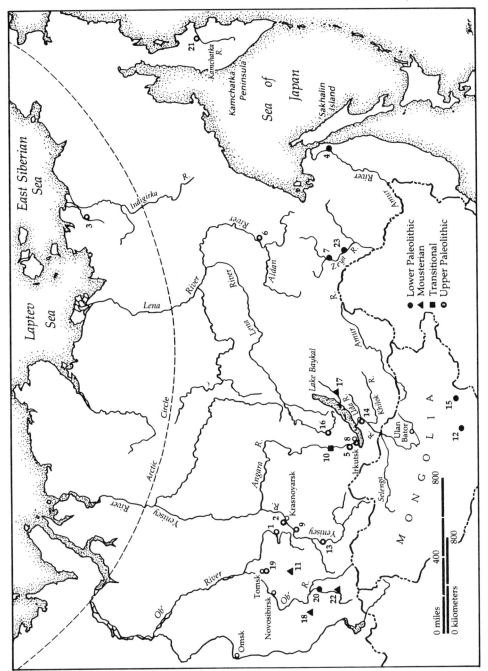

Map 1. Selected Paleolithic Sites

Map 2 Legend

Predominantly Neolithic Sites		Type*	Location		
No.	Name		Major River	°N	°E
1.	Balya Ozernaya	P	Angara	55°45′	103°10′
2.	Bazaykha	O	Yenisey	56° 0′	92°50′
3.	Bol′shaya Kada	P	Oka, Angara	55°20′	102°30′
4.	Ikh Tengerin Am	P	Tola, Selenga	47°45′	107° 0′
5.	Karakol	P	Katun, Ob′	50°40′	85°45′
6.	Khachurg	P	Tola, Selenga	47°55′	107°30′
7.	Kondon	O	Gorin, Amur	51°20′	136°30′
8.	Mugur Sargol	P	Yenisey	51°50′	92°10′
9.	Novoromanovo	P	Tom′, Ob′	55°18′	85°22′
10.	Ordinskoye I	O	Ob′	54°25′	81°55′
11.	Pegtymel′	P	Amguyema	Approx 68°	178°W
12.	Perviy Kamenniy Ostrog	P	Angara	55°12′	103°30′
13.	Sagan Zaba	P	L. Baykal	52°20′	105°45′
14.	Sakachi Alyan	P	Amur	48°45′	135°50′
15.	Samus′	O	Tom′ Ob′	56°45′	84°45′
16.	Shalabolino	P	Tuba, Yenisey	53°56′	91°30′
17.	Sheremyetovo	P	Ussuri, Amur	46°40′	134°05′
18.	Shigir	O	Pyshma, Ob′	57°10′	60°35′
19.	Shishkino	P	Lena	54°15′	105°20′
20.	Suchu Island	O	Amur	51°30′	140° 0′
21.	Suruktakh Khaya	P	Lena	61°00′	122°50′
22.	Tom′ R. Petroglyph (Pisanaya)	P	Tom′, Ob′	55°35′	85°30′
23.	Voznesenkoye	O	Khungari, Amur	50°15′	136°50′
24.	Vtoroy Kamenniy Ostrov	P	Angara	55°10′	103°30′
25.	Yaysk	O	Yaya, Chulym, Ob′	56°37′	86°22′
26.	Yelangash	P	Chuya, Katun, Ob′	49°55′	88°10′
27.	Yelanka	P	Lena	60°50′	122°50′

* P. Petroglyph
O. Other

Petroglyphic sub-regions:
A. Middle Lena
B. Angara
C. High Altay
D. Upper Yenisey (in Tuva)
E. Transbaykal
F. Lower Amur
G. Northeast Asia (Aldan-Maya)

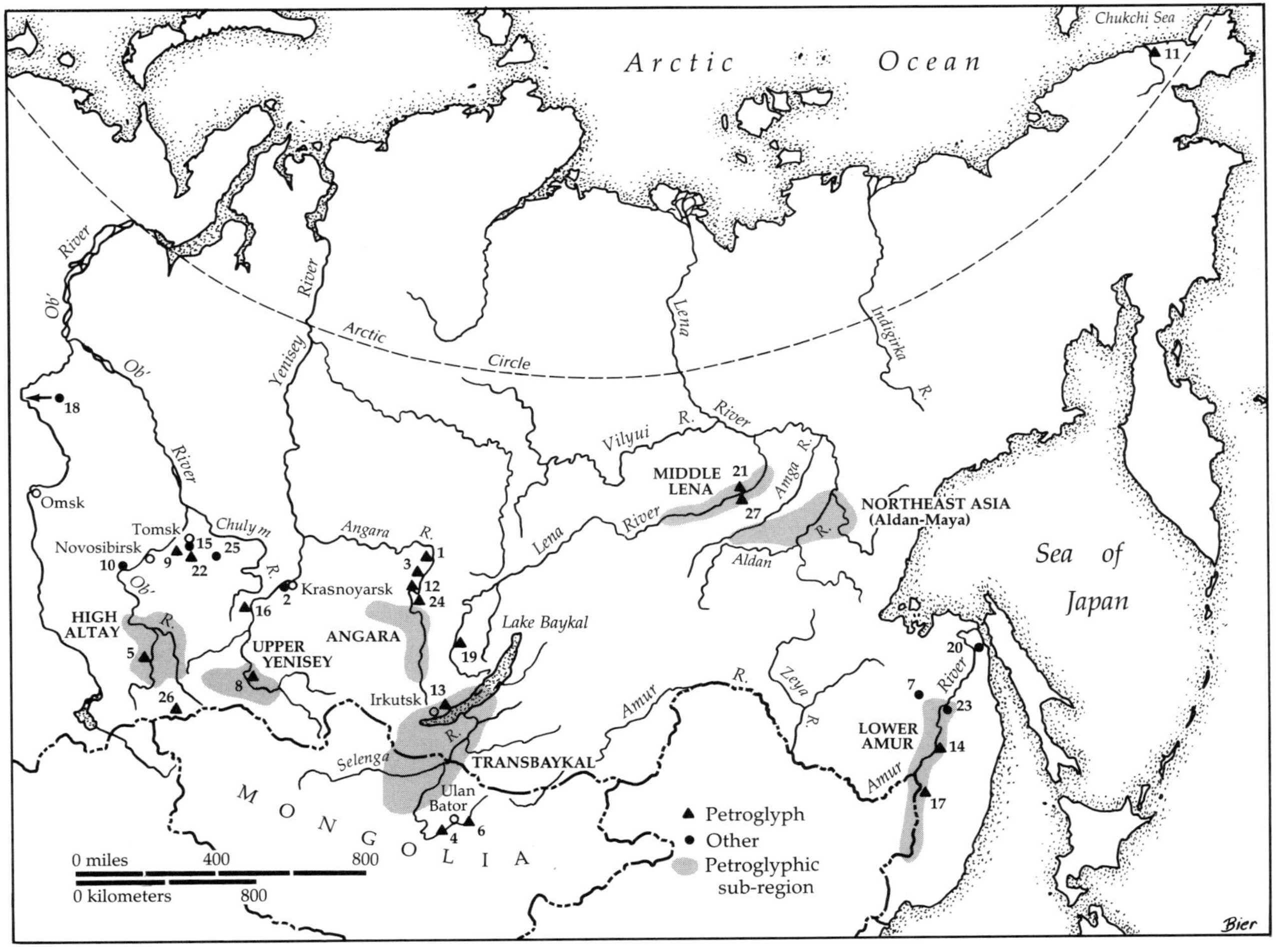

Map labels:

Bier

Chukchi Sea

Arctic Ocean

Sea of Japan

Indigirka R.

111

NORTHEAST ASIA (Aldan-Maya)

20
23
7
14
17

LOWER AMUR

River

Amur R.

Zeya R.

Amga R.

Aldan

Lena River

Vilyui R.

Lena R.

MIDDLE LENA

21
27

Arctic Circle

Lake Baykal

19

Amur

TRANSBAYKAL

1
12
24
3

ANGARA

Angara R.

13
Irkutsk

R.

Ulan Bator

4
6

M O N G O L I A

Selenga R.

Krasnoyarsk

2
16

UPPER YENISEI

8

Yenisey River

Chulym R.

Tomsk
15
25
9
22
10
Novosibirsk

Ob' R.

HIGH ALTAY
5
26

Ob River

Ob' River

18

Omsk

Petroglyph ▲
Other ●
Petroglyphic sub-region

0 miles   400   800
0 kilometers   800

Map 2. Selected Neolithic Sites

119

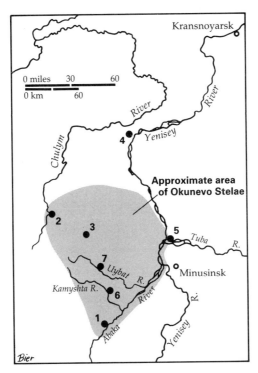

Map 3. Selected Eneolithic Sites

Map 3 Legend

		Selected Okunevo (Eneolithic) Sites		
Site		Location		
No.	Name	Major River	°N	°E
1.	Askyz	Abakan, Yenisey	53°10'	90°30'
2.	Belyy Ius R.	Chulym, Ob'	54°45'	89°45'
3.	Bira	Uybat, Abakan, Yenisey	53°50'	90°15'
4.	Chernovaya VIII	Yenisey	55°00'	91°05'
5.	Shalabolino	Yenisey	53°50'	91°30'
6.	Uybat	Abakan, Yenisey	53°30'	90°45'
7.	Verkhnebedzhinskaya steppe	Uybat, Abakan, Yenisey	ca. 53°40'	90°30'

Map 4 Legend

Site		Location		
No.	Name	Major River	°N	°E
1.	Bashadar	Bashkaus, Biya, Ob'	ca. 50°40'	88°00'
2.	Berel'	Irtysh, Ob'	49°50'	84°45'
3.	Bol'shaya Boyarskaya Pisanitsa	Yenisey	54°05'	90°55'
4.	Katanda	Katun, Ob'	50°07'	86°03'
5.	Kosh Agach	Chuya, Ob'	50°00'	88°40'
6.	Kudyrga	Bashkaus, Biya	51°00'	87°50'
7.	Kuray	Chuya, Katun, Ob'	50°10'	87°50'
8.	Lysaya Gora	Yaya, Chulym, Ob'	56°00'	86°15'
9.	Malaya Boyarskaya Pisanitsa	Yenisey	54°05'	90°55'
10.	Nekrasovo	Tyazhin, Chulym, Ob'	55°45'	88°50'
11.	Pazyryk	Bashkaus, Biya	50°44'	88°03'
12.	Serebryakovo	Tyazhin, Chulym, Ob'	55°35'	88°50'
13.	Shestakovo	Kiya, Chulym, Ob'	55°50'	87°59'
14.	Shibe	Charysh, Aley, Ob'	50°55'	85°10'
15.	Tisul'	Tyazhin, Chulym, Ob'	55°45'	88°10'
16.	Tom' River Petroglyph	Tom', Ob'	55°35'	85°30'
17.	Tuekta	Ursul, Katun, Ob'	50°50'	85°55'
18.	Yagunya	Tyazhin, Chulym, Ob'	55°30'	88°45'
19.	Yelangash	Chuya, Katun, Ob'	49°55'	88°10'

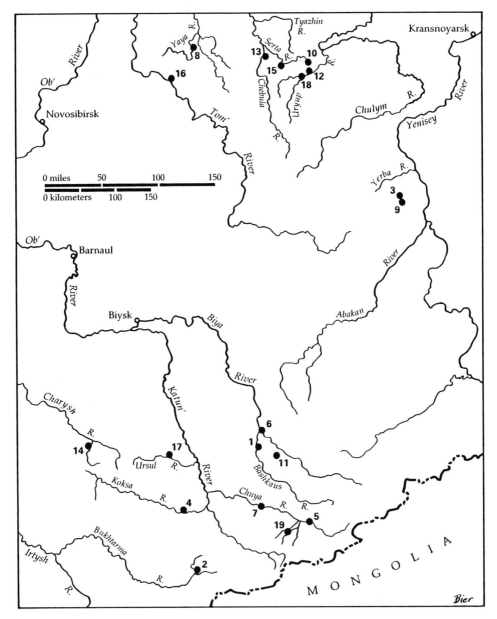

Map 4. Selected Scytho-Siberian Sites

123

Map 5 Legend

Site			Location		
No.	Name	Type*	River Basin	°N	°E
1.	Aydashinskaya Peshchera	HW	Chulym, Ob'	56°10'	90°20'
2.	Barsuchikha	H	Yenisey	(near Oglakhta)	
3.	Berkul' (Tyukovo)	W	Irtysh, Ob'	58°22'	68°25'
4.	Bokchar	W	Parbi, Ob'	57°08'	81°45'
5.	Bundyur	W	Iksa, Parbi, Ob'	57°35'	82°45'
6.	Karakol River	T	Katun, Ob'	50°40'	85°45'
7.	Khana Shuluun	T	(Orkhon), Selenga, L. Baykal	50°38'	106°35'
8.	Krivosheino	W	Ob'	59°30'	83°55'
9.	Kulay (Kulayka)	W	Iksa, Parbi, Ob'	57°35'	82°35'
10.	Lysaya Gora	HW	Yaya, Chulym, Ob'	56°00'	86°15'
11.	Makar Visyng Tur	W	N. Sos'va, Ob'	64°05'	65°45'
12.	Mankhay	T	Angara, Yenisey	52°30'	104°30'
13.	Murlinskiy klad	W	Irtysh, Ob'	56°45'	74°45'
14.	Nizhnaya Ivolga	H	Selenga, L. Baykal	51°45'	107°25'
15.	Noin Ula	H	(Orkhon), Selenga, L. Baykal	48°30'	106°20'
16.	Oglakhta	HT	Yenisey	53°55'	91°35'
17.	Shalabolino	HT	Yenisey	53°56'	91°30'
18.	Shestakovo	HW	Kiya, Chulym, Yenisey	55°50'	87°59'
19.	Sulek	T	Yenisey	55°45'	92°40'
20.	Tara River	W	Tara, Irtysh, Ob'	56°40'	74°45'
21.	Tabangutskoye Obo	T	Selenga, L. Baykal	50°35'	106°20'
22.	Tepsey	T	Yenisey	53°55'	91°30'
23.	Ust' Polui	HW	Ob'	66°40'	66°30'
24.	Uybat	HT	Yenisey	53°30'	90°45'
25.	Vasyugan	W	Vasyuga, Ob'	59°00'	80°30'
26.	Yelangash	T	Chuya, Katun, Ob'	49°55'	88°10'

* H. Hunnic-Tashtyk (first century B.C. to fifth century A.D.)
  T. Turkic (sixth to tenth century A.D.)
  W. Western Siberian Forest Medieval (first millennium A.D.)

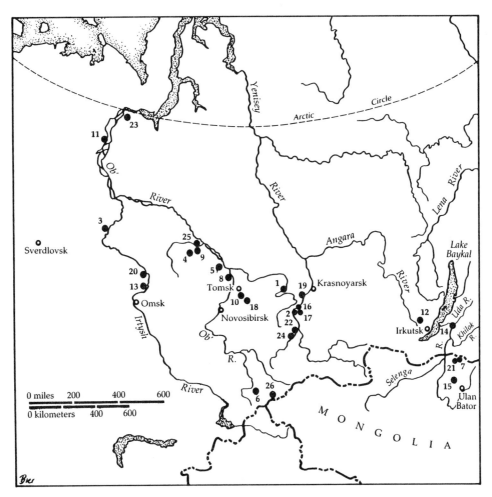

Map 5. Selected Medieval (Hunnic-Turkic) Sites

Map 6 Legend

			Location		
No.	Name	Age*	Major River	°N	°E
1.	Askyz river	E	Abakan, Yenisey	53°10'	90°30'
2.	Çatal Huyuk	N	Göksu, Mediterranean Sea	37°10'	33° 0'
3.	Chernovaya	E, S	Yenisey	55°00'	91°05'
4.	Chinga River	S	Yenisey	51°35'	92°35'
5.	Gobustan (Beyuk Dash)	N	Caspian Sea	40°10'	49°25'
6.	Kelermes	S	Laba, Kuban', Azov Sea	45°05'	40°00'
7.	Kulay (Kulayka)	W	Iksa, Porbi, Ob'	57°35'	82°35'
8.	Kunduz	S	Surkhab, Amu Darya	36°30'	68°50'
9.	Loz'va (Ivdel')	W	Loz'va, Tavda, Ob'	60°45'	60°25'
10.	Novocherkassk hoard	S	Don, Azov Sea	47°30'	40°08'
11.	Pazyryk	S	Bashkauz, Biya, Ob'	50°44'	88°03'
12.	Perm	W	Kama, Volga	58° 0'	56°20'
13.	Strettweg	S	Mur, L. Balaton, Danube	47°05'	15°25'
14.	Syda	E, S	Yenisey	54°20'	91°30'
15.	Tazmin (Bira R.)	E, S	Uybat, Abakan, Yenisey	53°50'	90°15'
16.	Tepsey	E, S, T	Yenisey	53°55'	91°30'
17.	Tokko	E	Chara, Lena	59°55'	119°55'
18.	Tutal'skaya pisanitsa	E, S	Tom', Ob'	55°45'	85°00'
19.	Ust' Tuba (see Tepsey)	E, S	Yenisey	53°55'	91°30'
20.	Uybat (see Tazmin)	E, S	Abakan, Yenisey	53°50'	90°45'
21.	Yelangash	S, T	Chuya, Katun, Ob'	49°55'	88°10'

* N. Neolithic; E. Eneolithic; S. Scytho-Siberian, including Hallstadt; T. Turkic (Early Medieval); W. West Siberian Forest Medieval

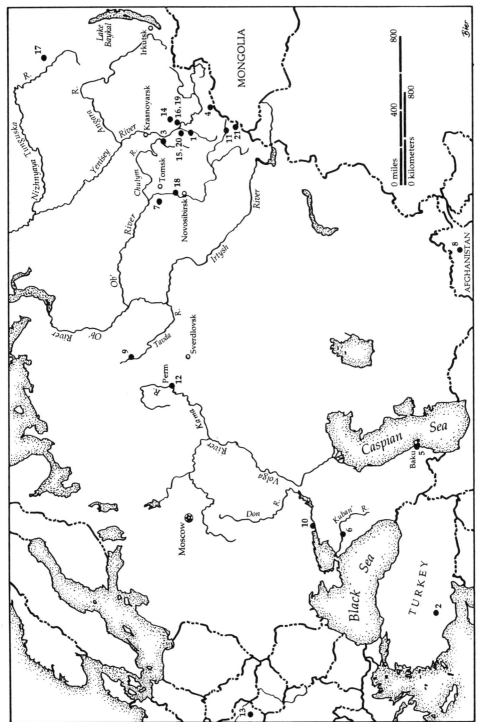

Map. 6. Selected Sites of Art and Mythology

127

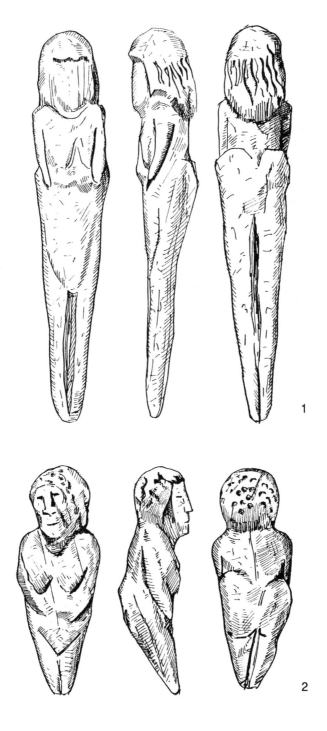

Figure 1. Statuettes of women from Mal'ta (1)
and Buret' (2) (Abramova 1962: pl. 46).

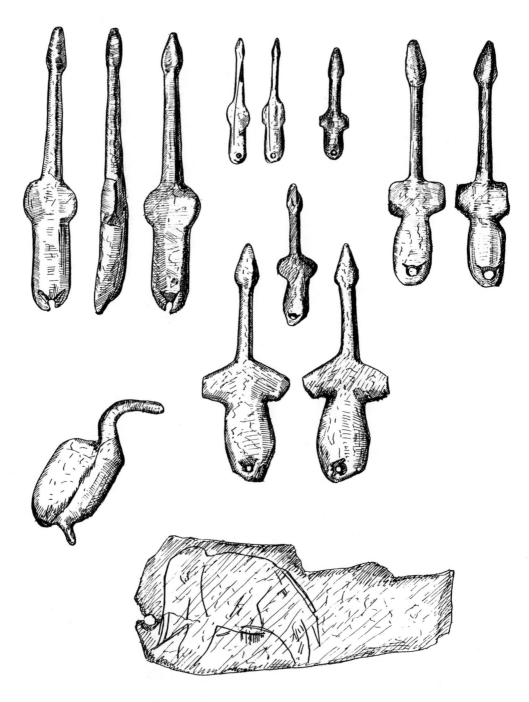

Figure 2. Bird figurines and an incised mammoth representation, Mal'ta
(Abramova 1962: pls. 50, no. 1; pl. 52; 53, no. 1).

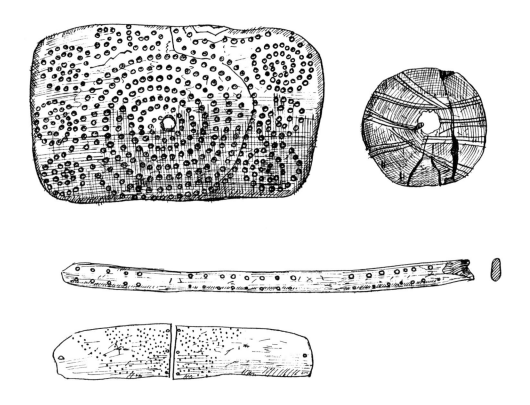

Figure 3. Incised bone plates, Mal'ta (Abramova 1962: pls. 50, no. 2; 54, nos. 11, 12).

131

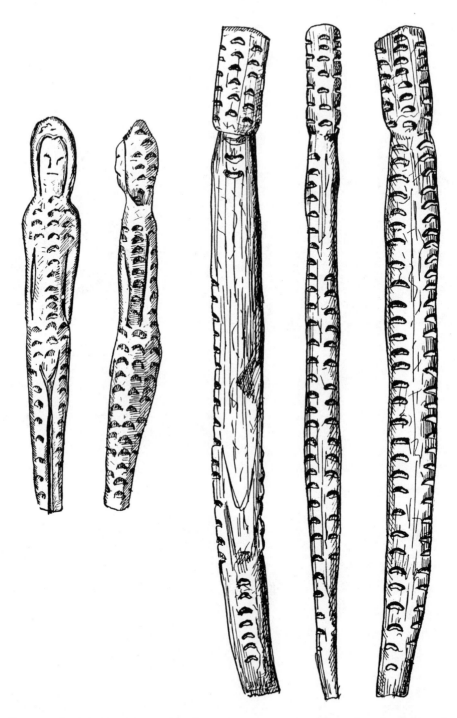

Figure 4. Incisions representing fur on a statuette from Buret' and an object from Mal'ta (Abramova 1962: pls. 53, no. 7; 57, no. 1).

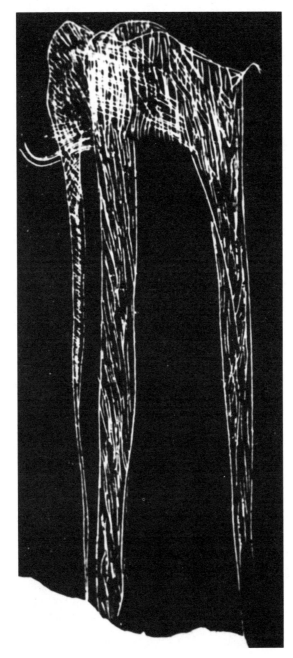

Figure 5. Engraving of a mammoth, Berelëkh
(Bader 1975).

Figure 6. Wide-mouthed vessel with complex spiral and banded ornament. Dark brown clay with smudges of black. Height 34 cm. Early Neolithic. Suchu Island, Amur (Okladnikov 1981: pl. 89).

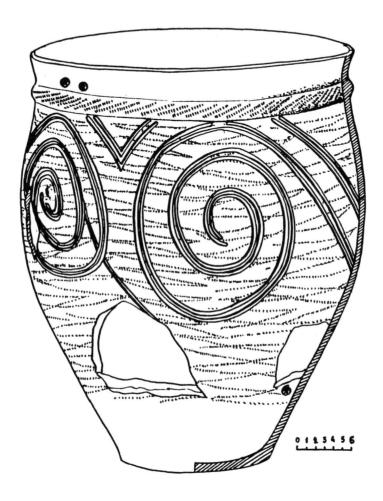

Figure 7. Incised spirals filled in with comblike stamp. Yellow-brown clay with traces of red pigment. Height 44 cm. Early Neolithic. Kondon, Gorin River, Amur drainage (Okladnikov 1981: pl. 88).

135

Figure 8. Potsherds with masks outlined by grooves and filled in with comblike impressions. Background burnished red. Height (left) 20.5 cm, (right) 33.5 cm. Early Neolithic. Voznesenskoye. L. Amur (Okladnikov 1981: pls. 18, 19).

Figure 9. Light-yellow clay. Figurine. Face realistic, torso schematic. Height 17 cm. Early Neolithic. Kondon (Okladnikov 1981: pl. 27).

Figure 10. Moose figurines from Bazaikha near Krasnoyarsk (1, 2), Shigir in the Urals (3), and the island of Gotland in the Baltic (4). Bone and antler (Okladnikov and Martynov 1972:181–83).

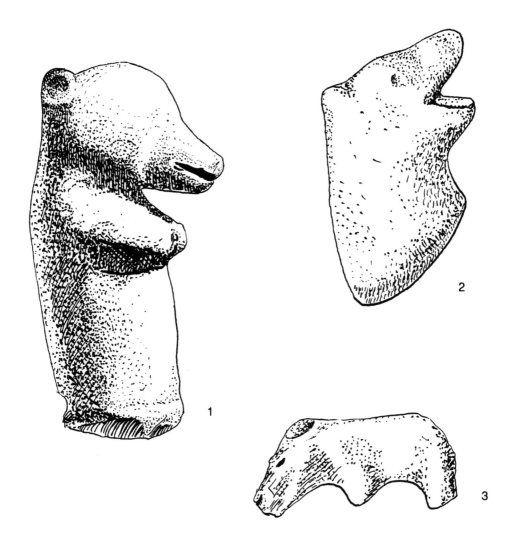

Figure 11. Bear figurines from Samus' in western Siberia (1), Sakachi-Alyan (2), and Suchu Island (3), the last two on the Lower Amur. Early Neolithic. A. I. Martynov.

Figure 12. The central group of figures on the Tom' River petroglyph. Neolithic (Okladnikov and Martynov 1972:70 insert; Martynov 1982: fig. 7).

Figure 13. A procession of boats, anthropomorphic beings, and deer. Shishkino. Painted. Bronze Age (Okladnikov and Zaporozhskaya 1959:98–108, no. 600).

Figure 14. Moose and anthropomorphic figure. Pecked. Balya Ozernaya (Angara). Neolithic (Okladnikov 1966:77–78, fig. 130).

142

Figure 15. Moose figures from Balya Ozernaya. Pecked. Balya Ozernaya (Angara). Neolithic (Okladnikov 1966:77–78).

Figure 16. Ibex and possible sun images. Yelangash, Gorniyy Altay (High Altay) (Okladnikov et al. 1979).

144

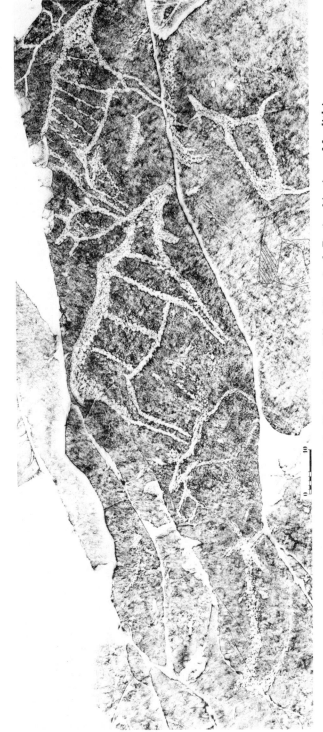

Figure 17. Moose figures. Pecked. Shalobolino cliffs, Minusinsk Basin, Yenisey. Neolithic.

145

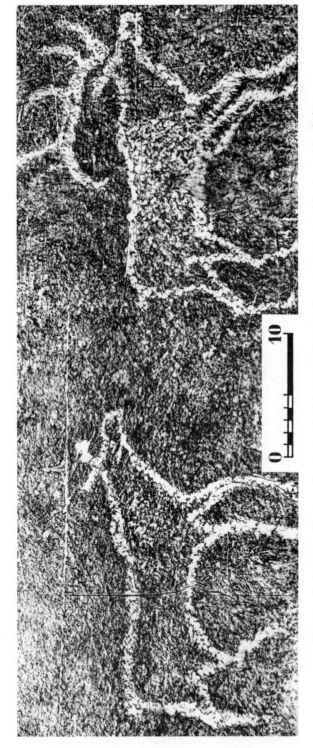

Figure 18. Moose figures. Pecked. Shalobolino Cliffs, Minusinsk Basin, Yenisey. Neolithic.

Figure 19. Moose figures. Pecked. Shalobolino Cliffs, Minusinsk Basin, Yenisey. Neolithic.

Figure 20. Anthropomorphic figures, masks, hunting scene. Mugur-Saragol, Upper Yenisey. Bronze Age (Devlet 1980).

Figure 21. Birds, anthropomorphic figures, and animal enclosures. Painted ochre. Ikh Tengerin Am and Khachurt, Tola River, Selenga drainage, Mongolia. Late Bronze Age (Okladnikov and Zaporozhskaya 1969–70: vol. 2, 51–54; Novgorodova 1984:90–94).

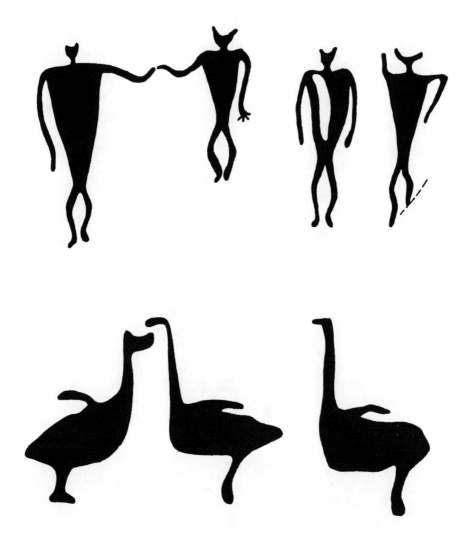

Figure 22. Human and bird figures from different compositions. Pecked. Sagan Zaba cliff, southwest Lake Baykal. Bronze Age (Okladnikov 1974: pls. 7, 16).

Figure 23. Mask and spiral figures on basaltic boulders. Deeply pecked. Sakachi Alyan, Lower Amur. Neolithic (Okladnikov 1971: pl. 33).

Figure 24. Anthropomorphic figures with "mushroom" headgear (top). Reindeer-hunting scenes. Pegtymel', Amguyema Basin, Chukotka. Late Bronze Age (Dikov 1971, 1979:157–60).

Figure 25. Anthropomorphic beings copulating with female moose: (1) Tom' River petroglyph, (2) Angara, Vtoroy Kamenniy ostrov. Neolithic (Okladnikov and Martynov 1972:67; Okladnikov 1966: pl. 38).

Figure 26. A magical scene of an anthropomorphic figure fertilizing female moose. Tom' River petroglyph. Neolithic (Okladnikov and Martynov 1972:70 insert).

Figure 27. Representation of a combined female moose/anthropomorphic figure, with another female moose and a phallic figure. Tom' River petroglyph. Neolithic (Okladnikov and Martynov 1972:70 insert).

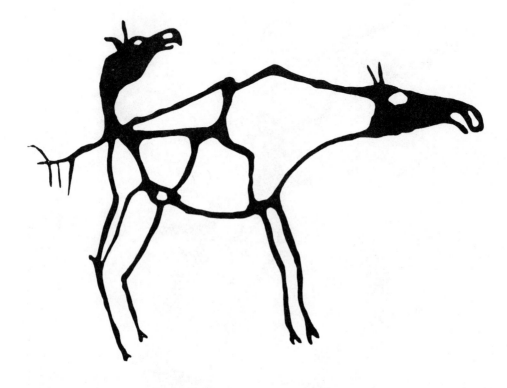

Figure 28. Birth of a moose calf. Tom' River petroglyph. Neolithic (Martynov 1982: fig. 8).

Figure 29. Hunting moose with a noose (1, 2) and with a surround and bows (3). Tom' River petroglyph. Neolithic (Martynov 1982: fig. 2; Okladnikov and Martynov 1972:123).

Figure 30. Killing moose with a harpoon or spear. Tom' River petroglyph. Neo-lithic (Okladnikov and Martynov 1972:64, 70 insert; Martynov 1982: fig. 2).

Figure 31. Hunting deer and ibex with bows. Mongolia. Unlocated. Neolithic.

Figure 32. Mass killing of moose at a river crossing. Tom' River petroglyph. Neolithic (Okladnikov and Martynov 1972:70 insert [reverse]).

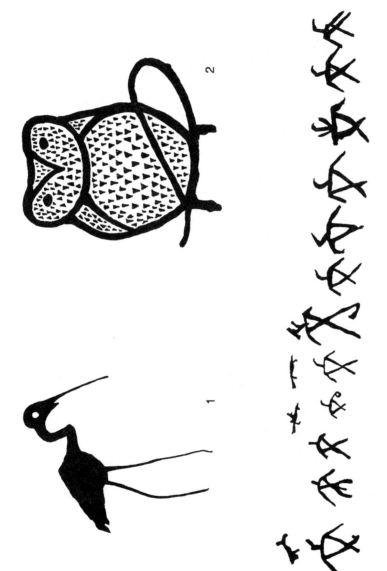

Figure 33. Sacred birds: (1) crane, (2) owl (Tom' River petroglyph), and (3) dancing bird-people (Suruktakh Khaya, middle Lena). Bronze Age (Martynov 1982: fig. 3; Okladnikov and Zaporozhskaya 1972:126).

Figure 34. Boat representations. Novoromanovo, Tom' River. Neolithic (Okladni-kov and Martynov 1972:138).

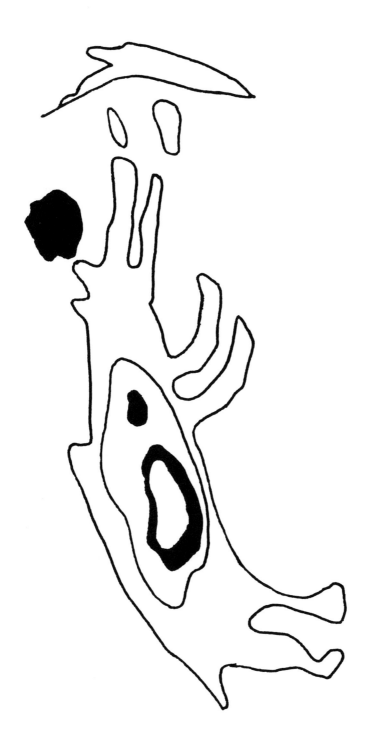

Figure 35. Fantastic creature, possibly representing the underworld. Tom' River petroglyph. Neolithic (Martynov 1982: fig. 13).

163

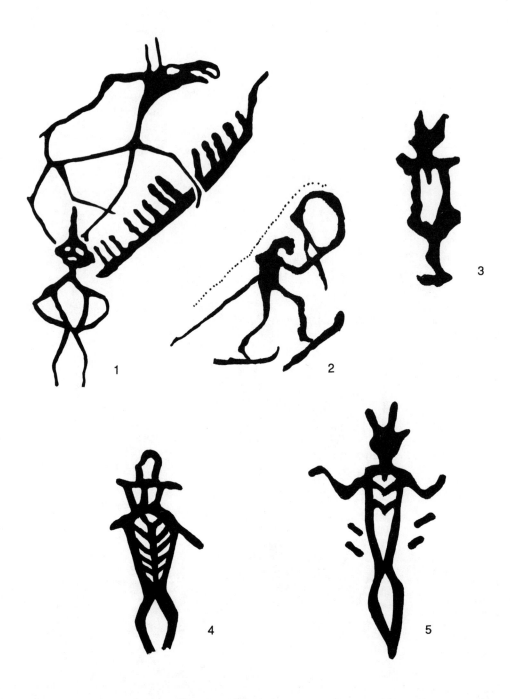

Figure 36. Anthropomorphic beings with animal-like features: (1, 2, 3) Tom' River petroglyph; (4), (5) Bol'shaya Kada, Angara. Neolithic (Okladnikov and Martynov 1972:60, 73, 87; Okladnikov 1966:302, 311).

164

Figure 37. Highly conventionalized anthropomorphic figures. Tom' River petro-glyph. Neolithic (Okladnikov and Martynov 1972:55, no. 69; 115, no. 244).

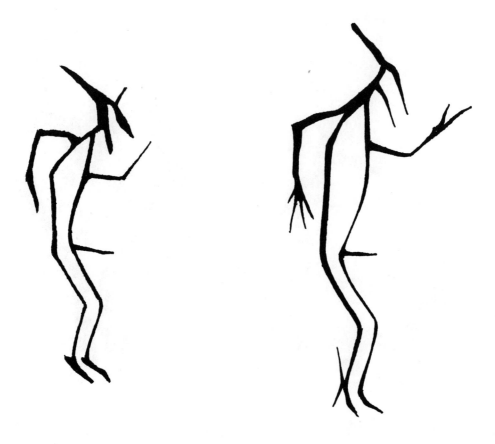

Figure 38. Birdmen. Tom' River petroglyph. Eneolithic (Okladnikov and Martynov 1972:188).

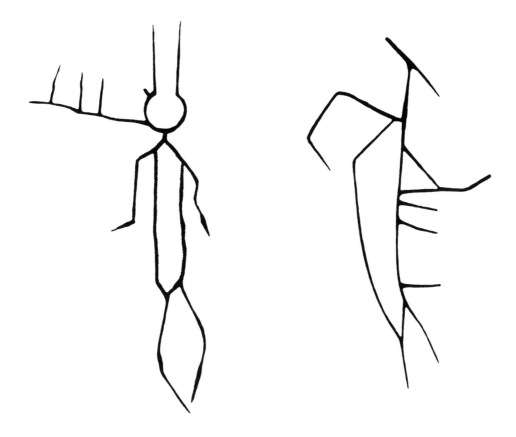

Figure 39. Highly conventionalized, dancing anthropomorphic figures. Tom' River petroglyph. Incised. Eneolithic, Samus' culture (Martynov 1982: fig. 10).

Figure 40. Ritual group of figures with birdlike hands. Mongolia. Unlocated. Eneolithic (Novgorodova 1984:44–49).

Figure 41. Anthropomorphic being with bird features and phallus. Painted. Perviy Kamenniy ostrov, Angara. Eneolithic (Okladnikov 1966:173, pl. 29).

Figure 42. Varieties of masklike petroglyphs at Sakachi Alyan, representational to highly conventionalized. Pecked. Neolithic (Okladnikov 1971:191, 209, 306, 193, 198, 164, 225, 313, 164, 170, 188).

Figure 43. Skull-like mask at Sakachi Alyan. Pecked. Neolithic
(Okladnikov 1971:205).

Figure 44. Skull-like masks with rays. Pecked. Sakachi Alyan. Neolithic (Okladni-kov 1971:222).

Figure 45. Masks with rays: (1) youthful appearance, Sakachi Alyan; (2) spiral conventionalized, Sheremetyevo. Pecked. Neolithic (Okladnikov 1971:173, 266).

Figure 46. Complex conventionalized masklike figures. Pecked. Neolithic. Sakachi Alyan (Okladnikov 1971:[1] 225; [2] 170).

Figure 47. Human mask image. Tom' River petroglyph. Pecked. Neolithic (Okladnikov and Martynov 1972:125, no. 272; 192).

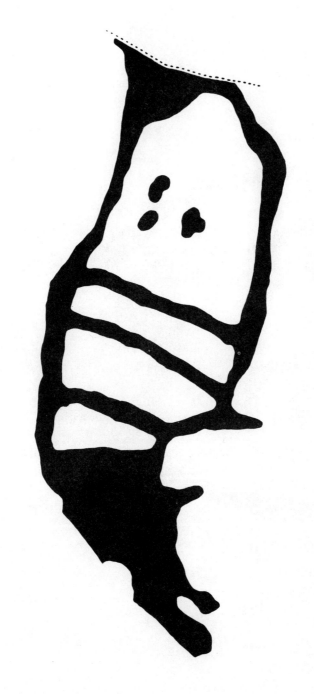

Figure 48. Conventionalized moose with human face on flank. Tom' River petroglyph. Neolithic (Okladnikov and Martynov 1972:69, no. 97).

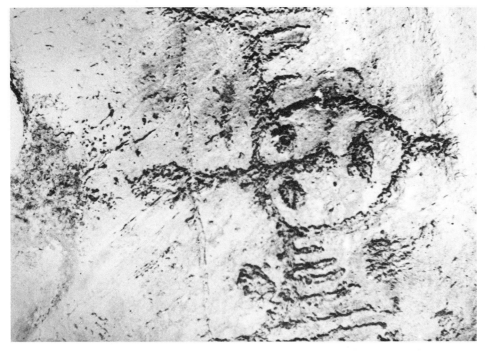

Figure 49. Elaborate portrait masks. Mugur Saragol, upper Yenisey. Early Bronze Age (Devlet 1976b: pl. 60).

177

Figure 50. The Tom' River petroglyph, a votive site. Sacred places of the past. Photo by A. I. Martynov.

Figure 51. The Tom' River petroglyph, a national treasure. Photo by A. I. Martynov.

Figure 52. Representation of a shaman. Charcoal painting. Historic Yakut. Ye-lanka, on Lena south of Yakutsk (Okladnikov and Zaporozhskaya 1972:225, no. 121).

Figure 53. Bull. Shalobolino, Yenisey River, Okunevo (Eneolithic).
A. I. Martynov.

Figure 54. Bull representations. Chernovaya 8, in Minusinsk Basin. Okunevo (Eneolithic) (Leontyev 1970:266).

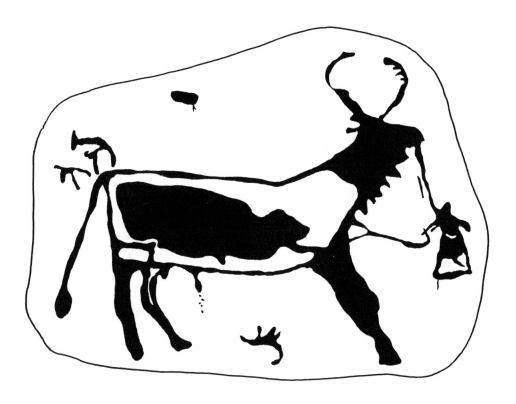

Figure 55. Bull progenitor. Early Bronze Age. Gornyy Altay (High Altay).
A. I. Martynov.

Figure 56. Patterns of decoration on steppe and forest-steppe pottery in the Late Bronze Age, primarily from the Minusinsk Basin (Maksimenkov 1978:67).

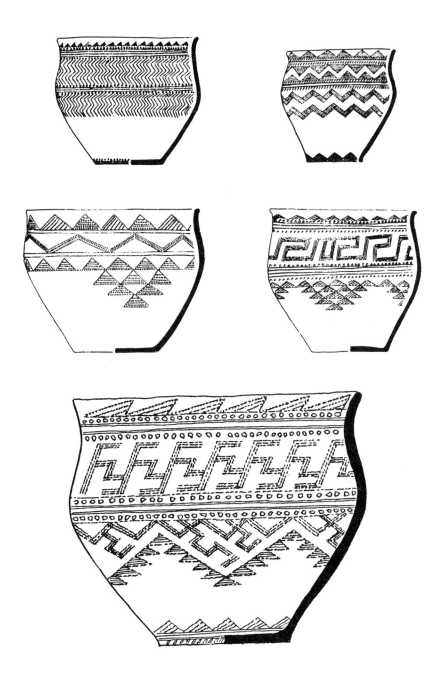

Figure 57. Shapes and decorative patterns in the Andronovo shouldered bowl (*gorshok*). A. I. Martynov (Kiselev 1951:75).

Figure 58. Shapes and decorative patterns in the Andronovo semicylindrical bowl (*banka*) (Maksimenkov 1978:65).

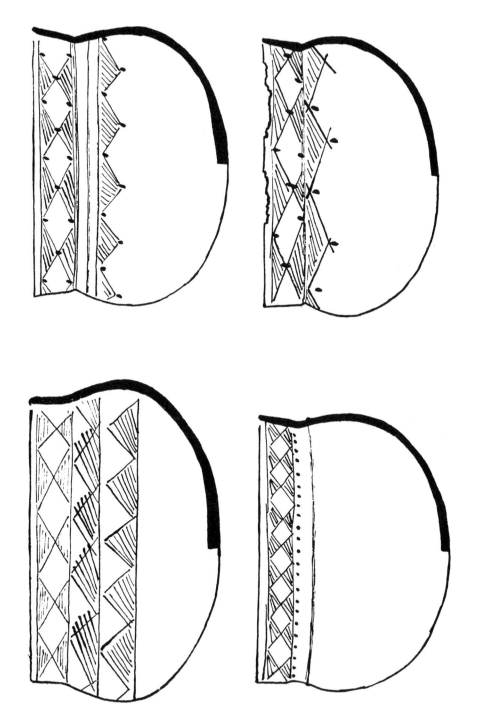

Figure 59. Shapes and decorative patterns in Karasuk pottery of the twelfth century B.C. A. I. Martynov.

187

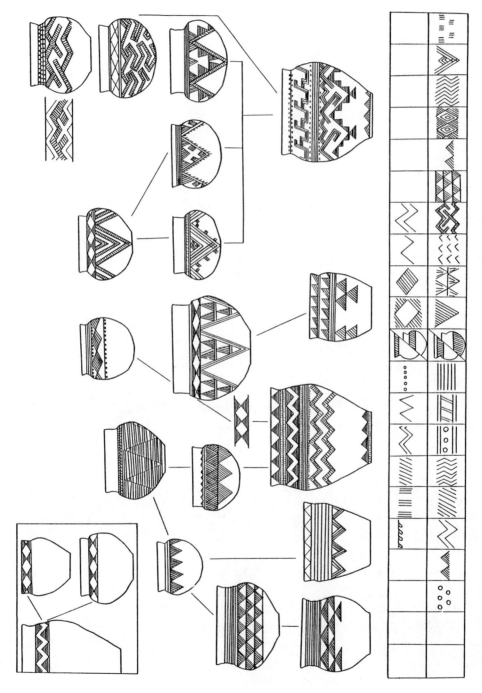

Figure 60. Andronovo/Karasuk decorative continuities and transformations (Maksimenkov 1978:115).

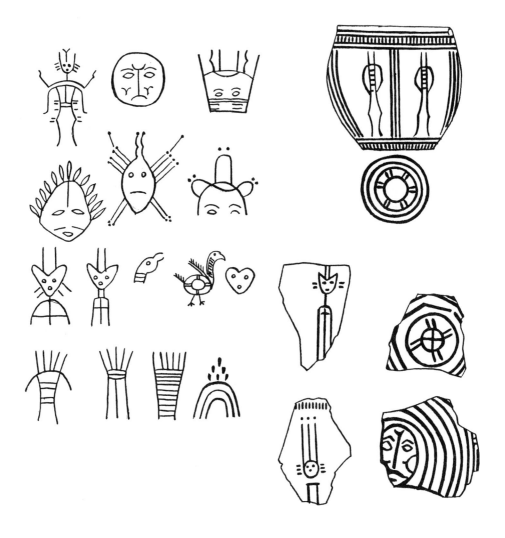

Figure 61. Decorative patterns on pottery of the Bronze Age Samus' culture (Matyushchenk 1973).

Figure 62. Plain Okunevo statues of the south Siberian Eneolithic: (1) Belyy Iyus River, Khakasia; (2) Inya River; (3) Malyy Iyus River (Vadetskaya et al. 1980).

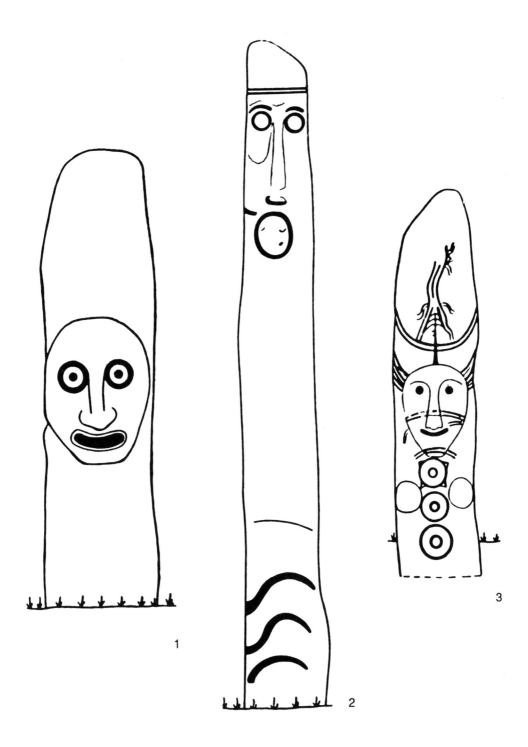

Figure 63. Okunevo statuary of south Siberia: (1) Uybat River, Minusinsk Basin; (2) Verkhnebedzhinskaya; (3) Bira River. Eneolithic (Vadetskaya et al. 1980).

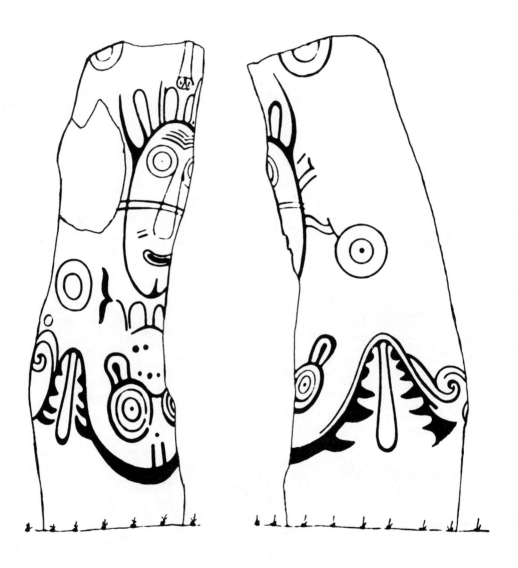

Figure 64. Complex Okunevo statues of the south Siberian Bely Iyus River. Eneolithic (Vadetskaya et al. 1980).

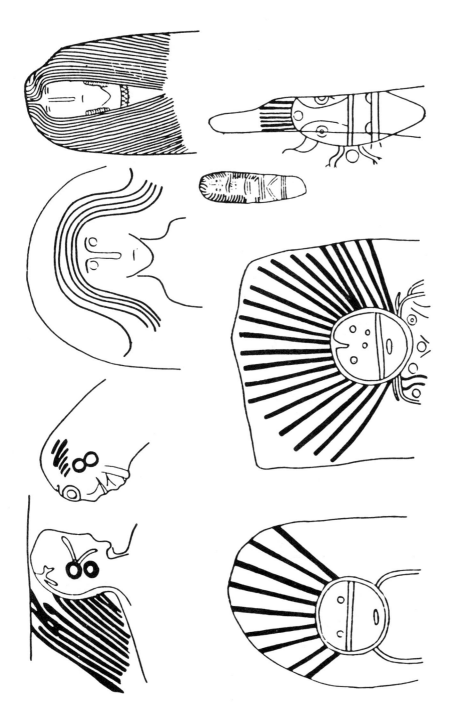

Figure 65. Hair and radiations from the heads of Okunevo statuary (Vadetskaya et al. 1980).

193

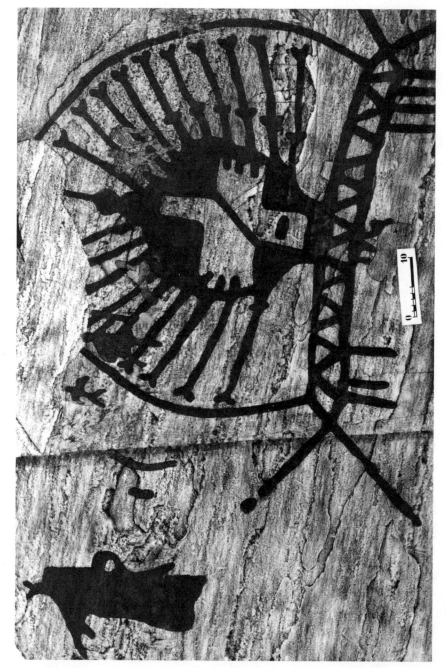

Figure 66. Red painted rayed figure. Petroglyph. Shalobolino, Yenisey. Okunevo. Eneolithic.

194

Figure 67. Representation of a solar deity. Okunevo Askyz River, Minusinsk Basin. Eneolithic (Vadetskaya 1967: pl. 5; Vadetskaya et al. 1980).

Figure 68. Wooden bas-relief saddle ornaments. Altay Animal Style (See also Rudenko 1953: pls. 80, no. 2; 81, no. 9).

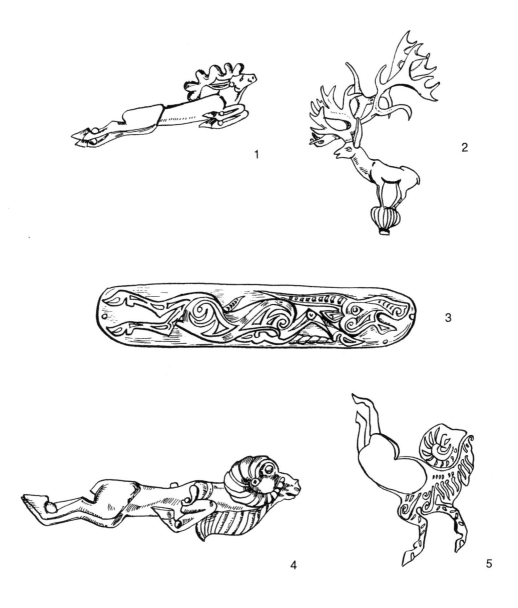

Figure 69. Bas- and full-relief figurines. Altay Animal Style: (1, 3, 4) wood; (2) wood and leather; (5) felt. (See also Rudenko 1953: pl. 79, no. 1; Gryaznov 1958, pls. 9, 29.)

Figure 70. Tiger attacking a moose. Leather appliqué saddle cover. Pazyryk (Rudenko 1953:273).

Figure 71. Attacks on herbivores. Leather appliqué saddle covers.
Pazyryk. (See also Rudenko 1953:275–77.)

Figure 72. Fantastic animal figures from arm tattoos of a princely burial in Kurgan 2. Pazyryk (Rudenko 1953:139).

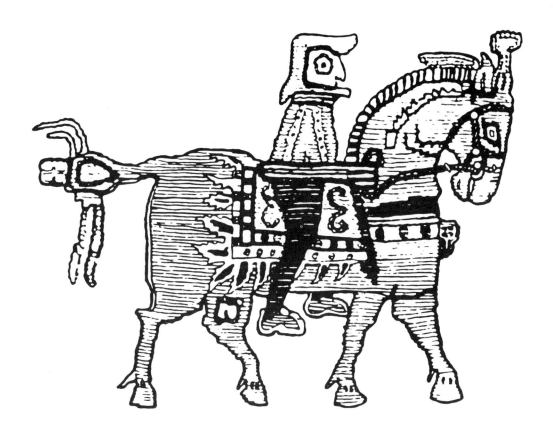

Figure 73. Horse and rider in procession. Detail from the border decoration of a pile carpet. Kurgan 5. Pazyryk (Rudenko 1953: pl. 16).

Figure 74. Rider. Detail from a scene with a goddess. Multicolored pile hanging. Kurgan 5. Pazyryk (Rudenko 1953: pl. 95).

Figure 75. Mythical eagle. Wood; full relief with leather ears. Kurgan 2. Pazyryk (Gryaznov 1958: fig. 32).

203

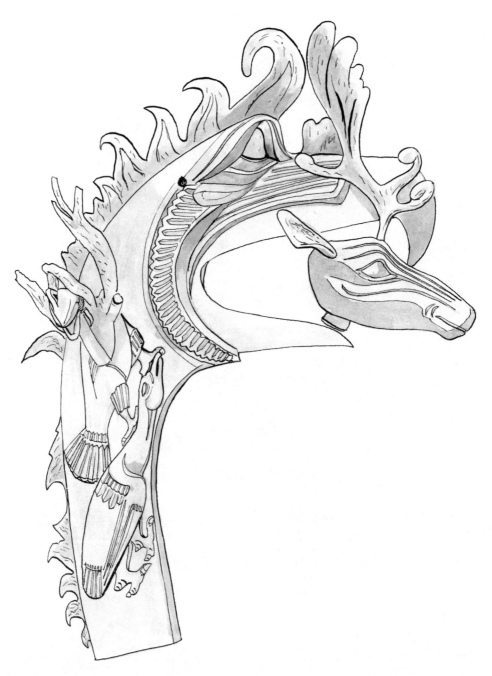

Figure 76. Moose in the maw of a griffin. Full relief, wood with bas-relief bird figure and leather mane. Kurgan 2. Pazyryk (Gryaznov 1958: fig. 37).

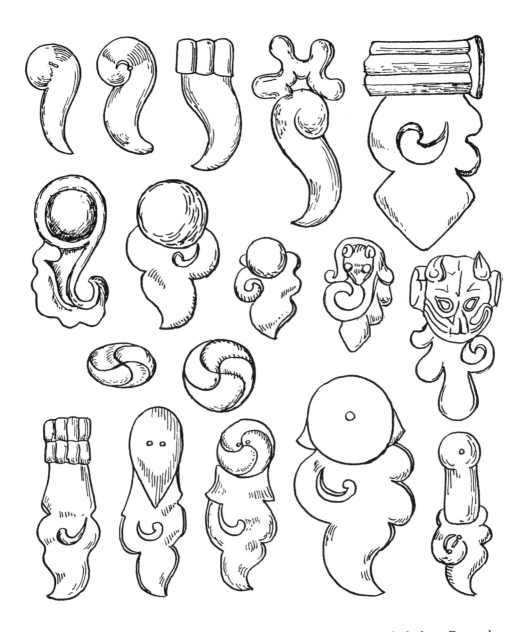

Figure 77. Wooden geometrical pendants. Probable solar symbols from Pazyryk, Bashadar, Tuekta.

205

Figure 78. Lotus and palmetto. Bridle ornament. Bone. Pazyryk (Gryaznov 1958: fig. 64).

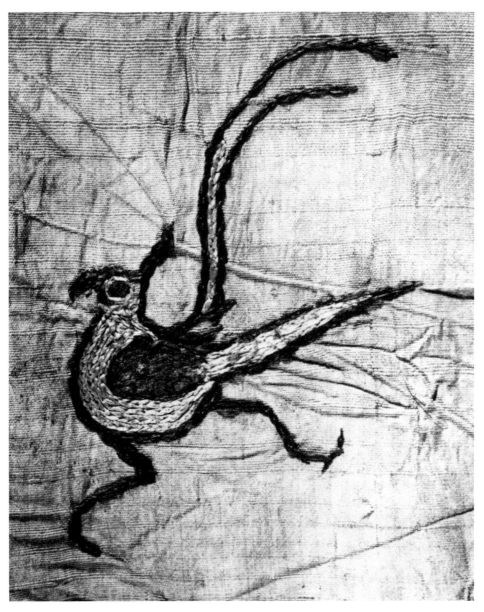

Figure 79. Phoenix embroidered on Chinese silk. Kurgan 5, Pazyryk (Rudenko 1953: pl. 118; Gryaznov 1958: fig. 53).

Figure 80. Greek-type face (*gorgoneion*) on bas-relief wooden saddle ornament. Kurgan 1. Pazyryk (Gryaznov 1958: fig. 12. Compare Boardman 1965, figs. 77, 105).

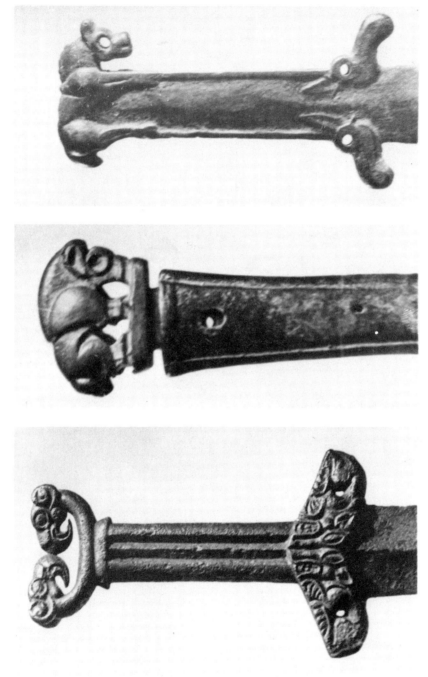

Figure 81. Bronze dagger hilts with animal figures. Tagar art from south Siberia and Mongolia. A. I. Martynov.

Figure 82. Reindeer emblems in forest-steppe Tagar art: Type 1 with S-shaped antlers. Yagunya, Tisul' (Martynov 1979: pl. 38).

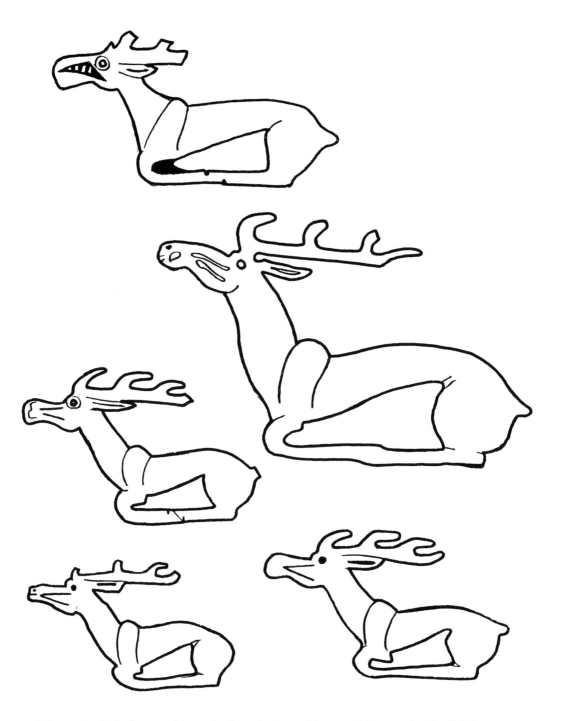

Figure 83. Reindeer emblems in forest-steppe Tagar art. Type 2A. Tisul' (Martynov 1979: pl. 39).

211

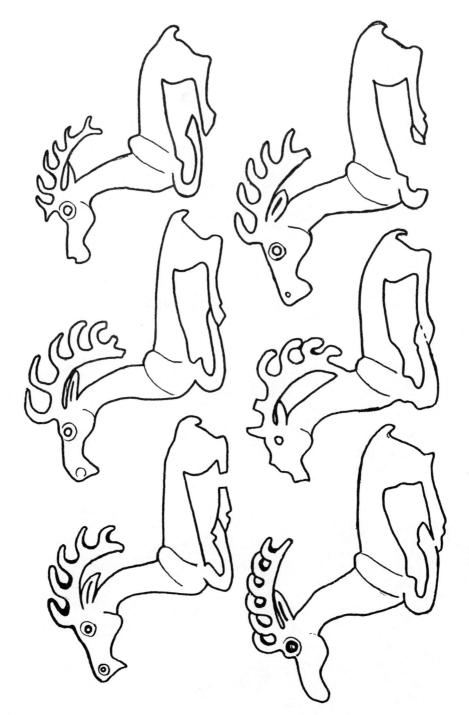

Figure 84. Reindeer emblems in forest-steppe Tagar art. Types 2B, C. Tisul' (Martynov 1979: pl. 40).

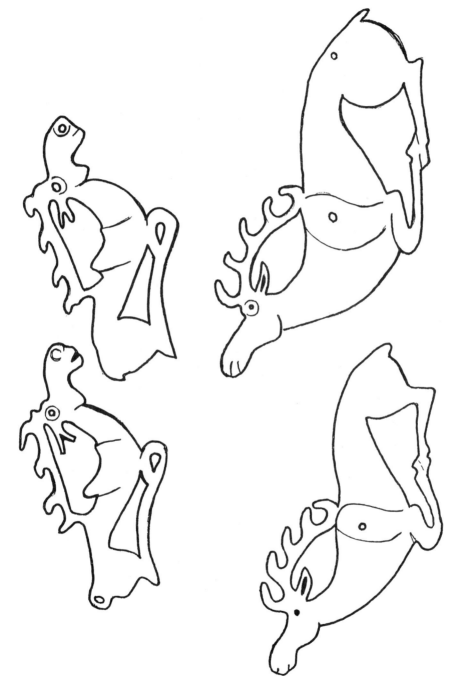

Figure 85. Reindeer emblems in forest-steppe Tagar art. Type 2D. Tisul' (Martynov 1979: pl. 40).

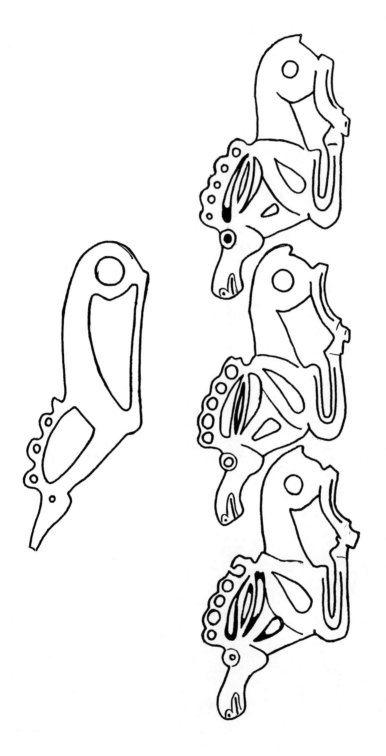

Figure 86. Reindeer emblems in forest-steppe Tagar art. Types 3A–D. Tisul' (Martynov 1979: pl. 41).

214

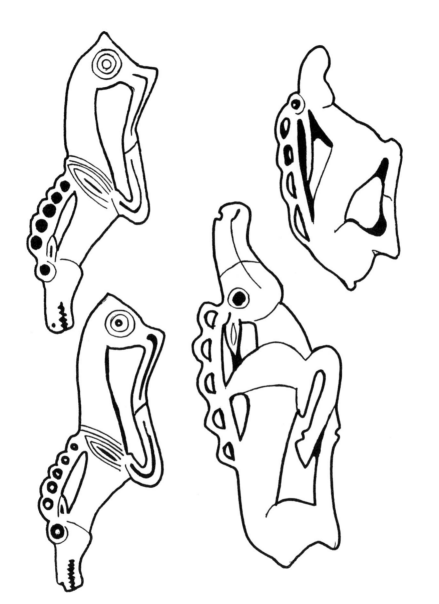

Figure 87. Reindeer emblems in forest-steppe Tagar art. Type 3E. Tisul' (Martynov 1979: pl. 41).

215

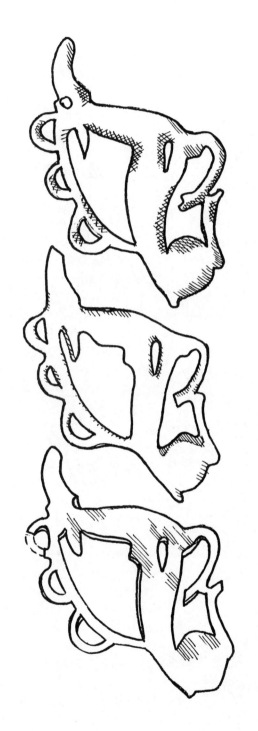

Figure 88. Reindeer emblems in forest-steppe Tagar art. Type 3H. Tisul', Yagunya (Martynov 1979: pl. 42).

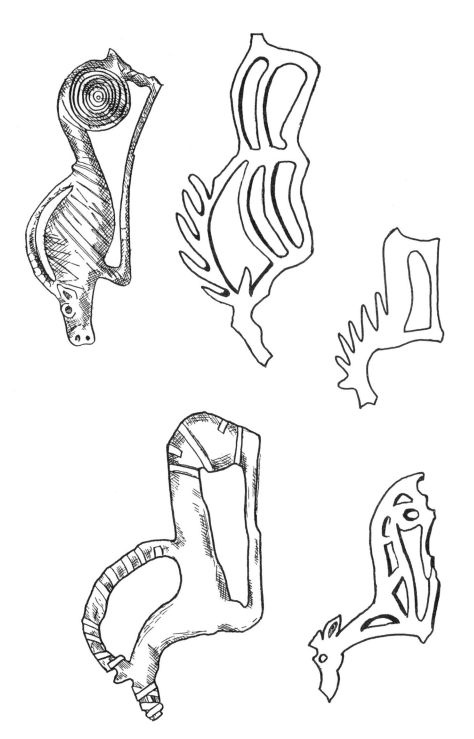

Figure 89. Reindeer emblems in forest-steppe Tagar art. Types 4–6. Tisul', Yagunya (Martynov 1979: pl. 43).

217

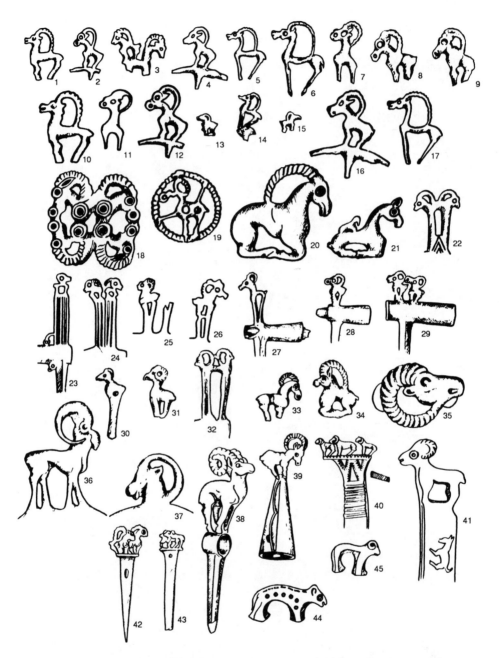

Figure 90. Ram figures in Tagar art: (1–9, 20) Yagunya; (10–12, 19, 21) Lysaya Gora; (22) Tisul'; (27–29); Barsuchikha I; (30–37) Minusinsk Museum; (39) Northern Kazakhstan; (40) Turbino (Kama River, European Russia); (41) Ordos (Inner Mongolia); (42, 43) Minusinsk area; (44, 45) central Asia, sacred images "farn" (Martynov 1979: pl. 44).

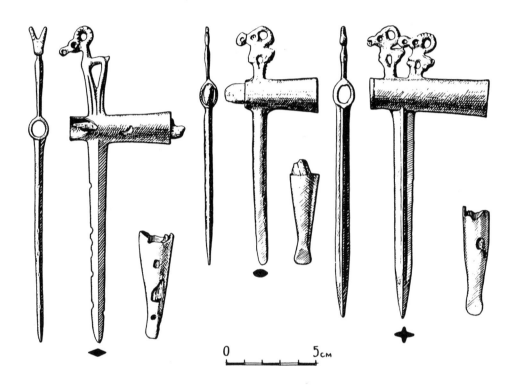

Figure 91. Tagar battle pickaxes with ram-headed butts. Barsuchikha.

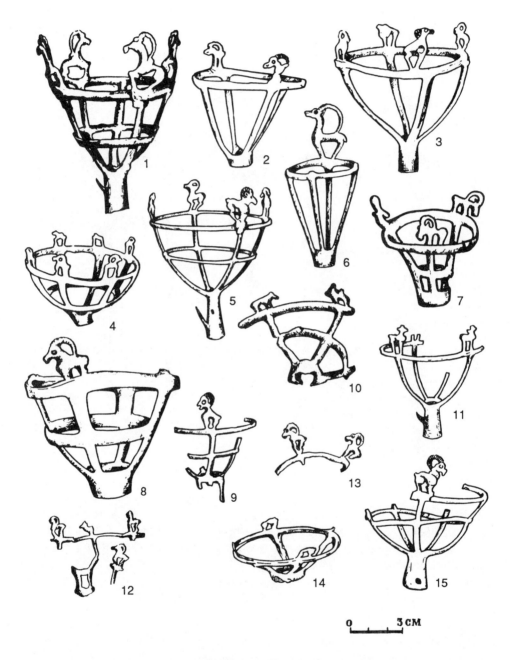

Figure 92. Tagar altars for sacred fires, with ram ornamentation: (1–5, 7, 10–13) Tisul'; (6, 8) Yagunya; (14–15) Nekrasovo cemetery (Martynov 1979:137–39).

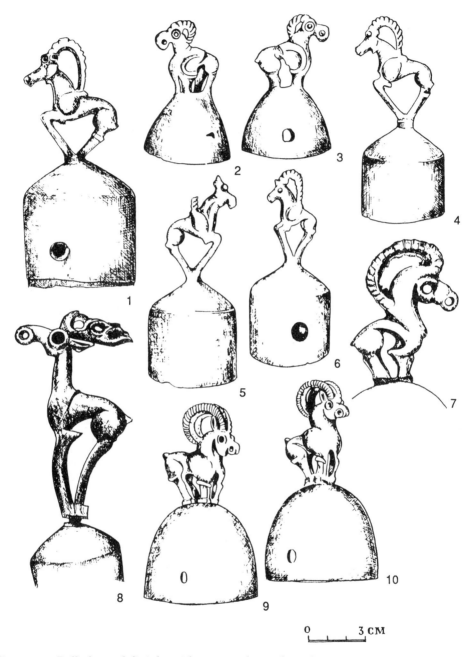

Figure 93. Bell-shaped finials with ram and reindeer decorations, Forest-steppe Tagar: (1–6) Tisul'; (7–10) Minusinsk Basin (Martynov 1979:122–23, pl. 45).

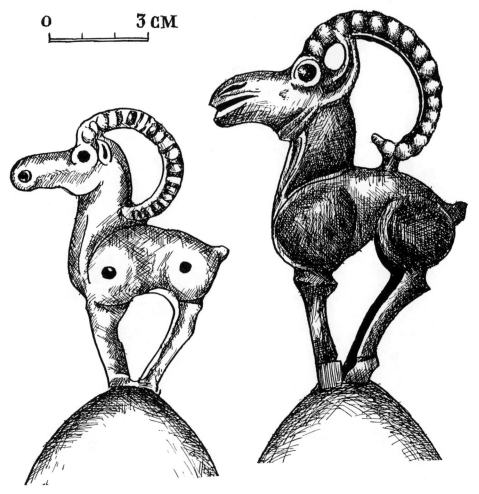

O   3 CM

Figure 94. Ram figures showing beading and finish, from bell-shaped finials.

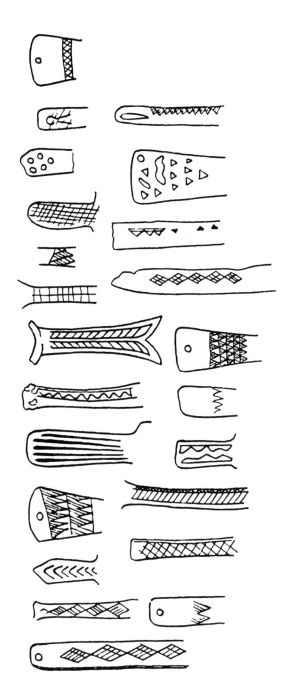

Figure 95. Geometric decorations on Tagar bronze objects (Martynov 1979: pl. 46).

Figure 96. Malaya Boyarskaya pisanitsa (Lesser Boyar Mountain pictograph). Punctate. Log-house types (Devlet 1976a: pl. 10).

Figure 97. Bol'shaya Boyarskaya pisanitsa (Great Boyar Mountain pictograph). Drawings of overview (top) and left portion (bottom). Punctate. Frieze is 9.8 × 1.5 m. Late Tagar (second century B.C.) (Devlet 1976a: pl. 5).

Figure 98. Bol'shaya Boyarskaya pisanitsa (Great Boyar Mountain pictograph). Drawings of the central (top) and right (bottom) portions. Punctate (Devlet 1976a: pl. 6).

226

Figure 99. North Asiatic solar animals from the following petroglyphs: Sakachi Alyan (1, 4, 5); Yelangash (2); Aldan River (3); Chankyr Köl, Altay (7, 8).

227

Figure 100. Winged solar reindeer on pile wool carpet. Kurgan 5, Pazyryk
(Rudenko 1953; pl. 116).

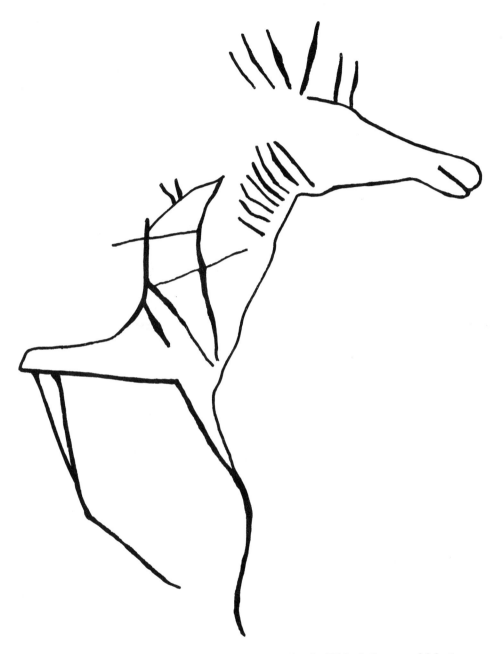

Figure 101. Solar reindeer. Tom' River petroglyph (Okladnikov and Martynov 1979: pl. 24).

Figure 102A, 102B. The hunt for the solar reindeer. Yelangash, Gorkyy Altay (High Altay) (Okladnikov et al. 1979).

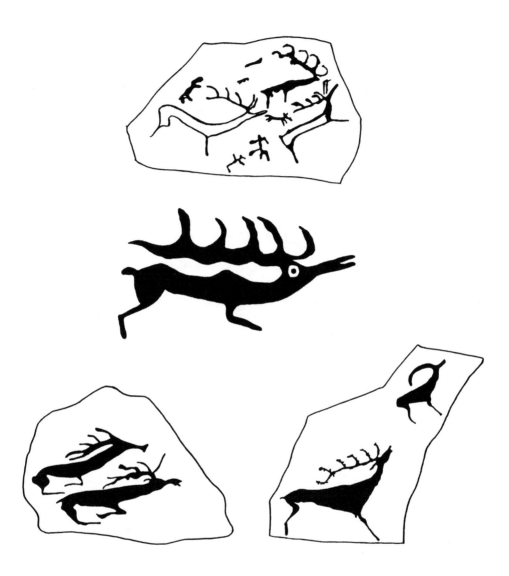

Figure 103. Reindeer representations in petroglyphs. Tagar art in south Siberia. Gornyy Altay (High Altay).

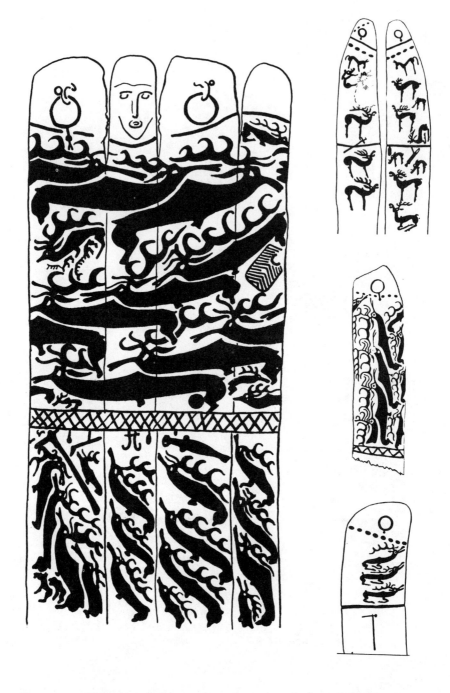

Figure 104. Reindeer flying to the sun on north Asiatic "deer stones."

232

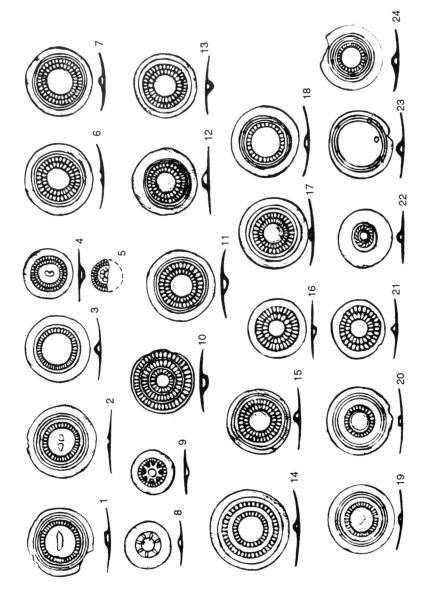

Figure 105. Solar badges representing circles of grain seeds: (1–2) Nekrasovo II; (3–24) Stepanovo hoard. Bronze. Late first millennium B.C. (Martynov 1979: pl. 53).

233

Figure 106. The Animal Style of the Hunnic period. Bronze. Second and first centuries B.C. South Siberia.

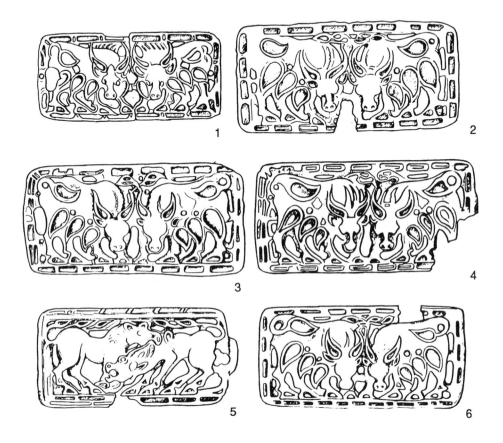

Figure 107. Belt plates depicting pairs of bulls (1–4, 6) and wild asses fighting (5). Hunnic. Minusinsk Museum. (See also Devlet 1980a: pls. 5, 6.)

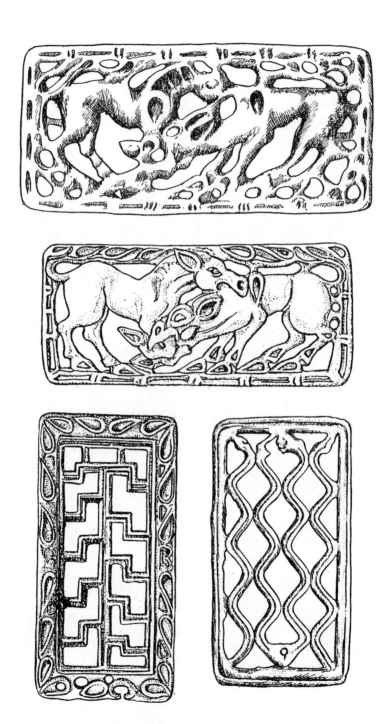

Figure 108. Open-work belt plates depicting wild asses fighting, geometrical ornamentation, and conventionalized snakes (See also Devlet 1980A: pls. 8, 10, 13, 16).

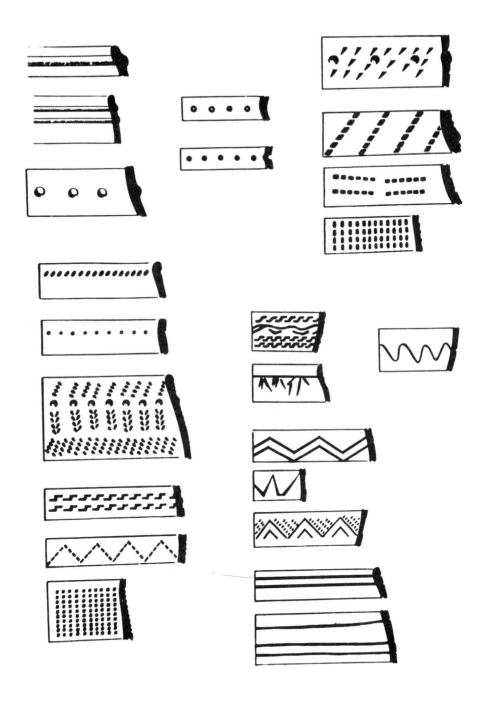

Figure 109. Pottery designs on Siberian Hunnic ware.

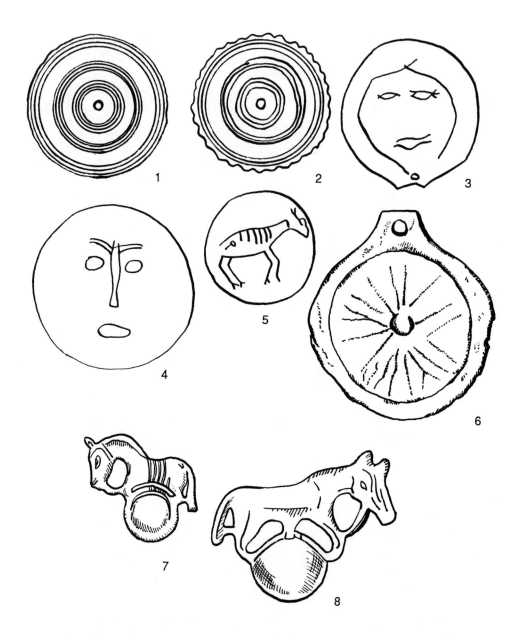

Figure 110. Medieval images of the sun: (1–6) bronze solar disks from the forested area of western Siberia, Ishim collection; (7–8) steeds carry the sun in their hooves (Aydashinskaya peschera).

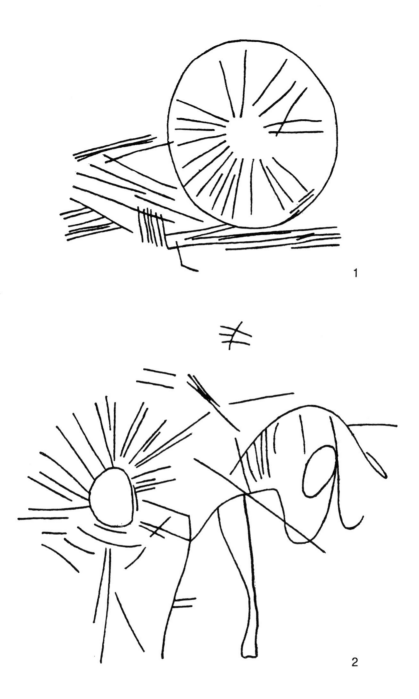

Figure 111. Medieval solar images on south Baykal petroglyphs: (1) Tabangut-skoye Obo; (2) Khana Shuluun (Okladnikov and Zaporozhskaya 1969–70: vol. 1, 140–41, pls. 36, 37).

Figure 112. Medieval warrior. Sulak petroglyph, Minusinsk Basin. First millennium A.D.

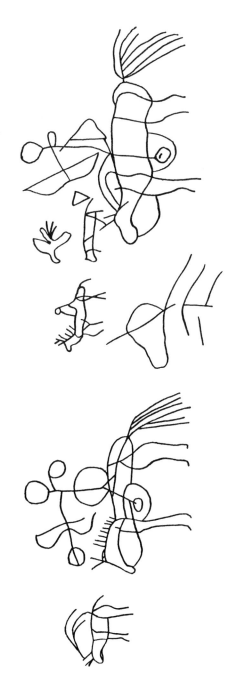

Figure 113. Mounted medieval hunters. Mongolian petroglyph. First millennium A.D.

241

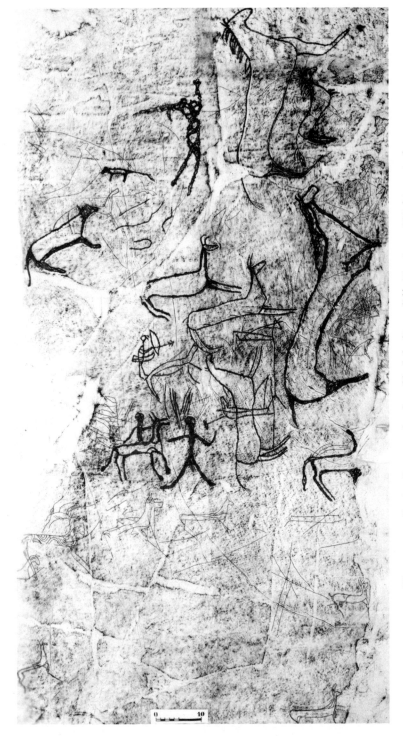

Figure 114. Incised petroglyphs. Shalabolino cliff, Yenisey. Türki period.

Figure 115. Medieval petroglyphs on the Karakol River, Gornyy Altay (High Altay): (top) young sheep; (bottom) rider and horse. Incised.

Figure 116. Incised medieval petroglyphs at Tabungutskoye Obo, south Baykal: (1) animal and lines; (2) composition of lines with possible felt tent; (3) mounted warrior, ram, horse, lines; (4) ram with sun images (Okladnikov and Zaporozhskaya 1969–70: vol. 1, 32, pl. 42).

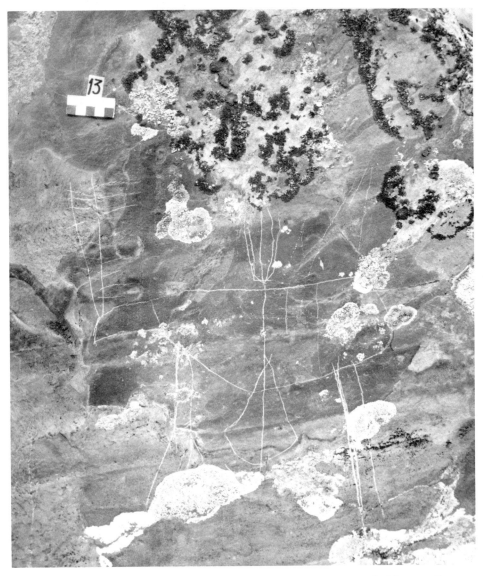

Figure 117. Medieval incised figure, possibly a shaman. Karakol River, Gornyy Altay (High Altay), Stone 13.

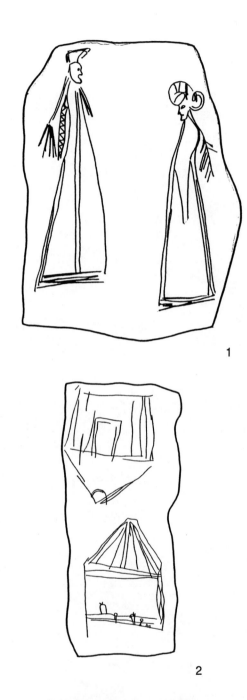

Figure 118. Medieval incised petroglyphs. Yelangash, Unit 8, Gornyy Altay (High Altay): (1) shamanistic figures; (2) housing (of two worlds?).

Figure 119. Charred wooden planks from sepulcher 1, Tepsey Kurgan, Yenisey. Beginning of the first millennium A.D. (Gryaznov et al. 1980).

Figure 120. Sculptured head of a man. Shestakovo cemetery, Siberian forest-steppe. Second to first century B.C.

Figure 121. Tashtyk death masks from Khakasia (Kiselev 1951:455; Kyzlasov 1960:
fig. 56). Minusinsk Museum.

Figure 122. Death masks. Minusinsk Museum.

Figure 123. Funerary busts. Tashtyk Uybat, Khakasia. (See also Kiselev 1953: pl. 43.)

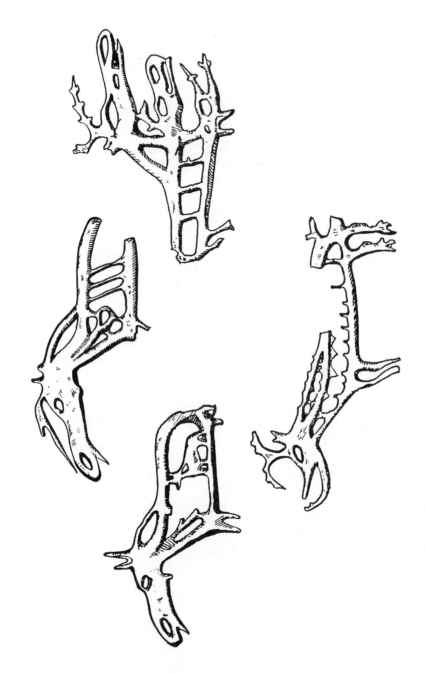

Figure 124. Kulay (Kulayka) cast bronze. Castings from the Murlinskiy hoard on the Irtysh are very similar (Chernetsov 1953:156, pl. 12, nos. 4, 5). Western Siberian early medieval forest art.

252

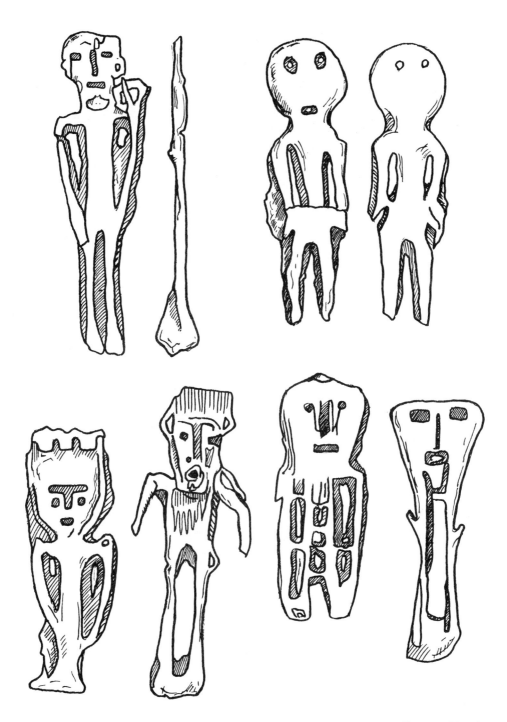

Figure 125. Anthropomorphic bronze figurines of the Stepanovo collection, Tom'
River area (Compare with the Berkal' figurine from near Tobol'sk on the Irtysh;
Chernetsov 1953:1177, pl. 24, no. 2). Western Siberian early medieval forest art.

253

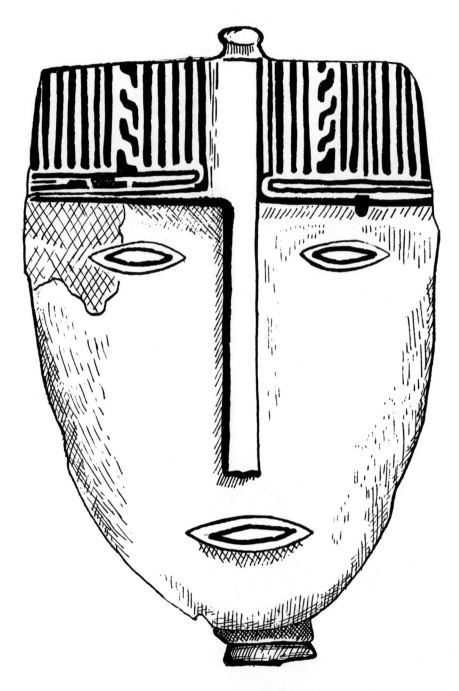

Figure 126. Bronze vase with the image of an ancient Finno-Ugrian, perhaps an ancestral spirit. First millennium A.D. Yelikayevo collection. Tomsk University (Compare the bronze mask from Makar Visyng Tur on the northern Sos'va in the Urals; Chernetsov 1953:149, pl. 9, no. 3.) Western Siberian medieval forest art.

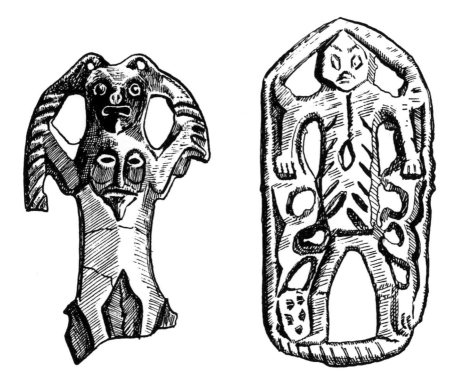

Figure 127. Bronze votive figures, "Sul'de." First millennium A.D. Yelikayevo collection. Tomsk University. (Compare the anthropomorphic figure with a human face in its chest from the Ust' Polui, at the mouth of the Ob'. Chernetsov 1953:141, pl. 6, no. 7.) Western Siberian medieval forest art.

Figure 128. Archaic type of Turkic portrait statue. Gornyy Altay
(High Altay). (Compare Yevtukhina 1952:72–73, fig. 2.)

Figure 129. Archaic (left) and later (right) types of Turkic portrait statuary. On right, note flask, sword belt, and Mongoloid features. Gornyy Altay (High Altay). (Compare Yevtukhina 1952:75–76, fig. 5.)

Figure 130. Late types of Turkic portrait statuary. Gornyy Altay (High Altay). (Compare Yevtukhina 1952:74–75, fig. 32.)

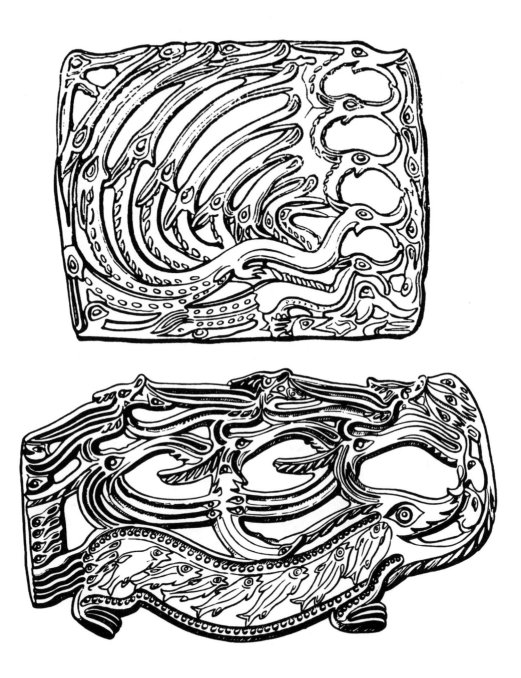

Figure 131. Concepts of the regeneration of life, of natural cyclicity in nature. Metal plates. Ural Animal Style (Perm). End of first millennium A.D.

Figure 132. The goddess of fertility with the branch of life in hand. Detail of a pile carpet hanging. Kurgan 5, Pazyryk. Fifth century B.C. (See also Rudenko 1953: pl. 95.)

Figure 133. Saka (central Asian Scythians) with switches in hand (they may be Mazdaic priests). Gold plaques from the "Treasure of the Oxus," an Afghan hoard supposedly from near Kunduz in Afghanistan. About fifth century B.C. (See also Dalton 1964:19–20, figs. 48–49.)

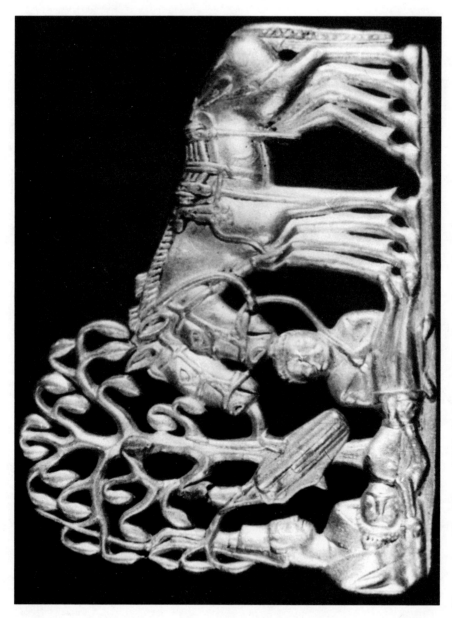

Figure 134. The Tree of Life linking the living and the dead. Gold open-work belt buckle. From the Siberian collection of Peter I. Scytho-Siberian, perhaps from the Altay. (See Rudenko 1962b: pl. 7, no. 7.)

Figure 135. Horses tethered to the World Tree. Petroglyphs, Tepsey, Yenisey. Tashtyk period.

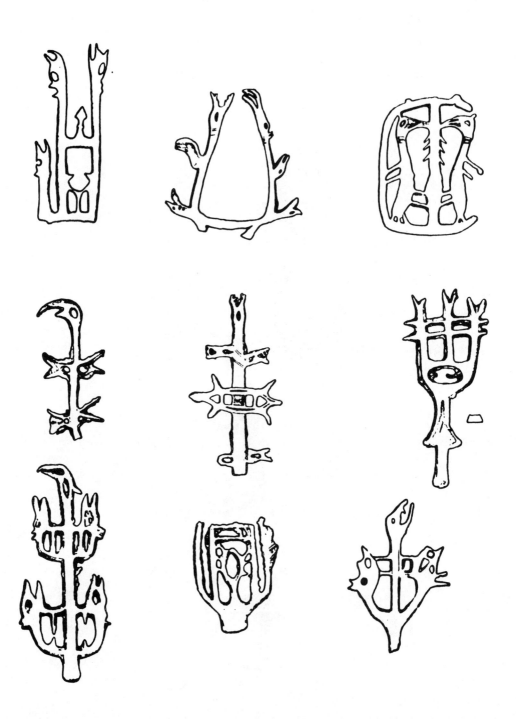

Figure 136. "Woody" bronze cast objects of the Kulay culture. Western Siberian medieval forest art. First millennium A.D. (For similar anthropomorphic and animal figurines from the Loz'va River in the Urals, see Chernetsov 1953:156–60, pls. 15, 16.)

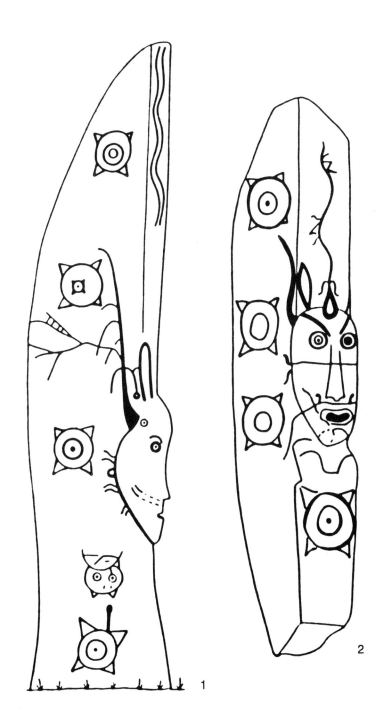

Figure 137. Images of an Earth Mother with emerging shoots: (1) Tazmin′ ulus, left shore of Bira [Byura] River, Minusinsk Basin; (2) Uybat chaatas, Minusinsk Basin. Okunevo Eneolithic. (For very comparable compositions, including shoots and four-pointed stars, see Vadetskaya 1967, figs. 5, 7.)

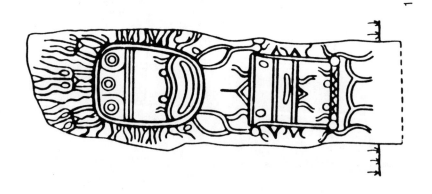

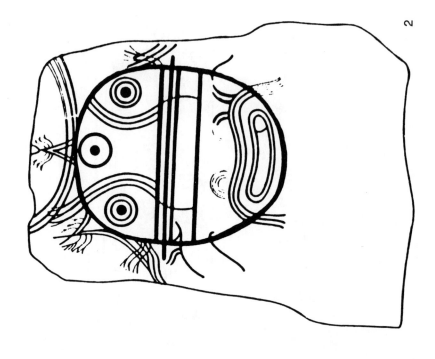

2

1

Figure 138. Fertility deities: (1) Tazmin ulus; (2) Chernovaya I, stela incorporated into Tagar-period *kurgan*. Okunevo Eneolithic. (See also, for left figure, Vadetskaya 1967, fig. 10.)

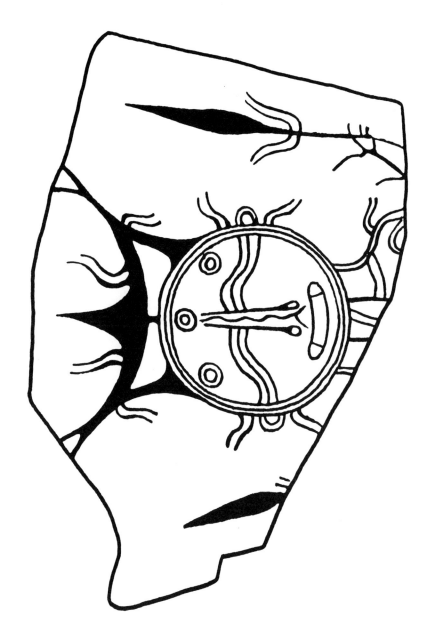

Figure 139. Fertility deity, "Deity with Spears," from Chernovaya VIII, Kurgan 4. Okunevo Eneolithic. (See also Vadetskaya 1967:22, fig. 17.)

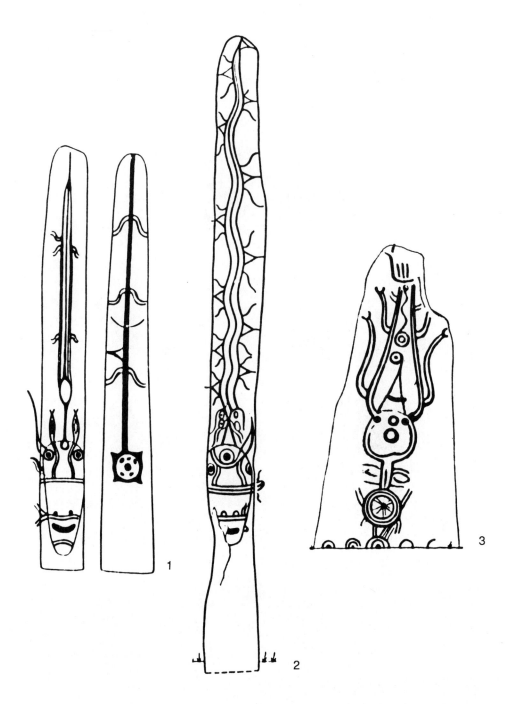

Figure 140. Fertility deities with trees growing from their heads: (1) sandstone gravestone in Khakasia; (2) Terentiy ulus, Khakasia; (3) Mount Chiti-Khys on left shore of Askyz River, on top of a Tagar *kurgan*. Okunevo Eneolithic. (See also Vadetskaya 1967: fig. 3.)

Figure 141. A deer in the maw of a griffin, with antlers tipped with griffin heads as sign of regenerated life. Kurgan 2, Pazyryk. Scytho-Siberian. (See Grayaznov 1958: pl. 38.)

Figure 142. The Tree of Life in the form of a ram with hypertrophied horns, tail, and penis ready for copulation—prolongation of life. Mongolian Scytho-Siberian. (Compare Novgorodova 1984: fig. 44, lower left.)

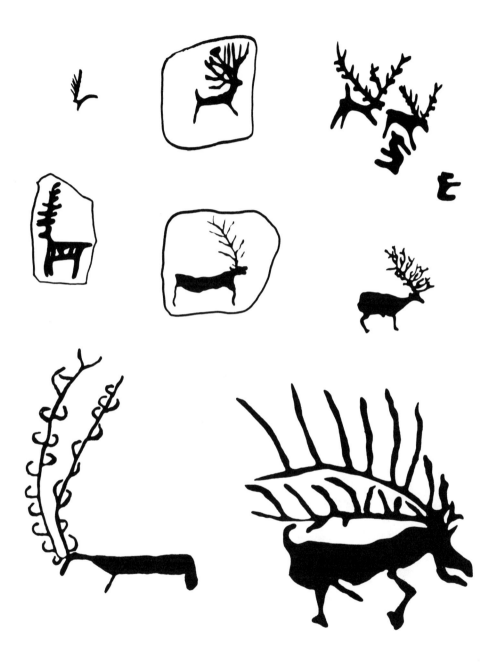

Figure 143. Exaggerated, luxuriously branching antlers as the Tree of Life. Altay, primarily Yelangash. Scytho-Siberian. (Compare Devlet 1976b:pl. 46, Chinga River, upper Yenisey.)

Figure 144. Images of ancestral mothers: (1) Ust' Tuba 3, Yenisey (from a tombstone); (2) Chernovaya (from a tombstone); (3) Syda, Minusinsk Basin (petroglyph). Okunevo Eneolithic. (See Vadetskaya 1970; ancestral mother pictures often showing successive births are prominent on Eneolithic Mongolian petroglyphs, especially Chuluut; Novogordova 1984:40–46.)

1

2

Figure 145. Images of half people, half animals: (1) Myandash-deva: half woman, half reindeer; (2) Myandash-paren': half man, half reindeer. Ural Animal Style, first millennium A.D.

273

Figure 146. Gold diadem from the Novocherkassk burial in the Ukraine, Tree of Life with attendant deer and a ram. Sarmatian (third to second century B.C.). (This theme in the form of a palm tree attended by two goats in heraldic pose is found on a ceremonial ax at Kelermes, a Scythian *kurgan* in the north Caucasus. A diadem similar to the one at Novocherkassk is also found here. Artamanov 1966: pls. 19, 26.)

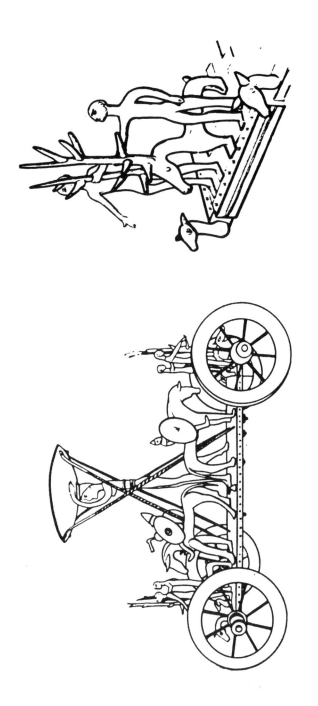

Figure 147. The solar cart of Strettweg, Graz, Austria. Hallstadt culture, sixth century B.C. In this bronze ritual vessel, found in a priestly burial, are combined solar, tree of life, and animal-cult symbols, as well as much ethnographic detail. (See Piggott 1968:181, pl. 26.)

275

References

The following abbreviations are used in the list of references.

AN   Akademiya nauk (Academy of Sciences)
AO   *Arkheologicheskiye otkrytyya* (Archaeological Discoveries) Annual
GE   Gosudarstvennyy Ermitazh (The State Hermitage), Leningrad
GIM   Gosudarstvennyy istoricheskiy muzey (State Historical Museum), Moskva
GMII   [Gosudarstvennyy] muzey izobrazitel'nykh iskusstv imena A. S. Pushkina (State Museum of Fine Arts, named for A. S. Pushkin), Moskva
INQUA   International Association for Quaternary Research
IOSRGO *Izvestiya Sibirskogo otdeleniya Russkogo geograficheskogo obshchestva* (Proceedings of the Siberian Division of the Russian Geographical Society)
Izd   Izdatel'stvo (Press)
KSIIMK *Kratkiye soobshcheniya Instituta istoriyi material'noy kul'tury* (Brief
(KSIA) Communications of the Institute for the History of Material Culture). Replaced by: *Kratkiye soobschcheniya Instituta arkheologiyi* (Brief Communications of the Institute of Archaeology)
LO   Leningradskoye otdeleniye (Leningrad Division)
MAE   Muzey antropologiyi i etnografiyi imeni Petra Velikovo (Museum of Physical Anthropology and Ethnography named for Peter the Great), Leningrad.
MAR   *Materialy po arkheologiyi Rossiyi* (Materials on the Archaeology of Russia)
MGU   Moskovskiy gosudarstvennyy universitet (Moscow State University)
MIA   *Materialy i issledovaniya po arkheologiyi SSSR* (Materials and Investigations on the Archaeology of the USSR) (Institut arkheologiyi AN SSSR)
SA   *Sovetskaya arkheologiya* (Soviet Archaeology)
SAI   *Svod arkheologicheskikh istochnikov* (Compilation of Archaeological Source Data). Moskva: "Nauka"
SE   *Sovetskaya etnografiya* (Soviet Ethnography)

SO   Sibirskoye otdeleniye (Siberian Division [Novosibirsk]).

TGU   Tomskiy gosudarstvennyi universitet (Tomsk State University)

Tr AN   *Trudy Akademiyi nauk Tadzhikskoy SSR* (Memoirs of the Academy of
TadSSR   Sciences of the Tadzhik SSR)

TrIE   *Trudy instituta etnografiyi* (Memoirs of the Institute of Ethnography)

ZRAO   *Zapiski russkogo arkheologicheskogo obshchestva* (Notes of the Russian
            Archaeological Society)

Abayev, V. I.
    1949   *Osetinskiy yazyk i fol'klor* (The Osetian language and folklore).
            Moskva: Izd AN SSSR.
    1958   *Istoriko-etimologicheskiy slovar' osetinskogo yazyka* [Historico-etymo-
            logical dictionary of the Osetian Language]. Vol. 1. Leningrad: Izd
            AN SSSR.
Abramova, M. N.
    1959   "Sarmatskaya kul'tura II v. do n.e.-I v n.e. (po materialam Nizhnego
            Povolzh'ya, suslovskiy etap)" (Sarmatian culture of the second cen-
            tury B.C.–first century A.D. [From Lower Volga materials of the
            Suslovo stage]). *SA* (1959) no. 1:52–71.
Abramova, Z. A.
    1962   "Paleoliticheskoye iskusstvo na territoriyi SSSR" (Paleolithic art in
            the territory of the USSR). *SAI* no. A 4–3. Moskva: Izd AN SSSR.
    1966   *Izobrazheniya cheloveka v paleolitecheskom iskusstve Yevraziyi* (The rep-
            resentation of human beings in Eurasian Paleolithic art). Leningrad:
            "Nauka" LO.
    1969   "K voprosu o zhenskikh izobrazheniyakh v modlenskuyu epokhu"
            (On the question of female representations in the Magdalenian
            period). *KSIIMK* 76:103–7.
Anisimov, I. F.
    1958   *Religiya evenkov v istoriko-geneticheskikh izucheniyi i problemy pervobyt-
            nykh verovaniy* (Evenki religion in historical-genetic studies and the
            problems of primitive beliefs). Moskva: Izd AN SSSR.
Anokhin, A. V.
    1924   "Materialy po shamanstvu u altaytsev" (Materials on shamanism
            among the Altay [Turks]). *MAE*, vol. 4, no. 2.
Anuchin, D. N.
    1982   "K istoriyi iskusstva i verovaniy u priural'skoy chudi" (On the
            history of art and religion beliefs in Cis-Uralic Chud). In *Materialy
            po etnografiyi Vostochnykh guberniy*, vol. 3. Moskva.
Anuchin, V. I.
    1914   "Ocherki shamanstva u yeniseyskikh ostyakov" (Materials on sha-
            manism among the Yenisey "Ostyak" [Ket]). *MAE*, vol. 2, no. 2.
Artamanov, M. I.
    1966   *Sokrovishcha skifskikh kurganov v sobraniyi Gosudarstvennogo Ermitazha*
            (The treasure house of Scythic Kurgan [remains] in the collections
            of the State Hermitage). Praga: Artiya.

1968   "Proiskhozhdeniye skifskogo iskusstvo" (The origins of Scythian art). *SA* (1968) no. 4.

1971   "Skifo-sibirskoye iskusstvo zverinogo stili (osnovnyye etapy i napravleniya)" (Scytho-Siberian art of the Animal Style: Basic stages and [developmental] directions). In *Problemy skifskoy arkheologiyi*. Moskva: "Nauka."

1973   *Sokrovischcha sakov* (Saka treasures). Moskva: "Iskusstvo."

Aseyev, I. V.

1980   *Pribaykal'ye v sredniye veka* (The Cis-Baykal in the middle ages). Novosibirsk: "Nauka" SO.

Bader, O. N.

1964   *Drevneyshiye metallurgi Priural'ya* (The most ancient metallurgists of the Cis-Urals). Moskva: Nauka.

1975   "Paleolitecheskaya gravirovka iz Indigirskogo Zapolyarya" (A Paleolithic engraving from the Indigirka [river], north of the Arctic Circle). In *Arkheologiya Severnoy i Tsentral'noy Aziyi*. Novosibirsk: "Nauka" SO.

Balfour, Henry

1893   *The Evolution of Decorative Art*. London: Rivington, Percival.

Bartol'd, V. V.

1897   "Otchet o poyezdke v Srednyuyu Aziyu s nauchnoy tsel'yu" (Report on a scientific trip to central Asia). Zapiski *AN*, series 8, vol. 1, no. 4. Sankt Peterburg.

Barzhenov, V.

1895   "Pogrebal'nyye obychai obdorskikh ostyakov" (Mortuary customs of the Obdorsk Ostyak [Khanty]. *Zhivaya starina* 5:487–92.

Begouen, M.

1925   *Les bijoux d'argile* (Clay jewels). Paris: A. Fayard.

1929   "La grotte des trois fréres" (The Cave of three brothers). *Mitteilungen über Höhlen-und Karstforschung* 3:97–101.

Bernshtam, A. N.

1952   *Istoriko-arkheologischeskiye ocherki Tsentral'nogo Tyan-Shanya i Pamiro-Alaya* (Historico-archaeological sketches of the central Tyan Shan and the Pamir-Alay) *MIA*, vol. 26.

Boardman, John

1965   *Greek Art*. New York: Praeger.

Bogayevskiy, Boris L.

1924   *Zadachi i metody izucheniya iskusstv: stat'yi B. L. Boguyayevskogo.* (Problems and methods in studying the arts: the essays of B. L. Boguyayevskiy). Gosudarstvennaya akademiya iskusstvoznaniya.

1934   "K voprosu o znacheniyi izobrazheniya tak nazyvayemovo 'Kolduna' v 'Peshchere trekh Bratyev' v Aryezhe vo Frantsiyi" (On the question of the meaning of the so-called "Sorcerer" in the "Cave of Three Brothers" at Ariege, France). *SE* (1934) no. 4:34–72.

Borodkin, Yu. M.

1967   "Materialy Neoliticheskogo Mogil'nika u s. Vas'kovo" (Materials on a Neolithic cemetery near Vas'kovo Village). *Izvestiya laboratoriyi arkheologicheskikh issledovaniy* 1:101–7. Kemerovo: Kemerovskoye knizhnoye izd.

Borovka, G. I.
   1928   *Scythian Art*. London. 1967 reprint; trans. V. G. Childe. New York: Paragon.

Bossert, Helmuth Th.
   1923   *Altkreta. Kunst und Handwerk in Griechenland, Kreta und auf den Kykladen während der Bronzezeit* (Ancient Crete. Art and Handicrafts in Greece, Crete and the Cyclades in the Bronze Age). Berlin: Wasmuth.

Calmeyer, Peter
   1964   *Altiranische Bronzen der Sammlung Bröckelscher* (Old Iranian Bronzes of the Bröckelsch Collection). Berlin: Museum für Vor-und Frühgeschichte.

Charnoluskiy, V. V.
   1965   *Legenda ob olenye-cheloveke* (The legend of the Reindeer-Man). Moskva: "Nauka."

Cheng Te-K'un
   1959–66 *Archaeology in China*. Vol. 1: *Prehistoric China*, 1959 (reprinted with corrections, 1966); Vol. 2: *Shang China*, 1960; Vol. 3: *Chou China*, 1963. Cambridge, England: W. Heffer and Sons.

Chernetsov, V. N.
   1964   *Naskal'nyye izobrazheniya Urala* (Representations on cliffs in the Urals). Moskva: "Nauka."

Chernikov, S. S.
   1965   *Zagadka zolotogo kurgana* (The mystery of the Golden Kurgan). Moskva: "Nauka."

Chernykh, Ye. N.
   1966   *Istoriya drevneyshey metallurgiyi Vostochnoy Yevropy* (History of the most ancient metallurgy of Eastern Europe). Moskva: "Nauka."
   1970   *Drevneyshaya istoriya metallurgiyi Urala i Povolzh'ya* (History of the most ancient metallurgy in the Urals and Volga [Regions]). Moskva: "Nauka."

Cherskiy, I. D.
   1872   "Neskol'ko slov o vyrytykh v Irkutske izdeliyakh kamennogo perioda" (Several words on objects of the Stone Period excavated in Irkutsk). *ISORGO* 3, no. 3:167–72.

Chindina, L. A.
   1977   *Mogil'nik Relka na Sredney Obi* (The Relka cemetery on the Middle Ob'). Tomsk: Izd TGU.

Chlenova, N. L.
   1967   *Proiskhozhdeniye i rannyaya istoriya plemen tagarskoy kul'tury* (Origins and early history of the tribes of Tagar Culture). Moskva: "Nauka."
   1971   *Skifskiy olen'* (The Scythic reindeer). MIA 115:167–205.
   1972   *Khronologiya pamyatnikov karasukskoy epokhi* (Chronology of sites of the Karasuk period). Moskva: "Nauka."

Dalton, Ormonde M.

1926   *The Treasure of the Oxus with Other Examples of Early Oriental Metal Work.* 2nd ed. London: British Museum.

Derevyanko, A. P.

1970   *V strane trekh solnts* (In the land of three suns). Khabarovsk: Khabarovskoye Knizhnoye Izd.

1975   *Mokheskiye pamyatniki Srednego amura* (Mohe sites of the Middle Amur). Novosibirsk: "Nauka" SO.

1981   *Plemena Priamur'ya I tys. n.e.* (Amur tribes of the first millennium A.D.). Novosibirsk: "Nauka" SO.

Devlet, M. A.

1964   "Keramika pozdnetagarskikh kurganov Krasnoyarskogo rayona" (Pottery of late Tagar kurgans [Burial Mounds] of the Krasnoyarsk region). SA (1964) no. 2:205–10.

1973   "O poyasnykh pryamougol'nykh azhurnykh plastinkakh s izobrazheniyem zhivotnykh iz Tsentral'noy Aziyi i Sibiri (On rectangular, open work, belt plates with animal representations from inner Asia and Siberia). In *Problemy etnogeneza narodov Sibiri i Dal'nego Vostoka.* Novosibirsk: "Nauka" SO.

1976a   *Bol'shaya Boyarskaya Pisanitsa* (The great pictograph of Boyar Mountain). Moskva: "Nauka."

1976b   *Petroglify Ulug Khema* (Petroglyphs of Ulug Khem). Moskva: "Nauka."

1980a   *Petroglify Mugur-Sargola* (The petroglyphs of Mugur Sargol). Moskva: "Nauka."

1980b   *Sibirskiye poyasnyye azhurnyye plastiny: II v. do n.e., – Iv. ne* (Siberian open-work belt plates: Second century B.C.–First century A.D.) SAI D4–7. Moskva.

Dikov, N. N.

1958   *Bronzovyy vek Zabaykal'ya* (The Trans-Baykal Bronze Age). Ulan Ude: Buryatskoye knizhnoye izd.

1971   *Naskal'nyye zagadki drevney Chukotki* (Puzzles on cliffs of ancient Chukotka). Moskva: "Nauka."

1977   *Arkheologicheskiy pamyatniki Kamchatki, Chukotki, i Verkhney Kolymy* (Archaeological sites of Kamchatka, Chukotka and the Upper Kolyma). Moskva: "Nauka."

1979   *Drevniye kul'tury Severo-Vostochnoy Aziyi* (Ancient cultures of northeastern Asia). Moskva: "Nauka."

Dzhafarzade, Isaak M.

1973   *Gobustan: naskal'nyye izobrazheniye* (Gobustan [Kobystan]: Representations on cliffs). Baku: "Elm."

Eding, D. N.

1940   *Reznaya skul'ptura Uraly* (The carved sculpture of the Urals). Trudy GIM, Vyp. X.

Formakovskiy, V. B.

1914   *Arkhaicheskiy period na yuge Rossiyi* (The archaic period in south Russia). MAR 34. Sankt Peterburg.

Formozov, Aleksandr A.
1966   *Pamyatniki pervobytnogo iskusstva na territoriyi SSSR* (Monuments of primitive art in the USSR). Moskva: "Nauka."
1969   *Ocherki po pervobytnomu iskusstvu* (Sketches of primitive art). MIA 165. Moskva: "Nauka."

Foss, M. E.
1952   *Drevneyshaya istoriya severa yevropeyskoy chasti SSSR* (The most ancient history of the European part of the USSR). MIA 29. Moskva: Izd AN SSSR.

Fraydenberg, O. M.
1978   *Mif i literatura v drevnosti* (Myth and literature in antiquity). Moskva: "Nauka."

Frazer, James George
1935   "Taboo and the Perils of the Soul." *The Golden Bough.* V. 3. 3rd ed. New York: Macmillan.

Frezer, Dzh. D. [Frazer, James George]
1980   *Zolotaya vetv'* (The golden bough). Moskva: Izd "Politicheskaya literatura."

Frolov, B. A.
1973   "Etnogeneticheskoye znacheniye sibirskikh analogiy iskusstvom paleolita" (The ethnogenetic meaning of Siberian analogies with Paleolithic art). In *Problemy etnogeneza narodov Sibir i Dal'nego Vostoka.* Novosibirsk: "Nauka" SO.

Frolov, B. A., and A. I. Spiranskiy
1967   *Issledovaniye drevnykh naskal'nykh izobrazheniyi v gornom altayae* (The investigation of ancient cliff representations in the High Altay). AO 1966, pp. 158–61.

Furtwängler, Adolf
1883   *Der Goldfund von Vettersfelde* (The Vettersfeld hoard of gold). *Programme zum Winckelmannsfeste* B. 43. Berlin: G. Reimer.

Gavrilova, A. A.
1957   "Raskopki Vtorogo katandinskogo mogil'nika" (Excavations of the second Katanda cemetery). *SA* 37:250–68.

Gening, V. F., R. D. Goldina, and V. A. Oborin
1970   *Pamyatniki Lomavatovskoy kul'tury* (Sites of the Lomavatova culture). In *Voprosy arkheologiyi Urala.* Sverdlovsk: Izd Sverdlovskogo universiteta.

Ghirshman, Roman
1950   "Notes iraniennes: Le trésor de Sakkez, les Origines de l'art Mède et les bronzes du Luristan" (Iranian Notes: The Sakkez treasure, Origins of Median art and the Luristan bronzes). *Artibus Asiae* 12: 180–206.

Gimbutas, Marija
1971   *The Slavs.* New York: Praeger.
1974   *The Gods and Goddesses of Old Europe, 7000 to 3500 B.C.: Myths, Legends, and Cult Images.* Berkeley: University of California Press.

1987   "Slavic Religion" In *Encyclopedia of Religion* 13:353–61. New York: Macmillan.

Gmelin, Johan G.
1751   *Reise durch Sibirien* (Travels through Siberia), vol. 1. Gottingen: A. Vandenhoecks.

Grach, A. D.
1961   *Drevnetyurkskiye izvayaniya Tuvy* (Old Turkic sculptured stelae of Tuva). Moskva: Izd. Vostochnoy literatury.

Gribova, L. S.
1975   *Permskiy zverinyy stil'* (The Perm Animal Style). Moskva: "Nauka."

Grishin, Yu. S.
1976   *Metallicheskiye izdeliya Sibiri epokhi neolita i bronza* (Neolithic and Bronze Age metal artifacts from Siberia). *SAI* no. B3–I2.

Grjasnoff, M.
1928a   "Fürstengräber in Altaigebiet" (Princely graves in the Altay Region). *Wiener Prähistorischen zeitschrift* 15:120–23.

Gryaznov, M. P.
1928b   "Raskopki knyazheskoy mogily na Altaye" (Excavation of a princely grave in the Altay). *Chelovek* (1928) nos. 2–4:217–19.
1947   "Pamyatniki mayemirskogo etapa epokha rannykh kochevnikov na Altaye" (Sites of the Mayemir stage of the epoch of early nomadism on the Altay). *KSIIMK* 18:9–17.
1950a   "Minusinskiye kamennyye baby v svyazi s nekotorymi novymi materialami" (The Minusinsk "Stone Peasant Women" in relation to certain new materials). *SA* 12:128–57.
1950b   *Pervyy Pazyrykskiy kurgan* (The first Pazyryk Kurgan [Burial Mound]). Leningrad: Izd AN SSSR.
1956   "Severnyy Kazakhstan v epokhu rannykh kochevnikov" (Northern Kazakhstan in the epoch of the early nomads). *KSIIMK* 61:8–16.
1958   *Drevnoye iskusstvo Altaya* (Ancient Art of the Altay). Leningrad: GE.
1961   "Drevneyshiye pamyatniki geroicheskogo eposa narodov Yuzhnoy Sibir" (The most ancient monuments of the heroic epic [tale] of south Siberian peoples). In *Arkheologicheskiy Sbornik GE*, no. 3.
1962   *Pazyrykskoye iskusstvo* (Pazyryk Art). Leningrad: Izd GE.
1979   *Kompleks arkheologicheskikh pamyatnikov u gory Tepsey na Yeniseye* (The complex of archaeological sites on Mt. Tepsey on the Yenisey). Novosibirsk: "Nauka" SO.

Gurina, N. N.
1967   *Mir glazami drevnego khudozhnika Kareliyi* (The world in the eyes of an ancient Karelian artist). Leningrad: "Nauka."

Haddon, Alfred C.
1895   *Evolution in Art as Illustrated by the Life-Histories of Designs.* London: Contemporary Sciences Series, v. 30.

Hällström, Gustaf
1938   *Monumental Art of Northern Europe from the Stone Age: The Norwegian Localities.* Stockholm: Thule.

Henning, W. B.
1945   "Sogdian Tales." *Bulletin of the School of Oriental and African Studies*
        11:477–79.
Iokhel'son, V. I. (Vladimir Jochelson)
1898   "Ocherki zverepromyshlennosti i torgovli mekhami v Kolymskom
        okruge" (Sketches of commercial hunting and the fur trade in Ko-
        lyma Okrug). In *Trudy Yakutskoy ekspeditsiyi: I.M. Sibiryakova t. X,
        vyp. 43*. Moskva: Vostochno-Sibirskiy Otdel Imperatorskogo rus-
        skogo Geograficheskogo Obshchestva.
Ivanov, S. V.
1934   "Sibirskiye paralleli k magicheskim isobrazheniyam iz epokhi pa-
        leolita" (Siberian parallels to magical representations from the Pa-
        leolithic Age). *SE* (1934) no. 4:91.
1954   "Materialy po izobrazietl'nomu iskusstvu narodov Sibiri XIX– nach.
        XX vv" (Materials on the fine arts of Siberian peoples in the 19th
        and early 20th centuries). *TrIE*, n.s., vol. 22.
1963   *Ornament narodov Sibiri kak istoricheskiy istochnik* (The ornamentation
        of Siberian peoples as a historical source). Moskva: Izd. AN SSSR.
1974   "Opyt istolkovaniya ritual'nykh i mifologicheskikh terminov, obra-
        zovannykh ot *kon*" (zhertvoprinosheniye konya i derevo asvattho v
        drevney Indiyi) (An attempt at deciphering ritual and mythological
        terms formed from "steed" [horse offerings and the asvattho tree
        in ancient India]. In *Problemy istoriyi yazykov i kul'tury narodov Indiyi*.
        Moskva: "Nauka."
1979   *Skul'ptura altaytsev, khakasov i Sibirskikh tatar (XVIII- Pervoya chetvert'
        XX v.)* (Sculpture of the Altayans, Khakas and Siberian Tatars: 18th
        to first quarter of 20th centuries). Leningrad: AN SSSR LO.
Ivanova, L. A.
1968   "O razlichnykh keramicheskikh traditsiyi afanas'yevskoy i okunev-
        skoy kul'tur" (On different ceramic traditions in Afanasyevo and
        Okunevo cultures) *SA* (1968) no. 2:251–54.
Jettmar, Karl
1964   *Die frühen Steppenvölker; der eurasiatische Tierstil. Entstehung und sozi-
        ale Hintergrund* (The early peoples of the steppe. The early Animal
        Style and its social background). Baden-Baden: Holle.
Khangalov, M. N.
1960   *Sobranie sochineniy* (Collected writings). 3 vols. Ulan Ude: Buryat-
        skoye knizhnoye Izd.
Kharuzin, Nikolay N.
1890   *Russkiye Lopari, Ocherki proshlogo i sovremennogo byta* (Russian Lapps:
        Sketches of past and present life-ways). *Izvestiya Obshchestva Lyubi-
        teley yestestvoznaniye, antropologiyi i etnografiyi*, vol. 66.
1905   *Etnografiya. Vol. 4: Verovaniya* (Ethnography, vol. 4: Belief [Sys-
        tems]). Sankt Peterburg: Gosudarstvennaya tipografiya.
Khazanov, A. M.
1964   "Religiozno-magicheskoye ponimaniya zerkala y sarmatov" (The

religico-magical concept of the mirror among the Sarmatians). *SE* (1964) no. 3:89–104.

Khlobystina, M. D.
1971   "Drevneyshiye yuzhno-sibirskiye mify v pamyatnikov okunevskogo iskusstva" (The most ancient South-Siberian myths [as presented] in monuments of Okunevo art. In *Pervobytnoye iskusstvo*. Novosibirsk: "Nauka" SO.

Khoroshykh, P. P.
1947   "Pisanitsy Altaya" (Pictographs of the Altay). *KSIIMK*, no. 4:26–34.

Kinzhalov, R. B.
1958   *Statuetka Izidi-Fortuny. K voprosu o pozdnem ellinisticheskom sinkretizme* (The Izidi-fortuna statuette: On the question of late Hellenistic syncretism). *Trudy GE*, Vol 1. Leningrad: Izd GE

Kirillov, I. I.
1980   "Predmety izobrazitel'nogo iskusstva paleoliticheskogo poseleniya Sokhatino IV (Titovskaya sopka)." (Objects of representative art of the Paleolithic settlement of Sokhatino IV, i.e., Titovskaya Knoll). In *Zveri v kamne (pervobytnoye iskusstvo)*. Novosibirsk: "Nauka" SO.

Kiryushin, Yu. F., and A. M. Maloletko
1979   *Bronzovyy vek Vasyugan'ya* (The Bronze Age of the Vasyugan'ye [Swamps]). Tomsk: Izd TGU.

Kiselev, S. V.
1951   *Drevnyaya istoriya Yuzhnoy Sibiri* (The ancient history of south Siberia). 2nd ed. Moskva: Izd AN SSSR.

Klyashtornyy, S. G.
1978   "Khram, izvayaniye i stela v drevnetyurkskikh tekstakh (K interpretatsiyi Ikhe-Khanyn-norskoy nadpisi)" (Temple, statue and stela in Old Turkic texts: Toward the interpretation of the Ikhe Khanyu Nor inscription). In *Tyurkologicheskiy sbornik*, pp. 250–53. Moskva: "Nauka."

Korostovtsev, M. A.
1976   *Religiya drevnego Egipta* (The religion of ancient Egypt). Moskva: "Nauka" Glav. izd. vostochnoy literatury.

Kosarev, M. F.
1970   "O khronologiyi i kul'turnoy prinadlezhnosti turbinskoseyminskikh bronz" (On the chronology and cultural affiliations of the Turbino-Seyma Bronzes). In *Problemy khronologiyi i kul'turnoy prinadlezhnosti arkheologicheskikh pamyatnikov zapadnoy Sibiri*. Tomsk: Izd TGU.

1974   *Drevniye kul'tury Tomsko-Narymskogo Priob'ya* (Ancient cultures of the Tomsk-Narym [Region] of the Ob'). Moskva: "Nauka."

1978   "O kul'te dereva u kulaytsev" (On the tree cult among the Kulay [people]). In *Ranniy zheleznyy vek Zapadnoy Sibiri*. Tomsk: Izd TGU.

1981   *Bronzevoy vek zapadnoy Sibiri* (The Bronze Age of western Siberia). Moskva: "Nauka."

Kubarev, V. D.
1978   "Drevnetyurkskiy pominal'nyy kompleks na D'yer-Tebe" (The Old

Turkic funerary complex at D'yer-Tebe). In *Drevniye kul'tury Altaya i zapadnoy Sibiri*, pp. 86–98. Novosibirsk: "Nauka."

Kühn, Herbert
1962–63 *Vorgeschichte der Menschheit* (Human Prehistory). B. I – III. Köln: M. DuMont Schauberg.

Kuznetsov, V. A.
1962 "Alanskiye plemena Severnogo Kavkaza" (Alanic Tribes of the North Caucasus). *MIA* 106. Moskva.

Kyzlasov, L. R.
1960 *Tashtykskaya epokha v istoriyi khakassko-minusinskoy kotloviny* (The Tashtyk Period in the Khakas-Minusinsk Basin). Moskva: Izd MGU.
1962 "Nachalo sibirskoy arkheologiyi" (The start of Siberian archaeology). In *Istoriko-arkheologicheskiy sbornik*. Moskva: Izd MGU.

Lapo-Danilovskiy, A.
1887 *Skifskiye drevnosti* (Scythian Antiquities). Sankt Peterburg.

Laufer, Berthold
1899 "Petroglyphs on the Amoor." *American Anthropologist* (n.s.) 1:749–50.

Lennrod, E. (Comp. and Ed.)
1956 *Kalevala. Karelo-finskiy narodniy epos* (Kalevala: The Karelo-Finnish national epic). Petrozavodsk: Gosizdat Karel'skoy ASSR.

Leontyev, N. V.
1970 "Izobrazheniya zhivotnykh i ptits na plitakh mogil'nika Chernovaya VIII." (The representation of animals and birds on slabs in the cemetery Chernovaya VIII). In *Sibir' i yeyo sosedi v drevnosti*, ed. V. E. Larichev, pp. 265–70. Novosibirsk: "Nauka" SO.
1978 "Antropomorfnyye izobrazheniya okunevskoy kul'tury (problemy khronologiyi i semantiki)" (Anthropomorphic representations of Okunevo culture [problems of chronology and semantics]). In *Sibir', Tsentral'naya i Vostochnaya Aziya v drevnosti, Neolit i epokha metalla*. Novosibirsk: "Nauka" SO.

Lipskiy, A. N.
1961 "Novyye dannyye po afanasyevskoy kul'tury" (New data on Afanasyevo culture). In *Voprosy istoriyi Sibiri i Dal'nego Vostoka*. Novosibirsk: Izd SO AN SSSR.

Litvinskiy, B. A.
1964 "Zerkalo v verovaniyakh drevnykh fergantsev" (The Mirror in the beliefs of the ancient [people of] Fergana). *SE* (1964) no. 3:97–104.
1972 *Drevniye kochevniki "Kryshi mira"* (Ancient nomads of "The Roof of the World"). Moskva: "Nauka."

Loehr, M.
1955 "The Stag Image in Scythia and the Far East." *Archives of Asian Art* 9:63–67.

Longfellow, Henry W.
n.d. *The Poems of Longfellow*. New York: Modern Library.

Longfello(w) (Henry W. Longfellow)
1956 *Pesne o Gaiavate* (Song of Hiawatha). Translated from English. In I.

A. Bunin, *Sobraniye sochineniy* 5:5–140. Moskva: Khudozhestven-
naya literatura.

Loud, Gordon, and Charles B. Altman
  1938   *Khorsabad*. Vol. 2: *The Citadel and the Town*. Oriental Institute Publica-
          tions, vol. 38, pt. 2. Chicago: University of Chicago Press.

Lundy, D.
  1974   "The Rock Art of the Northwest Coast." Master's thesis, Simon
          Fraser University, Vancouver.

Maksimenkov, G. A.
  1978   *Andronovskaya kul'tura na Yeniseye* (The Andronovo Culture on the
          Yenisey). Leningrad: "Nauka" LO.

Maksimenkov, G. A., and A. I. Martynov
  1968   "Okunevskaya kul'tura i yeyo sosedi na Obi" (The Okunevo culture
          and its neighbors on the Ob'). *Istoriya Sibiri*, vol. 1, pp. 165–72.
          Leningrad: "Nauka" LO.

Mannay-Ool, M. Kh.
  1970   *Tuva v skifskoye Vremya* (Tuva in Scythic Times). Moskva: "Nau-
          ka."

Martynov, A. I.
  1966   *Lodki v stranu predkov* (Boats in the ancestors' land). Kemerovo:
          Kemerovskoye knizhnoye izd.

  1970   *Ekho vekov* (The echo of centuries). Kemerovo: Kemerovskoye kniz-
          hnoye izd.

  1971   *Raskopki Nekrasovskogo mogil'nika tagarsky kul'tury* (Excavations of the
          Nekrasavo cemetery, Tagar Culture). Kemerovo: Izvestiya Labor-
          atoriyi arkheologicheskikh issledovaniy.

  1973   *Pamyatniki i otdel'nyye nakhodki predmetov skifosarmatskogo vremeni v
          Tomsko-Yeniseyskom lesostepnom rayone* (Sites and isolated artifactual
          finds of Scytho-Sarmatian time in the Tomsk-Yenisey forest-steppe
          region). Izvestiya Laboratoriyi arkheologicheskikh issledovaniy,
          no. 6. Kemerovo.

  1974   "Skul'pturnyy portret cheloveka iz Shestakovskogo mogil'nika" (A
          sculptured portrait of a man from Shestakovo Cemetery). *SA* (1974)
          no. 4: 231–42.

  1979   *Lesostepnaya tagarskaya kul'tura* (The Tagar Culture of the Forest
          Steppe). Novosibirsk: "Nauka" SO.

  1981   "Siberia before the Mongols: New Findings and Problems." *Journal
          of the Steward Anthropological Society* 12:441–506.

  1982   "The Tom' River Petroglyphs of Siberia." *The Musk Ox* 31:1–16.

Martynov, A. I., and V. V. Bobrov
  1971   *Serebryakovskiy mogil'nik* (Serebryakovo cemetery). Kemerovo: La-
          boratoriya arkheologicheskikh issledovaniy, no. 3.

Maslova, G. S.
  1951   *Narodnyy ornament Verkhnevolzhyskikh karel* (Folk ornamentation of
          the Upper-Volga Karelians). Moskva: Izd. AN SSSR.

Mat'ye, M. E.
  1940   *Mify drevnogo Egipta* (Myths of Ancient Egypt). Leningrad: GE.

1956   *Drevneyegipetskiye mify* (Ancient Egyptian Myths). Moskva: Izd AN SSSR.

Matyushchenko, V. I.

1961   *Samus'skiy mogilnik* (The Samus' Cemetery). Trudy TGU, vol. 150. Tomsk.

1963   *Yayskiy neoliticheskiy mogil'nik* (The Yaysk Neolithic Cemetery). Trudy TGU, vol. 165. Tomsk.

1973   *Drevnyaya istoriya naseleniya lesnogo i lesostepnogo Priob'ya. Chast' vtoraya. Samus'skays kul'tura* (Ancient history of the population of the forested and forest-steppe Ob' region. Part 2: The Samus Culture. In *Iz istoriyi Sibiri*, no. 10. Tomsk: Izd TGU.

Matyushchenko, V. I., and L. G. Igol'nikova

1966   Poseleniye Yelovka—pamyatnik vtorogo etapa bronzovogo veka v Srednem Priob'ye (Yelovka Settlement, A Site of the Second Stage of the Bronze Age on the Middle Ob') In *Drevnyaya Sibir'*. Novosibirsk: "Nauka" SO.

Maydar, D.

1981   *Pamyatniki istoriyi i kul'tury Mongoliyi VIII* (The historical and cultural monuments of Mongolia [no.] VIII). Moskva: "Mysl'."

Mazhitov, N. A.

1968   *Bakhmutinskaya kul'tura* (The Bakhmutovo Culture). Moskva: "Nauka."

Meade, Edward F.

1971   *Indian Rock Carvings of the Pacific Northwest*. Sidney, British Columbia: Grey's Publishing Co.

Medvedev, V. Ye.

1977   *Kul'tura amurskikh chzhurchzheney* (The Culture of the Amur Jurchen). Novosibirsk: "Nauka" SO.

Mellaart, James

1967   *Çatal Hüyük. A Neolithic Town in Anatolia*. New York: McGraw-Hill.

Melyukova, A. I.

1958   "Pamyatniki skifskogo vremeni lesostepnogo Srednego Podnestrov'ya" (Scythian period sites of the forest-steppe [zone] of the middle Dnestr). *MIA* 64:5–102.

de Menasce, J.

1973   "Persia: Cosmic Dualism." In *World Mythology*, ed. Pierre Grimal, pp. 189–206. London: Hamlyn.

Messerschmidt, D. G.

1962   *Forschungsreise durch Sibirien 1720–1727* (Exploratory travels through Siberia 1720–1727). Herausgegeben von E. Winter und N. A. Figurovskij. Teil 1. Tagebuchaufzeichnungen 1721–1722. Berlin: Akademie-Verlag.

Middendorff, Aleksandr

1860–69 *Puteshestviye na severe i vostoke Sibiri* (Travels in the North and East of Siberia). 2 vols. Sankt Peterburg.

Miller, G. F.

1937   *Istoriya Sibiri* (History of Siberia). Vol. 1 Moskva: Izd AN SSSR.

Miller, V. F.
1886   "Epigraficheskiye sledy iranstva na yuge Rossiyi" (Iranian epigraphic traces in south Russia). *Zhurnal Ministerstva Narodnogo Prosveschcheniya* (October 1886): 257–78.
1896   "Lada [Lady]" Entsiklopedicheskiy slovar' Brokgauz-Yefron 17:234–35. Sankt Peterburg.

Minns, Ellis H.
1913   *Scythians and Greeks: A Survey of Ancient History and Archaeology of the Euxine from the Danube to the Caucasus.* Cambridge: Cambridge University Press.
1944   *The Art of the Northern Nomads.* London: H. Milford.

Minorskiy, A. N.
1951   "Drevniye naskal'nyye risunki Gornogo Altaya" (Ancient cliff drawings of the High Altay). *KSIIMK* 36:184–89.

Mochanov, Yu. A.
1969a   "Dyuktayskaya Kul'tura i nekotoryye aspekty eye genezisa" (The Dyuktay Upper Paleolithic Culture and certain aspects of its genesis). *SA* (1969) no. 4:235–39.
1969b   "Paléolithique de l'Aldan et le problem du peuplement de l'Amérique" (The Aldan Paleolithic and the problem of the peopling of America). P. 153 of VIII Congrès. Paris: INQUA.
1977   *Drevneyshiye etapy zaseleniya chelovekom Severo-Vostochnoy Aziyi* (The oldest stages of the human settlement of northeast Asia). Novosibirsk: "Nauka" SO.
1978   "Stratigraphy and Absolute Chronology of the Paleolithic of Northeast Asia." In *Early Man in America*, pp. 54–66. Edmonton, Alberta.

Mochanov, Yu. A. et al.
1983   *Arkheologicheskiye pamyatniki Yakutiyi. Basseyny Aldana i Olekmy* (Yakut Archaeological Sites: Aldan and Olekma Basins). Novosibirsk: "Nauka" SO.

Mogil'nikov, V. A.
1970   "K voprosu ob etnokul'turnykh arealakh Priirtysh'ya i Priob'ya v epokhu rannego zheleza" (On the problem of ethnocultural areas of the Irtysh and the Ob' in the early Iron Age). In *Problemy khronologiyi i kul'turnoy prinadlezhnosti kul'tur Zapadnoy Sibiri.* Tomsk: Izd TGU.

Myagkov, I. M.
1929   *Drevnosti Narymskogo kraya* (Antiquities of Narym Kray). Trudy Tomskogo krayevedcheskogo muzeya. Vol. II.

Nashchekin, N. V.
1967   *Kosogol'skiy klad* (The Kosogol hoard). *AO* (1966):164.

Novgorodova, E. A.
1984   *Mir petroglifov Mongoliy* (The world of Mongolian petroglyphs). Moskva: "Nauka" Glav. red. vostochnoy literatury.

Okladnikov, A. P.
1945   "Paleoliticheskaya statuetka iz Bureti (raskopki 1936g)" (A paleo-

lithic statuette from Buret': 1936 excavations). In *Paleolit i neolit SSSR. MIA 2.* Moskva: Izd AN SSSR.

1950   *Bronzovoye zerkalo s izobrazheniyu kentaura naydennoye na ostrove Fad-deya* (A bronze mirror with the representation of a centaur found in Faddeya Island [n. of Taymyr Peninsula] *SA* 13:139–72.

1955   *Istoriya Yakutskoy ASSR.* Vol. I: *Yakutiya do prisoyedineniya k russkomu gosudarstvu* (History of the Yakut ASSR. Vol. 1: Yakutia up to its union with the Russian State). Moskva: AN SSSR.

1958   "Arkheologicheskiye raboty v zone stroitel'stve angarskikh gi-droelektrostantsiy" (Archaeological work in the construction zone of the Angara hydroelectric stations). In *Zapiski Irkutskogo oblastnogo krayevedcheskogo muzeya.* Irkutsk: Irkutskoye knizhnoye.

1959   *Shishkinskiye pisanitsy* (The Shishkino Pictographs). Irkutsk: Irkut-skoye knizhnoye izd.

1960   "Paleoliticheskiye zhenskiye statuetki Bureti" (Paleolithic female statuettes from Buret'). In *Paleolit i neolit SSJR.* Vol. 4. *MIA* 79:280–88. Moskva: Izd AN SSSR.

1964a   "Sibir' v drevnekamennom veke. Epokha paleolita" (Siberia in the Old Stone Age: The Paleolithic epoch). In *Drevnyaya Sibir'.* Ulan Ude: Buryatskoye knizhnoye izd.

1964b   *Olen'-Zolotyye roga* (The Reindeer with Golden Antlers). Moskva: "Nauka."

1966   *Petroglify Angara* (Petroglyphs of the Angara River). Moskva: "Nauka."

1967   *Utro iskusstva* (The Morning of Art). Moskva: "Iskusstvo."

1968   *Liki drevnego Amura: petroglify Sakachi Alyana.* (Images of the ancient Amur: The Sakachi Alyan petroglyphs). Novosibirsk: Zapadno-Sibirskoye knizhnoye izd.

1969   "Die Felsbilder am Angara-Fluss bei Irkutsk" (The Petroglyphs on the Angara River near Irkutsk). *Jahrbuch für prähistorische und ethno-graphische Kunst* 22:18–29.

1971   *Petroglify Nizhnego Amura* (Petroglyphs of the Lower Amur). Lenin-grad: "Nauka."

1972a   *Petroglify Sredney Leny* (Petroglyphs of the Middle Lena River). Leningrad: "Nauka."

1972b   "Ulalinka—drevnepaleoliticheskiy pamyatnik Sibiri" (Ulalinka—An ancient Paleolithic site of Siberia). In *Paleoliti i neolit SSSR,* vol. 7. *MIA* 185.

1974   *Petroglify Baykala: pamyatniki drevney kul'tury narodov Sibiri* (Petro-glyphs of the Baykal: Monuments of the Ancient Culture of Siberian Peoples). Novosibirsk: "Nauka" SO.

1981   *Ancient Art of the Amur Region.* Leningrad: Aurora Publishers.

Okladnikov, A. P., and A. I. Martynov

1972   *Sokrovishcha Tomskikh pisanits* (The treasures of the Tom' picto-graphs). Moskva: Iskusstvo.

Okladnikov, A. P., and A. I. Mazin

1976   *Pisanitsy reki Olëkmy i Verkhnego Priamur'ya* (Pictographs of the

Olekma River and the Upper Amur). Novosibirsk: "Nauka" SO.

1979 *Pisanitsy basseyna reki Aldan* (Pictographs of the Aldan River Basin). Novosibirsk: "Nauka" SO.

Okladnikov, A. P., Ye. A. Okladnikova, V. D. Zaporozhskaya, and E. A. Skorynina

1979 *Petroglify doliny reki Yelangash* (Petroglyphs of the Yelangash River Valley). Novosibirsk: "Nauka" SO.

1980 *Petroglify Gornogo Altaya* (Petroglyphs of the High Altay). Novosibirsk: "Nauka" SO.

1981 *Petroglify Chankyr köla, Altay. Yelangash* (Petroglyphs of Chankyr Köl in the Altay: Yelangash). Novosibirsk: "Nauka" SO.

Okladnikov, A. P., and V. D. Zaporozhskaya

1959 *Lenskiye pisanitsy: naskal'nyye risunki u derevni Shishkino* (Lena [River] pictographs: Cliff drawings near Shishkino Village). Moskva: Izd. AN SSSR.

1969–70 *Petroglify Zabaykalya* (Petroglyphs of the Transbaykal). Leningrad: "Nauka" LO.

1972 *Petroglify Sredney Leny* (Petroglyphs of the Middle Lena). Leningrad: "Nauka" LO.

Okladnikova, Ye. A.

1979 *Zagadochnyye lichiny Aziyi i Ameriki* (Puzzling masks of Asia and America). Novosibirsk: "Nauka" SO.

Oppenkheym [Oppenheim], A. L.

1980 *Drevnyaya Mesopotamiya* (Ancient Mesopotamia). Moskva: "Nauka."

Pallas, Peter Simon

1771–76 *Reise durch verschiedene provinzen des Russischen reichs* (Travel through various provinces of the Russian Empire). 3 vols. St. Petersburg: Gedruckt bey der Kayserlichen academie der Wissenschaften.

Petri, B. E.

1923 *Narodnoye iskusstvo v Sibiri* (Folk Art in Siberia). Irkutsk.

1927 *Sibirskiy paleolit* (The Siberian Paleolithic). Irkutsk: Izd Irkutskogo universiteta.

Piggott, Stuart

1968 *Ancient Europe from the Beginnings of Agriculture to Classical Antiquity.* Chicago: Aldine.

Piotrovskiy, B. B.

1962 *Iskusstvo Urartu VIII–VI vv do n.e.* (The art of Urartu in the VIII–VI centuries B.C.). Leningrad: GE.

Pletneva, L. M.

1978 "Tomskoye Priob'ye v kulayskoye vremya" (The Ob' near Tomsk in the Kulay period). In *Rannyi zheleznyy vek zapadnoy Sibiri.* Tomsk: Izd TGU.

Pletneva, S. A.

1967 *Ot kocheviy k gorodam* (From nomadizing to cities). Moskva: "Nauka."

1974 "Polovetskiye kamnyye izvayaniya" (Polovetsian sculptured stone stelae). *SAI* no. 1–2.

Pogrebova, N. M.
1950 "K voprosu o skifskom zverinom stile" (On the question of the Scythian Animal Style). *KSIIMK* 34:139–40.

Pospelova, G. A., Z. N. Gnibidenko, and A. P. Okladnikov
1980 "O vozraste poseleniya Ulalinka po paleomagnitnym dannym" (On the age of the Ulalinka settlement according to paleomagnetic data). In *Arkheologicheskiy poisk. Severnaya Aziya.* Novosibirsk: "Nauka" SO.

Potratz, Johannes A. H.
1963 *Die Skythen in Sudrussland. Ein untergegangenes Volk in Sudosteuropa* (The Scyths in South Russia: A Vanished People of Southeastern Europe). Basel: Raggi.

Putnam, E. W.
1887 "Conventionalism in Ancient American Art." *Essex Institute Bulletin* 18:155–67.

Radloff, W.
1884 *Aus Sibirien, Löse Blätter aus meinem Tagebuch* (Out of Siberia: Loose Leaves from my Diary). Vol. 2. Leipzig. (Reprinted Oosterhout, N. B. Anthropological Publications, 1968.)

Radlov, V. V.
1888 "Sibirskiye drevnosti" (Siberian antiquities). *MAR* 3. Sankt Peterburg.
1891 "Sibirskiye drevnosti" (Siberian antiquities). *MAR* 5. Sankt Peterburg.
1894 "Sibirskiye drevnosti." *MAR* 15:68–71.
1895 "Sibirskiye drevnosti. Iz putevykh zametok" (Siberian antiquities: From notes en route). *ZRAO* 7.

Rosenfield, John M.
1967 *The Dynastic Arts of the Kushans.* Berkeley: University of California Press.

Rostovtsev, M. I.
1918 *Ellinstvo i iranstvo na yuge Rossiyi* (Hellenism and Iranianism in south Russia). Petrograd: "Ogni."
1922 *Iranians and Greeks in South Russia.* Oxford: Clarendon Press.
1925 *Skifiya i Bospor; kriticheskoye obozreniye pamyatnikov literaturnykh, arkheologicheskikh* (Scythia and the Bosphorus: A critical survey of literature and archaeological monuments). Leningrad: Rossiyskaya akademiya istoriyi material'noy kul'tury.
1929 *Sredinnaya Aziya, Rossiya, Kitay: Zverinnyy stil'* (Inner Asia, Russia, China: The Animal Style). Praga: Seminarium Kondakovianum.

Rudenko, S. I.
1952 *Gornoaltayskiye nakhodki i skify* (Discoveries in the High Altay and the Scyths). Moskva: Izd AN SSSR.
1960 *Kul'tura naseleniya Tsentral'nogo Altaya v skifskoye vremya* (The culture

of the population of the central Altay in Scythic times). Leningrad: Izd AN SSSR.

1962a   *Kul'tura khunnov i Noinulinskiye kurgany* (Hiung Nu culture and the Noin Ula Kurgans [Burial Mounds]. Moskva: "Nauka."

1962b   "Sibirskaya kollektsiya Petra I" (Siberian collection of Peter I). *SAI* no. DZ–9. Moskva: Izd AN SSSR.

Rudenko, S. I., and N. M. Rudenko

1949   *Iskusstvo skifov Altaya* (Art of the Altay Scyths). Moskva: GMII.

Rybakov, B. A.

1982   *Yazychestvo drevnykh slavyan* (The Pagan Ways of the Ancient Slavs). Moskva: "Nauka."

Salmony, Alfred.

1933   *Sino-Siberian Art in the Collection of C. T. Loo.* Paris: C. T. Loo.

Sawencof, I. T.

1893   "Sur les restes de l'époque néolitique" (On remains of Neolithic Age). In *Congrès internationale d'archaeologie et antropologie: Deuxième session à Moscou.* Vol. 2.

Savenkov, I. T.

1910   *O drevnykh pamyatnikov isobrazitel'nogo iskusstva na Yeniseye* (On ancient monuments of representative art on the Yenisey). Trudy XVI arkheologicheskogo s'yezda v Chernigove. Moskva.

Savvateyev, Yu. A.

1970   *Zalavruga* (Zalavruga). Leningrad: "Nauka" LO.

Sbornik [Collective Work]

1970   *Tatary-mongoly v Aziyi i Yevrope* (Collective work: The Tatar-Mongols in Asia and Europe). Moskva: Nauka.

Schefold, K.

1938   "Der Skythische Tierstil in Sudrussland" (The Scythic Animal Style in South Russia). *Eurasia Septentrionalis Antiqua* 12:3–78.

Schmid, W.

1934   *Der Kultwagen von Strettweg* (The Cult Cart of Strettweg). Führer zur Urgeschichte Vol. 12 Leipzig: C. Kabitsch.

Semenov, Vl. A.

1982   "Pamyatniki afanasyevskoy kul'tury v Sayanakh" (Sites of Afanasyevo culture in the Sayan [canyon]). *SA* (1982) no. 4: 219–22.

Shavkunov, E. V.

1968   *Gosudarstvo Bokhay i pamyatniki ego kul'tury v Primor'ye* (The Pohai state and sites of its culture in the maritime region). Leningrad: "Nauka" LO.

Sher, Ya. A.

1966   *Kamennyye izvayaniye Semirech'ya* (Stone Stelae-Statues of the Semirech'ye [N.E. Kazakhstan]). Leningrad: "Nauka" LO.

1980   *Petroglify Sredney i Tsentral'noy Aziyi* (Petroglyphs of Central and Inner Asia). Moskva: Izd vostochnoy literatury.

1988   "On the Sources of the Scythic Animal Style." *Arctic Anthropology* 25:47–60.

Shilov, V. N.
1959   "Kalinovskiy Kurgannyy mogil'nik" (The Kalinovka Kurgan [Burial Mound] Cemetery). *MIA* 60:323–523.

Shimkin, D. B.
1967   "Preislamic Central Asia." *Canadian Slavic Studies* 1:618–39.

Shrenk [Schrenck], Leopold [von]
1899   *Ob inorodtsakh Amurskogo kraya* (On the natives of Amur territory). Vol. 2: *Etnograficheskaya chast'* (Ethnographic part). Sankt Peterburg: Imperatorskaya AN.

Shternberg, L. Ya.
1936   *Pervobytnaya religiya v svete etnografiyi* (Primitive religion in light of ethnography). Leningrad: Izd Instituta narodov Severa TsIK SSSR. *Materialy po etnografiyi*, vol. 4.

Sinitsyn, I. V.
1959   "Arkheologicheskiye issledovaniya Zavolzhskogo otryada" (Archaeological investigations of the Trans-Volga Team). *MIA* 60:39–205.

Skalon, K. M.
1941   *Izobrazheniye zhivotnykh na keramike sarmatskogo perioda* (The representation of animals on Sarmatian period ceramics). Trudy Otdela istoriyi pervobytnoy kul'tury, vol. 1. Leningrad: GE.

Smirnov, A. P.
1956   "Zheleznyy vek Bashkiriyi" (The Iron Age of the Bashkiria). *MIA* 58:5–107.
1966   *Skify* (The Scythians). Moskva: "Nauka."

Smirnov, K. F.
1951   "Arkheologicheskiye issledovaniye v rayone dagestanskogo seleniya Tarki v 1948–1949gg" (Archaeological investigations in the vicinity of the Dagestan settlement of Tarki in 1948–49). *MIA* 23:263–67.
1964   *Savromaty* (The Sauromatians). Moskva: "Nauka."

Spitsyn, A. A.
1901   "Glyadenovskoye gorodishche" (The Glyadenoro fortified settlement). *ZRAO* 12, no. 1–2.

Steblin-Kamenskiy, M. I.
1976   *Mif* (The Myth). Leningrad: "Nauka." Seriya iz istoriyi mirovoy kul'tury.

Stein, Marc Aurel
1887   "Zoroastrian Deities on Indo-Scythian Coins." *Oriental and Babylonian Record* 1 (August 1887): 15–159.

von den Steinen, K.
1894   *Unter den Naturvölken Zentral Brasiliens* (Among the primitive people of central Brazil). 2nd ed. Berlin: D. Reimer.

Stolpe, Hjalmar
1892   "Entwicklungserscheinungen in des Ornamentik der Naturvölker" (Indications of Evolution in the Ornamentation of Primitive People). *Mitteilungen der Anthropologischen Gesselschaft* 22 (n.s. 12).

Stralenberg, Philipp Johann
1730   *Das Nord und Östliche Theil von Europa and Asien* (The north and eastern part of Europe and Asia). Stockholm.

Talbot-Rice, Tamara
1957   *The Scythians.* London: Ancient Places and Peoples.

Tallgren, A. M.
1934   "Zum ursprungsgebiet des sogenanten skythischen Tierstil" (On the source area of the so-called Scythian Animal Style). *Artibus Asiae* 4:258–64.

Temir Sanaa
1940   *Zapisi po pamyati i podstrochnyye perevody P. V. Kuchiyaka* (Notes from memory and interlineal translations by P. V. Kuchiyak). Novosibirsk.

Tikhonov, B. G.
1960   "Metallicheskiye izdeliya epokhi bronzy na Srednom Urale i v Priural'ye" (Metal artifacts of Bronze Age from the central Urals and the Cis-Ural Area). *MIA* 90:5–115.

Toporov, V. N.
1969   "K rekonstruktsiyi indoyevropeyskogo rituala i ritual'nopoeticheskikh formul (na materiale zagovorov)" (Towards a reconstruction of Indo-European ritual and ritual-poetic formulas [from spells]). *Trudy po znakovym sistemam* 4:133–37.

Urayev, V. A.
1956   *Krivosheinskiy klad* (The Krivosheino Hoard). *Trudy Tomskogo oblast'-nogo krayevedcheskogo muzeya.* Vol. 5

Vadetskaya, E. B.
1967   *Drevniye idoly Yeniseya* (Ancient idols of the Yenisey). Leningrad: "Nauka" LO.

1970   "Zhenskiye siluety na plitakh iz okunevskikh mogil'nikov" (Women's silhouettes on Okunevo cemetery gravestones). In *Sibir' i yeyo sosedi v drevnosti. Materialy po istoriyi Sibiri,* ed. V. E. Larichev, pp. 261–64. Novosibirsk: "Nauka" SO.

Vadetskaya, E. B., N. V. Leontyev, and G. A. Maksimenkov
1980   *Pamyatniki okunevskoy kul'tury* (Monuments of Okunevo Culture). Leningrad: "Nauka" LO.

Vanelov, V.
1956   *Soderzhaniye i forma v iskusstve* (Content and form in art). Moskva: Iskusstvo.

Vasilevskiy, R. S. (ed)
1983   *Paleolit Sibiri* (The Siberian Paleolithic). Novosibirsk: "Nauka" SO.

Vasilyevskiy, R. S., and A. P. Okladnikov
1980   "Izobrazheniya medvedey v neoliticheskam iskusstve Severnoy Aziyi" (Bear representations in the Neolithic art of northern Asia). In *Zveri v kamne. Pervobytnoye iskusstvo.* Novosibirsk: "Nauka" SO.

Veselovskiy, N. I.
1915   "Sovremennoye sostoyaniye voprosa o kamennykh babakh ili 'balbalakh' " (The present state of the question of "Stone Peasant

Women" or "Balbal"). Zapiski Odesskogo obshchestva istoriyi i drevnosti, vol. XXII.

Vinogradov, V. B.
1961   "K voprosu ob izobrazheniyi zhivotnykh na sarmatskoy keramike" (On the representation of animals on Sarmatian Pottery). In *Arkheologicheskiy sbornik* NSO MGU. Moskva: MGU.

Volkov, V. V.
1967   *Bronzovyy i ranniy zhelezniy vek Severnoy Mongoliyi* (The Bronze and Early Iron Ages of northern Mongolia). Ulan Bator [The Mongolian Peoples Republic].

Watson, William
1962   *Ancient Chinese Bronzes*. Rutland, Vt.: Charles Tuttle.

Witzel, Maurus
1935   "Tammuz-liturgien und Verwandtes" (Liturgies to Tammuz and Related [texts]). *Analecta Orientalia*. Vol. 10. Roma: Pontificio instituto biblico.

Wood, Allen H.
1959   *The Gold Coin-Types of the Great Kushanas. Numismatic Notes and Monographs*. Varanasi: Numismatic Society of India.

Wymer, John
1982   *The Paleolithic Age*. London: Croom Helm.

Yevtyukhina, L. A.
1952   "Kamennyye izvayaniya Yuzhnoy Sibiri i Mongoliyi" (Stone sculptured stelae of south Siberia and Mongolia). *MIA* 24:72–120.

Zavitukhina, M. P.
1977   "K voprosu o vremeni i meste formirovaniya Sibirskoy kollektsiyi Petra I" (On the question of time and place in the formation of the Siberian collection of Peter I). In *Kul'tura i iskusstvo petrovskogo vremeni*. Leningrad: "Avrora."

Zelenin, V. K.
1936   *Kul't ongonov v Sibiri* (The Ongon [Household Fetish] Cult in Siberia). Moskva: Izd. ANSSSR.

Zielinski, Tadeusz
1922   *Religiya ellinizma* (Hellenistic Religion). Petrograd: "Akademiya."

Index

A Note on the Author and the Editors

ANATOLY IVANOVICH MARTYNOV graduated in 1955 from the historical faculty of the Moscow Pedagogical Institute. During 1960–63 he was an Aspirant at the Siberian Division, USSR Academy of Sciences, and in 1973 he received the doctorate in historical sciences for his thesis on the forest-steppe Tagar culture. He is Professor and Chairman, Faculty of Archaeology, Kemerovo State University. In 1980, Professor Martynov was a Senior Fulbright Fellow and Visiting Professor of Anthropology at the University of Illinois at Urbana-Champaign.

Engaged in archaeological research since 1953, he has excavated in the Ukraine, central Asia, and particularly Siberia. A specialist in the archaeology of the Eurasian steppes, Scythic south Siberia, and primitive art, he has excavated over three hundred sites and published more than one hundred scientific reports and papers. Among his best known studies are monographs on Yagunya (1973), the Tom' river petroglyphs (1972, with A. P. Okladnikov) and the forest-steppe Tagar culture (1979). His incisive volume on the Archaeology of the USSR (2nd ed., 1982) is a text of the USSR Ministry of Education. In the West, he has published in *Arctic Anthropology*, *The Musk Ox*, and the *Journal of the Steward Anthropological Society*. He is married to a fellow archaeologist, Galena S. Martynova.

DEMITRI B. SHIMKIN, born in Siberia and brought to the United States in 1923, was educated at the University of California, Berkeley (A.B., 1936; Ph.D., 1939). He served in the U.S. Army (1941–47), and with the U.S. Bureau of the Census (1953–60). He has taught at Harvard (1948–1953, 1964–65) and, since 1960, at the University of Illinois, where he is Professor Emeritus of Anthropology and Geography, and Professor of Public Health. An ethnologist and specialist in ecology, he has done fieldwork in Wyoming, Alaska, Mississippi, Bengal (India), Tanzania, and western Siberia. Among his publications are *Minerals: A Key to Soviet Power* (1953), *The Extended Family in Black Societies* (1978, with others), and *Clinical Anthropology* (1983, with Peggy Golde and others).

EDITH M. SHIMKIN, a graduate of George Washington University, was an editor and a specialist in archaeology. She was the author of, among other works, *The Upper Paleolithic of North Central Eurasia* (1978). She died in 1984.